And we know that God causes everything to work together for the good of those who love God and are called according to his purpose for them.

Romans 8:28

Finding Gideon

A Broken Dream, a Missing Horse, and the Faith of a Mustard Seed

Sarah Hickner

To Kathy,
Soli Deo gloria!
♥
Sarah Hickner

Book Cover by David Fassett www.davidfassett.com

For my parents, who didn't make me come home.

In the early 1980s, God created a girl. He knit her together, and in her DNA he included a little horse hair. For as long as I can remember remembering, horses have called to me. The mere sight of one stirs my soul and creates a yearning to do more, to be more, and to bury my face into their mane and inhale God's goodness.

This is a work of creative non-fiction. It reflects the author's memory, which is a funny thing that evolves over time. Some names have been changed to protect the identity of their bearers. Not everyone gets to be a hero.

Part 1

Chapter 1

Red disappeared, teleporting into another realm. There was no longer a horse underneath me; for half a breath I soared through the air, weightless. Brown dirt, Kentucky bluegrass, and morning sky blurred together like a toddler's watercolor painting. Gravity snatched me from the air, hurtling me onto the racetrack.

Life moved in fractions of a second between gaping darkness and sheer, brilliant clarity. The first blackout must have happened in the time it took to squeeze my eyes closed as I hit the ground, because the thought after *where is Red?* was *how am I on the track*? The thought fluttered away in the chaos like an erratic butterfly as my head turned just enough to see what was coming.

Red tumbled toward me in a somersault. A 1000-pound horse was about to roll over me. *This could be it, as in the "it" where my family lays roses on a casket decades before they should have to and I meet Jesus in person. If this isn't "it," I certainly might never walk again*. I squeezed my eyes shut for a breath. *Oh God*. A prayer, not a curse. Everything, black.

My eyes opened with Red on the other side of me and the realization that *I survived. That wasn't so bad* skimmed across my brain as my vision focused on a hoof surging toward my face. *This could be bad*. A blink. Darkness. A quick suck of air as the hoof of a panicking and flailing Red connected with my face, snapping my head back. Blank space. I heard nothing. It should have sounded like the solid hit of an axe on firewood. I felt no pain. I should have felt the agony like the flat side of a hammer smashing my face.

When my eyes opened and refocused, the light of early morning streamed in. Motion had stopped. Somehow I was cradled against Red's belly like a foal against their mom, and I longed to press against him for the comfort we both needed. Unfortunately, a panicked horse is dangerous, and after the tumble we'd just taken Red would likely scramble to get back on his feet. I crawled away from the warmth of his belly on hands and knees before he could flail and cause more damage with those lethal hooves.

Red, a gigantic two-year-old racehorse and my second mount of the day, lay midway between the inside and outside rails of the dirt training track. The trainer had told me to gallop him two times around, but we hadn't even made it to our first turn. Standing, spitting out blood and hard pieces of what must have been teeth, I turned toward the other side of the three-quarter-mile oval, where the trainer's box stood like a sentinel. It was a raised, covered platform where trainers could watch their horses progress during morning gallops. *Craig is there, and Robert. Surely they saw.* Like a kid standing at my mommy's feet, reaching up, begging for attention, for so many things I didn't know how to express, my eyes lifted to the stand. *Help.*

Two weeks. Craig hired me two weeks ago to work for him and his Thoroughbred training and racing operation, promising to teach me to exercise the racehorses. It was my dream come true.

Robert, a friend from home, had come to the training track today to watch me ride. *Did he see me fall? Am I the only person out here?* I leaned over, bracing my hands against my knees, and spit another stream of blood and teeth. *What should I do?* The world spun.

Where are the other horses and riders who are normally on the track? Is Red okay? Am I okay? God? Am I okay? The sound of hoofbeats pulled my attention back down the track. I turned my head to see another rider galloping toward us, and air filled my lungs a little easier. *I'm not alone. How is he getting his horse stopped so quickly? It's not like the racehorses have good brakes.* Eyes half-lidded, I watched the blood dribble from my face and land on the soft dirt, a pinkish color thanks to the saliva mixed in. The other rider flung himself off his mount and I recognized him—one of the few people here who had introduced himself to me. He was timid. *Is his name Ryan or Bryan?*

I stood and the world became more blurred watercolors. I knew this feeling. It was like in sixth grade when a horse lunged across his stall door, mouth gaping open like an alligator ready to attack. His teeth clamped down on my wrist before I could pull away, sending me into a vortex of shock and pain. I remember thinking *why am I dizzy?* just before I woke up amid moldy pieces of grain, mouse excrement, and spiders, with my riding teacher, Ms. Brenda, leaning over me with a rare look of concern.

I braced my hands on my knees again. *If I pass out now, will I choke on blood? Will I die?* I turned to Red to see him still lying down, but his head was up and alert. Ryan (or was it Bryan?) started toward me. Reins to a skinny, wary-eyed chestnut in his hand, his eyes flitted from Red to me in indecision. *I like him,* I thought. *He cares as much about the horse as he does me, as any good horseman should.* "Go to the horse," I mumbled, stumbling toward a soft-looking patch of dirt.

"Are you sure?" His eyebrows nearly touched his hairline on his leathery, crinkled skin, a common reward for a career with horses.

"Yeah, I've got to lie down before I pass out." I stretched out on my back, the lumpy safety vest hugging my torso and my helmet cradling my head like a pillow. Turning my head as far left as possible, I hoped if blackness overtook me, the blood would pour out of my mouth and not down into my lungs.

Oh God. Help.

"It looks like the horse's foot is stuck on the martingale," Ryan/Bryan yelled. I thought of the martingale, the piece of leather that stretched from between the horse's legs to his reins, and my stomach clenched with guilt. It had been too long. All these racehorses wore martingales much longer than Ms. Brenda had taught, but when I asked the groom about it he said it was good.

"Okay. Can you..." I paused to breathe and spit. Before I got the rest of my words out, Red was up. I wanted to rub his forehead under his forelock, like I did for my own horse when he was upset. I wanted to tell Red it would be okay. They lingered; one man and two confused young horses. *How long does it really take to get from the trainers' stand to the far side of the track?*

"Here comes Craig," Ryan/Bryan said. From the lift of his chin, it was clear I still had a few minutes to wait so I didn't turn to look. In the stillness, a thought popped into my head: *what if Mom and Dad make me go home?* I squeezed my eyes closed as reality sank in.

I don't want to go home. God, I just got here. I just got here. Please don't let my parents make me come home. And take care of Red. Help me, God. I don't want to go home.

Home. Where I had once laid on the floor of my parent's kitchen, kind of like I'm lying on the track now. I was holding it together now during this moment of physical trauma, but eight years before, I'd crumbled. Snot and tears smothered my face over simple words. Dinner that night had been a long-awaited moment.

For my entire twelve years of life, I had dreamed of having a horse of my own. I was a horse-obsessed girl. Every Christmas list to Santa or birthday list to parents mentioned a horse. When I saw a shooting star, 11:11 on the clock, or I squeezed my eyes shut to blow out candles, the wish was the same: a horse. Every day I pleaded with God to make this dream come true while sitting in a suburban Mississippi middle-class home. My dad was a CPA, my mom a teacher—neither knew nor cared anything about horses. We had neighbors every quarter acre who might have a pool, but certainly no backyard barns or fenced pastures.

On Saturday mornings, I woke before my older brothers, grabbed a blue windbreaker, and escaped to our tree seat. A treehouse would have been great, but we only had towering pines and two little cedar trees with paper-shred bark and sticky sap. My brother Joel did his best with what we had and wedged a piece of plywood between the branches on one cedar. He created a ladder by nailing wood scraps to the trunk and attached an old Easter basket to a rope so we could pull items up.

I read until the hot Mississippi sun evaporated the morning dew and my stomach demanded breakfast. Adventures on paper became my reality as I escaped a charging bull on a trail ride with my best friends, adopted a foal on Chincoteague Island at pony penning day, galloped down the final stretch at Churchill Downs to win the Kentucky Derby, and valiantly saved the beloved lesson ponies from a treacherous flaming barn. My heart was heavy with longing, and I begged God to make it real.

Dad successfully postponed "that horse problem" for several years, assuming it was a phase I would outgrow. "I'll get you a horse when you're twelve," he'd declared somewhere around my ninth birthday, when the whole family was worn out from my obsession.

I catapulted from bed on my twelfth birthday and pulled the slats of blinds apart for a clear view of the driveway. There was no horse tied to the mailbox. Throughout the school day, I stared at the door, waiting for mom to pull me out of class and deliver me to the lesson barn where a horse with a big red bow waited. School ended, and I rode the bus home as usual. I sat on the couch and restlessly watched cartoons, realizing my schoolteacher mom would obviously never pull me from class. *She'll deliver me to the barn as soon as she gets home from work*, I assured myself. But when she got home, she raced around doing laundry, cleaning the kitchen, and all the normal things moms do. It was a day of waiting, expecting.

At dinner, we sat around a table at the restaurant I chose, a perk of being the birthday girl, and my parents handed me a card. There had been many failed opportunities to surprise me with a horse, but I held onto a twinge of hope as I slid my hand underneath the seal of the envelope, tearing the flap open. Maybe the note would say, "Surprise! You're the proud owner of your very own horse!"

Before I could read it, a hundred-dollar bill slipped from the folded cardstock and fluttered to the table.

I pasted on the biggest smile I could, though it seemed the entire world could see it didn't reach my eyes. The server was clearing the dirty dishes when I worked up the courage to say something. "I really appreciate the money, but, uh, I thought you said when I turned twelve I could get a horse. And I'm even taking lessons."

Mom gave Dad a sideways glance, which I interpreted as *you really screwed up when you made that promise*. He paused, looking at her to be saved. She looked back at him, her lips sealed tight. After a gaping silence in which my heart tried to work its way out of my chest, he responded. "Well, Sarah, I'll tell you what. When you get all A's on your report card, we'll get you a horse." The cloud of disappointment lifted a tad and there was a slight upturn in the corners of my mouth. "Deal," I smiled. I normally made mostly A's with a B or two mixed in. It was time to buckle down.

A few months later, we sat at the kitchen table for dinner. It was a rare evening when Nathan wasn't at football practice and Joel wasn't at work. The entire family was present. I proudly stretched my arm across the table to hand my dad an orange envelope containing my newest report card. This was it! The moment I had waited my entire life for!

The envelope was sealed and I wasn't sure of the results, but I had worked extra diligently this semester. And for the last few weeks, every time Mom picked me up from my riding lesson, Ms. Brenda would walk over to the car and tell her all about this horse named Misty, who was perfect for me. Mom would nod, neither confirming nor denying that Misty was in my future. But I knew, if my report card was perfect, she had to be.

Dad bent each side of the brass envelope clasp forward, lifted the flap, and slid a folded piece of paper out. He read each grade aloud, a report card routine that usually produced glares from my brothers. I was the annoying, goody-two-shoes baby sister. But tonight, there was somber silence around the table. He made it to the bottom of the list and I gulped a relieved breath—all A's with glowing comments from my teachers! Tilting in my seat to hear Dad's next words, I watched him lean forward, dropping his eyes to the table for a second. *Dad must be preparing to speak! He must be readjusting because this is the moment he finally says, "Let's get you a horse!"*

He slowly reached into his back pocket and fished out his money clip, flicking a hundred-dollar bill on the table in front of me and congratulating me for a job well done. I mumbled a "thank you" as I studied the woodgrain of the table, tore the corner off the napkin, and processed. My family dispersed, leaving me alone, glued to the chair in a trance.

God, I'm sorry I'm being so selfish. I prayed, willing the tears to stay in my eyes. Horse girls were tough. Horse girls didn't cry. *How many kids would be upset over a hundred-dollar bill for good grades? But it was supposed to be a horse, God! It was supposed to be a horse! HE PROMISED ME A HORSE!* My calm, collected, find-a-way-make-a-way self crumpled from the kitchen chair onto the fake wood floor to cry over Dad's fake promise and my fake hope for a dream I apparently wouldn't reach any time soon. I stretched across the floor, hair falling around my face, and rested my head on my forearms while my body lurched with dramatically loud hiccups.

This was surely the final refusal. I had done everything I knew to do, and there was still no horse. My tears were those of a relentlessly positive girl who had lost hope, like a volcano that sat happily dormant for a lifetime until it was forced to erupt. For a moment I wasn't worried about my big brothers making fun of me, my determination to be a tough horse girl who didn't cry, or my lifelong goal of trying to impress my parents to get a horse. There would be no horse. I was just erupting.

Nathan strolled in, twitching his head to flick his perfectly highlighted hair out of his eyes. He glared at me, wallowing in my puddle of sorrow, and with exasperation, demanded an explanation for my hysterics. I set my jaw and narrowed my eyes at him from the floor, trying to decipher why he was asking, weighing his intentions. I couldn't find any malice, so I hiccupped my way through a tale of broken promises and heartache.

"Crying won't fix it," he deadpanned.

"What?" I whimpered. *What is he talking about? Why won't he just leave me alone?*

"Crying won't fix anything. You've got to get up and do something about it. Go into Mom and Dad's room and talk to them about it." Underneath the harsh tone, there was a slight inflection to his voice, and I wondered if possibly my mean older brother really cared.

"O ki *hiccup* kay," I pushed out while trying to decide whether there was any truth to this wisdom. Hadn't I done everything there was to do already? In the pause, we stared into each other's matching blue eyes, and I realized he had a solid point.

I lay on the floor stewing until he stepped over my prone body and walked out of the house, slamming the door like an exclamation point. He didn't need to actually witness me heed his advice. When I was sure he was gone, I slowly stood, threw up a prayer, and made my way down the hall to my parents' bedroom with swollen eyes and an occasional shoulder lurch from a sharp inhale. I tapped my knuckles against their white door.

"Come in," Mom said.

My parents gave each other knowing looks. I surveyed the jury who would decide my fate. Dad looked simultaneously irritated and nervous while Mom took it all in with her trademark resting (scary) teacher face, which gave nothing away. My chest lifted as I gathered myself enough to talk.

"I came to talk about my report card," I said.

"Okay," Mom responded with a nod to go ahead.

Shaking on the inhale, I spilled. "Dad said... and Ms. Brenda... and all A's... and the hundred-dollar bill... and I really appreciate it, but it's not a horse. I have money saved up. With the money from tonight, I can give you $600, and that means you just need $400, and her board is only $225 a month."

"So, you have $600?" Mom asked.

"With the money from tonight, yes!" I declared with slightly more confidence, chin jutted.

"Okay. Go get your money while your dad and I talk about it."

"Really?" A question and exclamation in one. I sounded breathy as I raced from the room with hope pounding in my chest.

I clenched years of birthday and report card money in my sweaty hand as I strode back into their bedroom. The muscles of my mouth twitched into a delicate grin, unsure if this was really happening.

Within minutes, Mom picked up the phone by their bed and punched in Ms. Brenda's number. "Hey Brenda, it's Janet," she said. "Tell us about this horse you think would be perfect for Sarah."

After a brief conversation, she hung up the phone. Dad looked overly serious, probably panicking over the money pit he'd just walked into. The corner of Mom's mouth tilted into the barest hint of a grin as I counted my cash into her hand. I tried not to laugh, or twirl, or do anything less than what a mature horse owner would do. Because the next day when we got to the barn, Mom was handing over the money and we were signing a bill of sale to purchase my very first horse, Misty.

Chapter 2

"Sarah?! Oh God, Sarah, are you okay?" Craig's face popped into my sky view as he leaned over me.

Everyone from the trainers' box had made it to the far side of the track where I lay dazed. Craig, Robert, and a third guy squinted at me, trying to survey the damage. Stoically I allowed them—invaded, embarrassed, and helpless—I couldn't do anything to push them away. My teeth were jagged shards next to gaping, gummy, bleeding spaces in my mouth. They pushed on swelling lips that oozed blood. When I was a kid, my dentist, Dr. Boteler, finished every appointment saying, "Sarah, you have such beautiful teeth!" My insides shriveled at the thought. I never believed him, convinced they were too big, like Chiclets.

A search party was underway for the shiny bits of bone that were unceremoniously ejected from my mouth. People milled about, scuffing their feet in the dirt that must have told its own tale of the fall. Someone called an ambulance. Robert hung close, my safety blanket, a piece of home. I met him back in Mississippi through a mutual friend who knew I wanted to ride racehorses in Kentucky. Robert took me under his wing like one of his own nearly grown kids and gave me my first gallop on his horse, Gigi.

We trailered her to a backcountry track in the middle of nowhere, Louisiana. I had pulled the stirrups up as short as they would go, like the jockeys I'd seen on TV. When the gray mare started galloping, I couldn't find balance by hovering over her like the other rider on the track. I tried clinging to her mane, leaning forward, and sitting back, but none of it worked. Halfway through the gallop, I took my feet out of the stirrups and sat, legs dangling as if I were bareback. Her muscles expanded and contracted beneath my blue jeans. I was a tad embarrassed and overwhelmed, but grateful. I fell in love with the little gray mare.

Craig rubbed his hands along Red's body, checking for obvious injuries, before asking Ryan/Bryan to deliver the horse to the barn. The trio walked away from the chaos, heads lowered.

Bored and curious riders trekked around the oval to see the holdup. They lined up and leaned over me one at a time, blocking the wide, blue sky I was laying under. They squinted to see the damage under the darkness of their shadows, then brought hands to their mouths and rushed off like they were fighting to hold breakfast in.

I wanted to shout and wave my arms. *Hello. I'm a human here! Not a corpse on the side of the road.* The other rider from Craig's barn was part of the procession. She didn't talk to me. I was a spectacle, a crunched car on the freeway. We had ridden together for two weeks. She was on a horse next to me the first time I truly galloped, hovering over the horse's withers, hands pressed into his neck as the hoof beats created music that matched the melody of my heart.

I wanted to punch her in the nose to see if she would notice me then. Instead, I shifted my eyes to the side as if I were the problem and sank into a numb calm. Vacant. I imagined my spirit lifting from my body and looking at the scene from above, like in movies. Then it hit me... what if I was more hurt than I felt. Didn't people sometimes have life-threatening injuries after an accident and not realize it? *I'll not imagine my death.*

We waited for the ambulance. Occasionally Craig leaned over and assured me it would be okay. I nodded and tilted my head to the side to spit out more blood. Robert hovered over me but didn't say much. Sweat streamed from his graying sideburns.

They'll do surgery at the hospital and have me back to normal in a couple days. It'll be okay. God, please don't let Mom and Dad bring me home, I pleaded.

I thought about the summer school class at the University of Louisville I would probably miss this week. Who would take care of my dog Sandi who waited at my apartment? How would I break the news about the accident to my parents and boyfriend, Joey? Or would someone else have to?

I wished I were with Gideon. We had the relationship I'd always dreamed of when I imagined having a horse. It took four tries, three other horses I loved but outgrew. Misty had sounded like a match made in Heaven to twelve-year-old me. I mean, she shared the name of the hero in my favorite childhood book! But she repeatedly found ways to drop me until one day she threw me onto a slab of concrete. Ms. Brenda declared it was time to move on.

Henry was next. He was a handsome chestnut with a white star who loved having a girl of his own. When I stepped off the school bus at Herald Farms, I'd walk out to the pasture and do our whistle. It started low until I narrowed my lips and finished with an ear-piercing shrillness. He would lift his head, eyes wide, and trot across the great big pasture to see me. But I grew as a rider and wanted to be a competitive barrel racer.

On the way home from another disaster of a run, Ms. Brenda turned to me, her hot pink Wet 'n Wild lipstick highlighting the downturn of her lips. "I know you love that horse, but if you want to be a great rider, it's time to move on. When you're learning to ride you outgrow horses. Your family can only afford to keep one horse, which is fine. It's part of life. You need to choose between keeping Henry or becoming a better rider." I loved that horse, but I dreamed of being good enough to ride *all* the horses.

So, Henry went to a new home and Dixies Sugarbars entered my life. Dixie was a beautiful bay roan quarter horse mare. She had a stunning coat of white and red hair covering her body, like someone had sprinkled her with salt and cayenne pepper. But her legs, mane, and tail were dusty black. She was awe-inspiring to look at and as hard-headed as they come. When she ate, she attacked her grain, then pinned her ears, circling the stall and threatening the walls, flies, or anything else that would even consider approaching her food.

In ninth grade, drawn by the allure of the jumper world, I left Ms. Brenda's and moved Dixie to the local hunter/jumper farm, Winterview. My horse hated it. She was miserable and challenged everything I asked her to do. Simple things like cantering a circle became an argument. She careened around the arena like we were at the Indy 500, and when I demanded she slow down, she hopped around like an angry rabbit. Sometimes she planted her feet and refused requests as simple as backing up.

I called Ms. Brenda in tears. She had taught me everything I knew and I needed her advice. After talking me through my woes, she asked if I could farm sit for a week at the end of the month. "Hey, while you're here, there's a chestnut horse you should look at. He'd fit in real well over at the hunter/jumper barn. Looks just like the kind of horse they want. Someone abused him around the barrels and he's so anxious he needs to change jobs."

"Okay, I'll come farm sit and check him out when I'm there." I wasn't eager to be rid of Dixie, but I'd give this horse a chance.

"We call him Easy," Ms. Brenda followed up. "You know, there's power in your words." If I'd heard that once from Ms. Brenda, I'd heard it a thousand times. *There's power in your words.*

The end of the month arrived, and it was a busy week with thirty horses to care for after school. There was hardly time to slow down around the chestnut, but one day I pulled my barrel saddle out and took a few minutes to try him. We walked and jogged around the sand arena. It was just the two of us at a barn that normally bustled with activity, and melancholy happiness settled over us. Sitting on a horse who seemed happy to have a rider, the frustrations over Dixie lightened. He would fit well at the jumper barn with his long legs and lean, muscular body. He was drool-worthy, with white stockings stretching from his hooves to his knees and a big white blaze covering the middle of his forehead down to the edge of his bottom lip. Riding hadn't felt right in months, but this felt good. Change was in the air.

The next week, Ms. Patti, the trainer at Winterview Farm, hooked up her horse trailer and drove the fifteen miles to Herald Farms. Winterview was picturesque and well-maintained. Evenly-spaced trees lined the road to the barn and a paddock by the sign housed very well-fed, expensive jumping horses. At Herald Farms, the place where I spent years becoming a horsewoman, the edge of the property featured a house trailer. Four long, narrow, boggy paddocks held muddy horses teetering on dry mounds in the center of their fields. Their hair was matted from being rained on and air drying, and I silently cursed them for not hiding under the sheds.

Biting my tongue, I focused my eyes on my knees and my mind on the trade papers, not wanting to cause or draw any insult to this sad-looking farm. Just because I left didn't mean I didn't love it. I signed the trade papers while Ms. Patti unloaded Dixie, my heart heavy and slow as I handed her off to Ms. Brenda. I had prayed over this and it felt right—not easy, but right.

The chestnut horse with four stockinged legs, a white blaze, and a little white around the edge of his eyes stood on a mound of old hay. A ten-foot-wide ditch crossed the center of his paddock. It smelled like hot mud and horse poop as the sun shone on us. Little birds swooped and chirped in the sky above.

Halter on my shoulder, I surveyed the massive amount of slop and regretted how bogged my boots would soon be. Taking a reluctant breath, I stepped through the gate into the shallow mud on the edge of the paddock. As I lifted my foot to move into the deep muck, I heard a sucking sound from the other side of the ditch. I glanced up to see that the chestnut had abandoned his dry mound and was lurching toward me.

The mud sucked at his feet, making each step a monumental effort. When he got to the ditch, he dropped his head and blew a loud snort at the water, creating a spray of tiny droplets and little rings that expanded until they disappeared. He looked up at me and then back to the ditch. Shifting his weight from one leg to the other and looking at me nervously, he rocked back on his haunches and leaped across the expanse of water, into my life.

I never left the spot by the gate as he walked up and touched his forehead to my elbow. "Hey, Easy." I slipped the halter over his head as my heart grew. I whispered into his ear while we walked to the trailer, "Welcome to my family! We're going to have fun! And I think we should change your name. What do you think?" He bumped his forehead into my arm again and a smile stretched across my face.

A bond snapped into place. The next day, I wrote "Gideon" on his stall when I came to visit, and when he saw me, he rushed to the door to say hello. He blew a gentle wind into my face, and I returned it. We soaked up each other's presence. I was his safe place, and he was my dream come true.

Chapter 3

"I found it!" Robert bent over, then thrust what must have been my tooth in the air. He was too far away to see, but Craig and the other guy rushed to him excitedly. Did it matter? It felt like a souvenir, a shark tooth found at the beach. The find boosted their morale and gave them something to focus on beyond the pitiful girl laying silent and broken on the track. Eventually they returned to pacing and complaining about how long the ambulance was taking. Craig came and went, checking on Red and the other horses in the barn, then coming back to check on me.

Will the ambulance ever get here? I wondered. The jagged points of broken and newly crooked teeth pushed against my lips. *How did this happen? How are my real teeth as bad, or worse even, than freaking Bubba teeth?* They poked into the swollen skin inside my mouth, where there was a gap of empty, bloody gums. *Is it better to lose teeth or for them to be broken?* I sighed. *I'm messed up. Things aren't right.* My heart pounded faster until it pulsed in my ears and even my fingertips. *I can't escape this. This happened to me, my body, my face. And what if Mom and Dad force me to come home? Could I even blame them? I couldn't. But I don't want to go home. Riding racehorses in Kentucky is all I want to do. God, please don't let them make me go home.*

What if it was ending here? What if years of dreaming, scheming, and sacrifices were useless thanks to this one fluke accident? I wasn't ready to go. I'd only been galloping for two weeks. I didn't know what was next, but I knew I wasn't ready to give up. Everything had been at my fingertips. My determination had paid off, and I was good at this. But I wasn't sure if the choice was mine. I could control and ride out a lot of things, but a horse disappearing from underneath me wasn't one of them.

Silent tears streamed down my face, creating salty streaks in the dirt and wetting the hair by my ears as I lay on the ground. *I don't want to go home, God! Please don't make me go home.*

The shift of energy drew the men back to me like a fish on a line, some natural inclination toward a damsel in distress. They leaned over and peered down, all their eyebrows in nearly-comical matching slants. I wanted to spit in their faces to make them turn away. I hated the way my tears perked them up and changed the tone of their collective voice. I hated that I needed them.

I turned my head to spit blood and let the moisture from my eyes become part of the track. So much for tough horse girls not crying.

The ambulance arrived. EMTs leaped from the truck and raced toward me, shooting questions at the men as if they had been there and knew what happened. As if I hadn't. They set an orange board beside me and voices came from every direction about how to transfer me safely onto it. *This is ridiculous*, I thought. *I'm only lying down so I don't pass out.* But they didn't want to risk anything. *What if something broke in my back and I can't feel it?* I realized. *The horse did roll over me.*

Anxiety crept up my body, an itchy flush making its way to my neck and face. *What if adrenaline is masking something worse than busted teeth?* They removed my safety vest and helmet and strapped me to the stiff orange board. They wrapped a brace that would fit a six-four linebacker around my neck. I considered asking for a kid's size, but not fitting into something so basic to humanity added to my humiliation. *Could this neck brace separate my head from my body*? My brother's football career flashed in my mind. If I had expected anyone in the family to be carted to an ambulance in a neck brace, he was it. Though, I was glad it wasn't him.

The EMTs set everyone abuzz, a blur of urgent conversations I no longer cared about. *Just get me to the hospital and get this over with.* My southern hospitality and perpetual hopefulness slipped into the dirt underneath the orange board.

The talking heads discussed which hospital to take me to. *Honestly, y'all, aren't all hospitals good? Get the show on the road.* Craig demanded they not take me to the closest one because it was next to the prison. *What's the big deal? Are convicts just running around loose in the ER?* I didn't care where they took me as long as they got me there soon and did some kind of surgery to make this all go away so I could get back to dream-chasing.

They hefted me up into the ambulance and the double doors closed, blocking Robert and Craig's pinched faces from view. It was just me, an EMT with beautiful dark brown hair, and a lot of machines. I had wondered what the inside of an ambulance looked like. It simultaneously met my expectations and shocked me. There was so much equipment jammed into this tiny space.

The EMT asked me questions, probably a method of distraction. Every time I moved my mouth to speak, the wrongness of it made me never want to open my mouth again. But she was also unexpectedly comforting. She didn't wince or fret, yet I could feel her care. I was broken, but still human.

"Do you have any family around?" I could tell she assumed I did.

"No, I just moved here a couple weeks ago from Mississippi. Both my brothers and my parents still live there. I hope they don't make me come home."

"Why would they make you go home?" She seemed genuinely concerned.

"They didn't really want me to come up here. But I've been wanting to ride on the track for forever. So I transferred up for my junior year of college." My eyes drifted closed while I talked. I wanted to shut it all out. The beeps, clicks, and rattles of the gurney against the floor were sweeping me into a vortex. I was in the center as it spun out of control, and this EMT girl was keeping me grounded.

"So, what does that make you? Twenty-one?"

"I'm twenty," I mumbled, remembering a book I read that had sparked this dream to gallop racehorses. I was probably eleven or twelve when I read it. The book had a jet-black Thoroughbred on the cover, a girl in jockey silks on his back. I had stared at the picture, getting lost in what-ifs, and my heart had clenched with want. The main character had an accident on the track and broke her back. She had a long and tumultuous but ultimately victorious comeback and, of course, won the big race on her favorite horse.

Regardless of the danger, the book planted a seed of desire to gallop racehorses on the track, and from then on nearly every horse-related book I read was about racing. They each watered the seed until it grew into a beautiful, gigantic tree with deep roots that was impossible to move, so I built my life around it. I knew in my gut I would end up in the hospital at some point while chasing this dream, just like the girl in the book. I just didn't expect it to happen this soon.

But I also didn't expect the journey here to take so long. The plan had been simple enough.

The summer after my junior year of high school, I contacted colleges, set up appointments to visit campuses, and with my mom's help, booked flights. The anchor of our trip was a day at the races. While scouring a magazine called *The Backstretch*, I found a Saturday horse race that fit in perfectly with my college tours.

We flew into Louisville to start a large loop through the state. First stop, Churchill Downs. There were simply no words. For years I had watched the Kentucky Derby on TV, pored over articles about it in newspapers, and read books that took place on this track. It was the biggest fangirl moment of my life. The Twin Spires pointed toward Heaven and my heart lifted with them. This was my destiny.

We walked through the parking lot and I spent half a roll of film taking pictures of the track on the other side of the fence. Lacing my fingers through the wire, I pressed my head against the metal, straining for a closer look at the starting gates and dirt. I envisioned myself on a racehorse, breaking from the green mechanical padded doors. I snapped photos of the empty gates before Mom offered to take my picture in front of them.

We continued to the main entrance and Dad walked up to the ticket seller. "Hey, we're here for the races," he said.

The guy behind the glass leaned into his little microphone. "That'll be eight dollars."

"Eight dollars? That's it? We've got two adults and one almost-adult. I think she qualifies as a kid still," he said with a chuckle as he gestured to me. Mom and I had our eyebrows to our hairlines in shock.

"Yessiree! Three dollars for adults, two if you're under eighteen on stakes day!" None of us knew what stakes day meant, but we smiled and nodded.

Dad counted out the bills to pay while I walked in slow circles. When I had my ticket I flew through the front entrance, greeted by a fenced-off area where horses were being led around an oval. Bright-colored saddle towels with numbers matched the smocks of the walkers. Some horses swaggered like they owned the place and others jigged around in a nervous trot. Immediately I decided the ones who strutted would win. I leaned against the fence, breathing in the smells of concession food mixed with horses. *This must be what Heaven smells like, minus the hot dogs.*

A bright bay horse with bulging neck muscles walked past me, making eye contact, and I gasped. *Get over here!* he said. *You belong with us!* His handler smiled at me and my stomach fluttered. I lifted my hand in a tentative wave.

Jockeys were tossed onto their mounts and disappeared through a tunnel under the stands. We raced in the same direction looking for seats. I didn't want to miss a single second. I had imagined a crowd like I'd seen on TV for the Derby, but instead it was sporadic race fans, dressed casually, studying programs and holding squares of paper that must have had something to do with their bets. The horses danced around the track to warm up. I forgot to breathe as I watched the parade of glistening young Thoroughbreds, led by gussied-up lead horses, and all the horsemen on their backs. I longed to be one of them.

A bell rang and the field of racehorses exploded from the gates. A lump rose in my throat as my heart kicked up to match the frantic rhythm of hoofbeats that shook the ground. The track caller sped along, updating us stride by stride as the field moved to the far side of the track, nearly out of sight. I strained to see them, eventually settling for watching on the big screen, until a blur of movement appeared at the turn of the track. The field of horses stampeded toward us, coming down the home stretch. I leaned over the railing and snapped picture after picture. The air was electric as they made their final rally right in front of me, throwing clods of dirt in the air.

It was real, and I was here. I could stick my hand through the fence and touch a piece of the actual Churchill Downs track.

My dad struck up a conversation with a petite woman with dark brown curly hair who appeared to be in her mid-40s. Dad regaled her with the tale of my dream to ride racehorses and how we were in town to tour schools. Her eyes twinkled in excitement. "Would you like a tour of the racetrack?"

She introduced herself as Trish and whisked me away.

We went back to the small area at the front of the track where I first saw the horses being led around. Trish explained that it was called the "paddock."

"But a paddock is where we turn horses out to graze," I countered in confusion.

"True! But at the track, it's what they call this area where the horses are walked around and saddled. They have some different lingo here." Her eyes crinkled at the corners when she talked. "You'll get used to it."

"Okay!" I replied as I rushed to keep up with her.

"Want to go in?" Her devious grin said she already knew the answer.

Everyone in there appeared to be connected to a horse—trainers, grooms, jockeys. "Are we allowed?"

"They know me! It won't be a problem!" She pulled an official-looking sticker from her pocket. "Put this on," she said before she winked to the security guard and flashed a badge. He became the footman, opening the door to Cinderella's magical carriage. I stepped down, one, two, three steps, and paused. I was no longer a peasant watching the ball from the outside. I was part of it, and I had to pause and take a breath.

"Come on!" My fairy godmother grinned at the awe emanating from my face.

I rushed across the dirt path between the horses and joined Trish on the grassy center of the oval. "Pretty cool, huh?" She bumped my arm.

My voice finally came to me. "This is incredible. Thank you so much!"

Making eye contact with a horse in the paddock.

The horses circled—princes and princesses dancing around us. Someone in a green blazer broke the trance, yelling, "Riders up!" Jockeys were popped up onto horses' backs before exiting the paddock and heading toward the track. It was time for the race.

The crowd that had pressed to the paddock fence disbursed in a rush toward the betting windows and the other side of the track. I started toward the gate we came through.

"Do you want to follow the jocks?" Trish's question startled me. Surely the tunnel was forbidden to anyone on foot.

"Uh, are you sure?" I didn't want to sound like a broken record, but...

"Yeah, it's fine! Come on, we gotta hurry if you want to see the horses." We jogged to the same opening the horses had exited through.

Trish knew everyone and they loved her. From the walkers who tossed their bibs into a laundry basket once their horses danced toward the track, to the outrider on a stocky mare who followed the herd, they chatted and laughed. A jockey walked alongside us and I tried not to stare. As he and Trish chatted, I decided maybe she wasn't a fairy godmother. She was the unofficial mayor of Churchill Downs. People clamored to bask in the glow of her joy and kindness.

The horses in front of us reached the end of the tunnel, prancing onto the track in anticipation. While they warmed up, Trish walked me across the edge of the track, through the winner's circle to an old-time analog scale. "This is where the jockeys weigh in with their saddles after the race." She nodded a greeting to an older gentleman in a green blazer.

"You want to step on the scales?" the man asked.

A grin stretched across my face and I looked to Trish for confirmation. "Get up there!" she gestured toward the scale. "Give it a try! Here, give me your camera and I'll take a picture!"

I stepped up. The numbers swirled beneath a needle and I turned to Trish and smiled, feeling completely cheesy but utterly thrilled.

Stepping onto the scales.

The bell rang, and horses exploded from the gate. "Come on!" Trish dragged me away. "Let's watch the race over here! Most people like to be up high, but the real horsemen watch the race by the rail, where the dirt can fly up and hit us."

"Yes! I love being on the rail. You can feel the vibrations when the field runs by."

"Here they come! Get your camera ready!" she shouted over the din of screaming fans. I leaned over the rail and snapped picture after picture as the horses approached and thundered past us. The crowd escalated until the horses passed the finish line. Little white squares of paper, previously gripped between the fingers of hopeful bettors, fluttered to the ground as heads tipped forward to study the racing program for the next race. Sporadic victors clutched winning tickets and raced to collect money.

Trish and I lingered around the winner's circle to catch a close-up view. When the horse pranced back for a picture, they invited us to stand in the circle and be in the win photo. *Is this even real?*

The winning horse and rider getting ready for the photo.

Still wide-eyed, the tired horses marched away with their handlers to the other side of the track where warm stalls waited, and a buzz of anticipation filled the air. The headlining race of the day, the Stephen Foster with a purse of $831,000, was next. "Do you want some jockeys to sign your program?" Trish asked.

"Sure!" and we were off. We stood by the door to "the jocks' room," and when a jockey walked up, she handed him my program and asked if he could get some signatures.

"Sure, I'll pass it around to the guys!" His eyes crinkled at the corners when he looked at me, and I was awestruck. I didn't follow jockeys or know any of their names. But ten minutes later they cracked the door and passed my program back. Trish gave them a warm thank you and wished them luck while I gawked. Every jockey in the upcoming race had autographed my program.

Trish pointed out each signature, telling me about the winningest jockey of this year's meet, who won the Derby, and more. I clutched my program to my chest, wanting to cry over this simple and beautiful thing. But we were moving too fast for emotions.

"I've got one more place to take you," Trish shared. "You watch the Derby on TV, right?"

I followed her up the escalators as I told her about watching it at home and reading the write-ups in the local paper the next day. It was the only day Dad pulled the sports page for me. It was the only day I cared what the newspaper had to say. We went through doors marked for employees and soon stood in a room filled with wall-to-wall sound equipment, overlooking the entire Churchill

Downs racetrack. Trish introduced me to one more friend, the guy who calls the races over the loudspeaker, including the Kentucky Derby.

They chatted while I marveled, searching my brain for questions and coming up empty. Really, I didn't care about asking questions, I just wanted to be here.

We made our way to the rail, fangirled over our favorite horses, jumped and screamed, and took more pictures as they battled down the homestretch, and then it was done. The clock struck midnight. Time to go.

Trish delivered me to my parents and we showered her with gratitude for creating such a magical day, before making our way to the exit.

On our way out, Mom and Dad gratified me with a trip through the gift shop. While they waited to pay for our souvenirs, I slipped out of the air-conditioned building to stand in the sun. The bright rays warmed my pebbled skin and a heaviness settled in my chest. It went down my body, through my feet, into the ground of the legendary Churchill Downs. I didn't leave a shoe on the front steps—I left a piece of myself, hoping I'd be back soon to reclaim it, but knowing deep down it might not be so easy.

CHAPTER 4

I WATCHED THE EMT's eyes follow the monitors as she asked questions about my life and told me track accidents kept them quite busy. "Why don't you find a more tame hobby?" she suggested. I almost laughed. Most people didn't get it.

She chatted as my mind drifted—half with her, half somewhere else. Anywhere but here. In the middle of a cheery sentence, mid-word, she fell silent. I tore my eyes from the ceiling to see why and noticed an absence of happy creases by her eyes, her mouth transformed into a thin line. "Sweetie, I'm going to need you to take steady, deep breaths." Her eyes focused on a machine to my left. I tried to turn my head but I was trapped. Panic built. Before I could get too desperate, she spoke, gentle and urgent. "Deep breath in! Great, now breathe out. Breathe in! Breathe out."

My heart hammered in my chest as I attempted purposeful, deep breaths. Her brows furrowed, glancing between me and the machines. "Breathe in, breathe out."

My brain raced. *Am I dying? I don't feel like I'm dying. Just breathe. Am I dying? God? I guess if I'm dying I'll see you soon? I'm not sure I'm ready to die. But who is? Help me, God. Am I dying? If I don't die, can I please stay in Kentucky?*

"Breathe in! Breathe out..." As if a switch flipped, the muscles in her face relaxed and she continued our conversation.

I guess I'm not dying.

We rocked back and forth when the ambulance turned into a gas station. O*kay, I'm definitely not dying or they wouldn't be stopping here,* I thought.

"I'm going to run in and get some milk to help preserve this tooth," the driver hollered before I heard the door open and close.

"Does that really work?" I asked the EMT. I'd heard of this, but logically it seemed unlikely.

"I don't know," she answered with a shrug. "But it's worth a shot to try to save that tooth for you."

I wouldn't argue with that. The door clicked and the ambulance lurched as the guy climbed back into the driver's seat. "I got milk!" He poured some into the cup that held my tooth.

"What hospital do you want us to take you to?" he asked. The Jewish hospital was nearby. From the interstate you could see its stunning chandelier. I didn't know much about hospitals, but I knew I wasn't Jewish. Did it matter? Back home we went to the Baptist hospital. Did we go because we were Baptist? Surely any place created to help hurt and sick people would take me. A wave of shame hit hard. I felt judgy. Naive. I was pretty sure it didn't matter. There's no way it mattered. But what if it did? Was there an authority figure standing at the door with a clipboard, asking, "Are you Jewish?" I'd embarrassingly mutter, "No," and the EMTs would load me back into the ambulance, grumbling about what an idiot I was.

That couldn't be how it worked, but what if it was? I stewed until the driver yelled, "We drove past the Jewish hospital. Where do you want to go?"

I stared at the ceiling and mumbled. They tossed out names. Eventually I said, "Just take me to the university hospital." It seemed neutral enough. A safe option. It was close to campus and my apartment.

The EMTs hefted me out on the gurney and wheeled me through the ambulance-only entrance. Pain radiated through my neck and my back ached against the unbending plastic. *I wonder if my body is actually injured.* Robert raced to me, interrupting the thought.

"Sarah, I've got your mom on the phone. I told her everything. Do you want to—"

"Let me talk to her." I needed her to hear my voice, to know I was well enough to talk. This is what I did when I got hurt. Robert held the phone to my ear.

"Hi, mom! So I think I'm going to be fine, but I had an accident on the track. I can't really talk because we're just getting into the hospital."

"Do you need us to come up?"

"No, I think it's okay," I lied. *Yes*! my mind screamed. *But if they come they might take me home. I won't risk that. Plus, I'll have surgery and this will all be over within a day or two. God, please help calm my parents' nerves. And don't let them come get me.*

"Well, let me talk to the doctor or someone," Mom said.

"I love you." Robert took the phone and handed it to the EMT, who talked to Mom before handing it back.

As Robert promised Mom he would take care of me, my eyelids drooped. I drew into myself and blocked out the world. *Can this be over with already? Can they just roll me in and fix me up?* The EMT leaned over my shoulder, her dark brown curls grazing my face. "Don't worry, sweetie. I talked to your mom and she said they won't make you come home."

My cheeks tinged pink and I wondered if I was less with it than I thought. I didn't realize I had shared that fear out loud.

"Thank you." I drew the words out, hoping she heard the sincerity.

The wheels of the ambulance gurney rolled to a stop inside a curtained room. There were several "rooms" made with walls of fabric. A bustling nurses' station stood in the center of it all. They leaned over computers, wrote on clipboards, and tossed things on the counter before hurrying off to another patient.

"We're going to need to lift you and move you over to the hospital gurney, okay sweetie?" the female EMT said, her eyes filled with apology.

"That's fine," I replied. *Why does she need to apologize? This is her job.*

With one EMT at my head and the other at my feet, they 1, 2, 3'd and lifted swiftly and gently, transferring me, the orange board, and the neck brace of misery to the hospital gurney.

"I need to fill out paperwork, but I'll drop back in to check on you before I go," the girl promised. The driver waved and nodded as he wheeled the rolling bed away.

And then I was alone. Trying to distract myself from the pain that spread along my back and neck, I zoned in on the conversation next door. Two nurses asked a man questions, but his voice slurred and he repeated himself. *It can't be later than 9 a.m. I don't understand. Is he drunk from last night? Is it drugs? How old is this guy? He sounds older, like maybe in his 50s. Is he homeless?* My mind painted an image of a white man with flushed red skin, a week of stubble, and greasy dark brown hair that nearly touched his eyes.

A familiar face popped in. "Sweetie, I filled out the paperwork. I've got to get back on the road, but I wanted to say bye and wish you the best." Her brows furrowed and her eyes glistened with guilt I didn't understand. Her compassion touched me, but the sooner she left the sooner the nurses would show up and get me fixed. *It will be fine,* I told myself as I bid her farewell and again thanked her for her help. Her warmth was still in the room when Robert ducked in. He rocked back and forth, glancing around. *Is he nervous?*

"Well, Sarah, everything is taken care of. I've got to go check on my horses and I decided I'm going to go ahead and get back home to Mississippi when I'm done, so I've got to get going."

"Okay," I replied, trying to understand what was going on, why his plans had changed so suddenly, and what the hurry was.

"Thank you, Robert." An awkward tension filled the space between us. He needed to go. I needed these nurses and doctors to make this better. He wished me luck, told me to call if I needed anything, and ducked out.

In this hive of activity, I was completely alone. Closing my eyes, I filled my lungs with as deep a breath as I could. The straps holding me onto the orange board restricted my lungs. Pain momentarily consumed me as I slowly let the breath out. *Nurses will be here soon.*

I'm in a hospital in Louisville, Kentucky, I reminded myself. I couldn't decide which was more significant, being in a hospital or in Kentucky. Was I still living my dream if I was simply in Louisville? Or did I need to be on the back of a racehorse? Somehow Kentucky had become as much a part of the dream as the horses—like I couldn't have one without the other.

Three weeks before, my truck sagged with the weight of furniture, clothes, and the gold shag rug I'd saved from my grandparents' trash bin. Gideon rode behind in a two-horse trailer. Suitcases filled the space for a second horse. Mom and my new dog, Sandi, sat next to me, staring ahead as rain drummed the roof and windshield, making it hard to see. I crept out of the Winterview Farm parking lot on our way to Kentucky, thrilled to finally be driving toward my dream.

My brother Joel swore that if we drove fast, the forward movement would create an air pocket and keep things in the back of the truck dry. I really hoped he was right. Everything needed to be moved into my third-floor apartment that evening.

I wasn't sure if I believed in luck, but maybe this was like rain on a wedding day, a sign of good things to come.

With a white-knuckled grip on the steering wheel, I drove north on I-55. The CD player rotated between No Doubt, Shane & Shane, and Jack Johnson. Every song held a memory, from being fifteen feet away from Gwen Stefani at Voodoo Fest in New Orleans, to watching the sunrise on the back of my friend Lauren's boat when we were out early to catch the good water. If I focused too much on what I was leaving behind, I'd turn around. I loved my life—my family, friends, church, all of it. There was just one thing they couldn't give me—the chance to gallop racehorses.

I knew little about the racing industry, but it didn't take a master to know there was a ton of racing in Kentucky. My apartment and the University of Louisville were less than five miles from *the* Churchill Downs. I could wake up early, work at the track, then head to class by 10 a.m. It took about fifteen phone calls before I found a trainer who would teach me to gallop. He said to call when I got to town. There was a lot riding on a five-minute phone conversation, but all I could do was trust that Craig would be good on his word. If he wasn't, surely someone else would help me out.

The rain pounded so loud we could barely hear the music, much less converse. I had a lot to say to my mom and she probably had a lot to say to me, but the unspoken words drifted around us in the hum of the rain. *I love you. Thank you. Leaving doesn't mean I don't love you. I see your love for me by the way you're helping me leave home and a scholarship for this crazy dream.*

They hadn't wanted me to move to Kentucky. If my dad had his way, I would have graduated from their Alma Mater, Mississippi College, and gone to medical school. But I guess they'd learned that when I truly wanted something, stopping me was like stopping a runaway horse. They showed their support in their own subtle ways. Mom was driving up with me to help get me settled, and Dad had gone with me to get Sandi. He was meeting us in a couple days.

Focusing enough to drive in a downpour helped keep my mind on what was directly ahead. Three hours in, the rain broke. My brain was mush and my hands shook. We needed a break. Mom and I discussed getting Gideon out. This was my first long drive with a horse and if my nerves were frayed, he was probably exhausted as well.

We pulled into a vacant lot next to a gas station in rural Tennessee. I undid the latches on the trailer so the ramp could drop to the ground, and Gideon turned his head just enough to see me in his peripheral vision. He was definitely looking forward to getting off the trailer. Southern summer heat combined with post-rain humidity clung to our skin as Gid carefully backed down the ramp, getting all four feet onto solid ground. He took a deep stretch, straightening his front legs and poking his haunches in the air like a cat after a good nap. He lifted his magnificent head into the air, ears forward, taking in his surroundings. Then he put his head down and tore into the grass. We relaxed in the sun as rain lifted from the ground in a hazy steam. Mom and I chatted about our to-do list and checked on my things. Everything felt damp but not waterlogged.

Thirty minutes later, energized by the rest with our nerves calmed, I tugged on Gid's lead rope. "Come on, Gid! It's time to go." We had become lunchtime entertainment for a group of workers who sat on the curb eating. With awkward, polite nods to the guys, I pulled again on the rope to lift Gid's head from the grass and get him loaded in the trailer. He lifted his head, planted his feet, and refused to budge.

It took over an hour, maybe even two. I used every tactic and technique I had ever learned to get that horse back in the trailer, all while the crowd of guys sat and watched, drinking mega cans of Arizona tea. I sweated, prayed, fought tears, and muttered curse words. I scanned the horizon, thinking of our long drive to Gideon's new barn in Indiana and about what would happen if he didn't get back in the trailer. Then I realized that unless he ran away from me, which he probably wouldn't do, he'd eventually walk up the ramp.

The gawking onlookers dispersed, bored or needing to get back to work, and I took a deep breath. However long it took, it would happen. Eventually, Gid exhaled a deep sigh before clip-clopping his way into the trailer. I yelled to Mom, who quickly latched the butt bar that would keep him secure in his compartment. Once the bar was in place, I tied him to the trailer with a quick-release knot. Then Mom and I lifted the heavy ramp while Gideon jerked tendrils of hay from the hay net, completely chill as if he hadn't just cost us an hour or more.

Taking a quick walk around the trailer to make sure everything was closed, I threw up a prayer of gratitude under my breath. Lesson learned. *Never* take a horse off a trailer in the middle of a road trip unless I'm planning to stay the night.

A couple hours later than planned, we dropped Gideon at his new home in Indiana. I'd found this farm on the internet and it was affordable. The owner swore it would take only thirty-five minutes to get from his barn to downtown Louisville, but it was close to an hour later when we finally pulled up to my apartment.

Dad joined us a day later. We visited Churchill Downs, unpacked my things, made sure I was set to start classes at U of L, and ate at local restaurants. Meals were quiet and tense, and I worried my parents would change their minds at any moment. I had persisted, believed, and set this plan into motion, but now that it was happening, it felt unreal.

After three short days, we stood in my tiny corner bedroom saying goodbyes. They hugged me, Mom cried, and Dad didn't say much. He was probably hiding a pile of his own emotions. Then they went down the rickety stairway to their car and drove away.

The apartment felt empty. Quiet.

I felt empty.

In my visions of Kentucky, there were horses, racetracks, and bluegrass. I hadn't imagined the moment my parents walked out of my apartment to drive back to their lives while I stayed in a new place with approximately four acquaintances. Sandi pressed her nose against me. It was Sandi, Gideon, and me—ready to take on the world. I tried to pump myself up, but my heart stayed heavy. I wanted to lie down. Instead, Sandi and I hopped into my blue GMC Sierra and headed to Indiana to see Gid.

Chapter 5

"Sir, we understand you have a stomachache, but you can't just leave! Sir! Sir!" I imagined the flushed faces of frustrated nurses trying to keep the drunk guy from walking out, and I couldn't decide if this was funny or infuriating. The nurses' station was a flurry of activity that still hadn't made it to my room. I wondered what time it was. How long had I been here? No clock hung from the fabric walls and straps still held me down, rendering me unable to check my phone. It felt like 10 a.m.—when people are no longer drowsy from an early morning and not quite tired from the day. Ten o'clock energy is demanding and urgent, and so was every hospital worker darting around the triage area.

I was hurting but surely they would get to me soon. A doctor would arrive, the angels would sing, and they would remove me from the board and neck brace and rush me to surgery. I was supposed to be with Robert today, watching his horse run. If she won, we would have gone to the winner's circle together for the photo. It would have been the ultimate of track experiences. Instead I was strapped to this board of misery. I searched the doorway for someone who could relieve me from my torture devices.

I'll be after the guy next door. I can wait. The world doesn't revolve around me.

The drunk guy left, replaced with someone being peppered with questions about their leg. I could hear wheels hum past my curtain, followed by padding footsteps of what must be a family member as the guy was rushed to x-rays. My mind drifted, imagining scenarios in which a person broke their leg: falling down the stairs, a car accident, being attacked by someone with a crowbar. I landed on a soccer game incident. *How can a broken leg be more urgent than a possible broken back? If they aren't worried, they wouldn't have me strapped down.* My thoughts ratcheted my anger. *If you aren't worried, unstrap me!* I wanted to scream! My skin itched and a lump built in my throat. *I need to get free.*

I inhaled deeply, trying to calm the tension that threatened to explode. A vision of my guts dripping from the curtains, a literal explosion of self, danced across my mind and I coaxed my thoughts to a different route.

It's fine. You're fine. You're safe, I told myself. *God, get their attention. Get them to help me, please.*

The guy with the broken leg returned from x-rays and a load of concerned staff came and went on his side of the curtain. Then he was gone and someone new took the room.

Maybe the world doesn't revolve around me, but it's my turn! I should scream and cry like they'd expect a girl in my situation to do. That might get their attention.

As I pondered giving in to my emotions, a couple women in scrubs peeked into my room. One asked in a curt tone, "Do you have any pain or reason to believe you have a back injury?"

My nostrils flared as I grasped at composure. *Stay calm and polite.* The last thing I needed was to piss off the people who were here to help. But my voice shook with anger when I replied. "Yes! My back hurts and my neck hurts." They shared a dismissive look, but I continued, "I honestly can't tell if I'm injured or if it's because you've left me strapped to a board in an oversized neck brace for *hours!*" Their eyes rolled. I wanted to howl and rip the curtains from the walls and throw things until they actually saw *me. If they keep me strapped down much longer, they'll really need these straps,* I thought as I slipped further into a pit of rage. I tried my hardest to remain calm and polite. I needed to be released. Free.

The nurses walked away.

I couldn't clench my jaw. I couldn't throw things. I wouldn't yell or scream. So instead, tears made the short trip from my eyes to the hair above my ears. I seethed at my vulnerability.

"We're taking you to x-rays," someone said a few minutes later. With a nurse on each end of the gurney, they unlocked the wheels and rolled me away. I closed my eyes and focused on breathing. My body hurt. I couldn't understand why these ladies were so frustrated with me. I slipped into a fog.

When I returned, they yanked at the straps that held me captive. Pain radiated down my spine, and my muscles screamed as they tilted me to the side and pulled the board away. It hurt so much. It felt so good. Maybe my back was broken. Maybe I didn't care if they would just get that thing off me.

"Now you need to take off your clothes and put on this gown," a nurse snapped. I looked her in the eye, pausing so she could take in every bit of my brokenness, pain, and frustration. I imagined taking my jeans off by myself: unbuttoning, shimmying to get them over my hips, and then bending over to get them past my feet. My muscles felt stuck in the shape of the orange board.

"I'm not sure I can," I replied, hating that I needed help, and despising even more that the only people available to give it seemed to loathe my existence. I glared like a wounded stray dog, willing to do whatever it took to defend myself, to hold on to at least a piece of my pride. The nurses looked me up and down before the hardness in their features lifted the smallest degree.

"We'll help you," the lady on the left replied.

"Please don't cut my jeans. They're my favorite." My voice softened with the plea.

Soon, little white circles were stuck to my skin under the hospital gown, wires connecting them to monitors. I was still in the curtain room, but at least I was on a bed in a nearly sitting position. The nurses strode to the exit and informed me a doctor was on the way. I believed them. They left.

A hospital mattress with a thin blanket wasn't the Four Seasons, but it was a vast improvement over the orange board. I listened to the activity around me, thinking about everything going on at the training track, wondering how Red was, and waiting for someone to come fix me so I could get back to my new life. Signs saying, "NO CELL PHONE USAGE IN THIS AREA" seemed to yell every time I considered pulling out my phone. Eventually I hid it beside my leg and quickly shot a text to my roommate. "Had a riding accident. In ER at U of L. Can you walk Sandi?" I messaged Craig to update him, as well as my family and Joey.

What a difference between what was happening here and what was probably happening at Mississippi College. The cool sheet tempered the heat of my body, and when my eyes closed, I could see my friends. They were smiling, hugging, and walking across the bright green quad toward the science and math building. I didn't regret leaving, but that didn't stop me from tasting a slight bitterness when I imagined the bubble of joy and love that had been MC.

I fought so hard not to go there. I almost laughed. God must have a sense of humor.

I had this crazy fantasy of riding racehorses, but there were a few problems. There were no racehorses anywhere near where I lived. They only existed in books and on TV during the Triple Crown races. I would have to wait to pursue my dream until after high school. I also planned to go to vet school. That meant after college, I would dive headfirst into tough curriculum and clinicals. Then I'd have a career and maybe a family. I had one window to make the dream happen and it was during my four years of undergrad. I knew nothing about horse racing other than that it happened in the Bluegrass State, so I set my sights on the University of Kentucky.

Every single test in high school suddenly held hope for my future. A good grade meant scholarships and chasing dreams; a poor one meant being stuck in Mississippi, likely going where my parents went—Mississippi College. There wasn't anything wrong with MC, except it wasn't in Kentucky and there wasn't a racetrack down the street.

Throughout high school, I played sports, auditioned for plays, won art awards, held a position in student government, and kept good grades in advanced classes. I just knew with that kind of resume and a 30 on my ACT, the University of Kentucky would beg me to grace their campus and gladly pay my way. "Honestly, aside from Ivy League schools, who wouldn't?" I told my mom as I put the finishing touches on my admissions essay. When she looked at me, her eyes shone with sadness and hope.

Letters started arriving from schools—some asking me to apply, some acceptance letters, and something from the University of Kentucky. It was a simple cream-colored envelope with the logo in the top left corner. All the other mail spilled onto the table as I stared at the envelope. I held it, the smooth texture of the paper beneath my fingertips a premonition. Time slowed. I slipped my finger under the edge of the flap and gently pulled it up. If this was what I hoped it was, I would put it in a scrapbook or frame it. But if it was what I hoped for, wouldn't it come in a linen envelope at least? Wouldn't it be exquisitely textured under the pads of my fingers? I slid the paper out and unfolded it, scanning the words.

The University of Kentucky was pleased to offer me $600 a semester toward my books.

I bit the inside of my lip and blood rushed to my head. The letter made it sound like such a gift, but it was a joke. An insult. Out-of-state tuition at the University of Kentucky was close to $30,000 a year. The dream was slipping through my fingers. I threw the letter on the table and went to the barn, tears burning my already hot cheeks.

The next day, I built up my courage, picked up the kitchen phone, and dialed the number at the bottom of the letter. "The University of Kentucky, this is Stacy speaking!" came through the receiver in a sing-song voice, like she was Snow White singing to her animal friends on a cloudless day.

I inhaled a steadying breath. "Hi Stacy, my name is Sarah. I'm calling about the $600 scholarship offer I received in the mail this week."

"Oh, wonderful Sarah! Congratulations!" she said, as if I had won the lottery. As if $600 was even enough to park my car for a year, which it probably wasn't.

"Yeah, well, thanks!" I tried to match her cheerful tone. "The thing is, I'm coming from Mississippi, so that's not going to be very helpful considering out-of-state tuition."

"Oh yes, I see your point. But it should be more than enough to cover your books!"

"Uh huh. Well see, I made a 30 on my ACT. I scored almost perfect on the reading portion. I have nearly a 4.0 GPA in the most advanced classes my school offers. I was wondering if maybe y'all could review my application or something? Because $600 a semester isn't enough to get me to your school." I shocked myself with my bravery and was grateful Stacy couldn't see the tangled mess of my insides.

"Wow, that's all really impressive!" she said like a cheery robot on autopilot. "But $600 is the best we can offer you."

"Okay." My hands shook and I hoped she couldn't hear it in my voice. I tried to sound confident, like I didn't need them to make my dream come true. "The University of Kentucky will regret this. You're missing out on a really great applicant," I blurted before hanging up the phone. Defiance that they couldn't see my worth warred with utter despair. *What now?*

I didn't want to go to Mississippi College. I didn't want to follow in my parents' and brothers' footsteps. I was a trailblazer.

One weekday afternoon I drove home from school and pulled up to the mailbox, hoping for surprise scholarship letters from anyone other than MC. The heavy iron front of the mailbox clunked open and I peered into the half cylinder. The light bounced off kelly green wrapping paper. I'd heard about this wrapping paper from friends—friends who were excited and hopeful for their future because of what it contained. I could still see the spark in one of my friend's eyes when she bounced into class two days earlier telling us about her green envelope. My hands shook and red splotches climbed up my neck onto my face. I reached into the mailbox and pulled the gaudy envelope into my lap. Slowly my fingers found a seam and peeled open the flap, my heart growing hollow as the rubber cement stretched into tiny strings and gave way. I read the letter.

"Congratulations! We at Mississippi College are excited to offer you a leadership scholarship!" It was the highest scholarship MC offered.

Sitting in my blue pickup truck in front of my house, I melted into a red-faced, snot-nosed, crying mess of broken dreams. It wasn't fair. I had worked so hard, believed so big, and here I was—trapped by a life-changing scholarship I couldn't refuse. This plus the scholarship from the state meant an education at a highly regarded private college would be nearly free. A girl from a middle-class family didn't turn down a free ride to such an excellent school unless there was something just as good or better offered to her. And there wasn't.

This was the hundred-dollar bill flicked to the table, when all my heart wanted was a horse at the mailbox.

My dad excitedly announced to everyone he saw that I would follow in his footsteps and attend Mississippi College. I came along behind him and set everyone straight. Nothing was set in stone. I took every detour I could find, applying to

Mississippi State and even lining up a roommate. I just wanted to blaze my own trail.

It didn't matter. No one beat Mississippi College's offer.

Mom and Dad cornered me in the kitchen one night after dinner. I was the last to finish eating. When I turned to leave the table, there they were. Mom was a bit ashen. Dad was red. My pulse picked up at the idea of confrontation. Maybe they wanted the best for me, I got that. But what about what I wanted for myself? How come no matter how hard I tried, this wasn't coming together?

"You're not going to Mississippi State," my dad said. "You've got the highest scholarship Mississippi College offers on the table. It's a great school. You can go there and do pre-med or pre-vet and go on to be a brain surgeon or a... a horse vet."

God help me, I prayed. I looked at them, scrounging for anything. "I'll make you a deal." The idea popped into my head the very moment I said it. The words were a white flag that felt like a bullet to the leg. "I'll go to Mississippi College, but only if you promise me that if I still want to go to Kentucky in two years, I can do it." My eyes were full, but I fought the tears. Tough horse girls don't cry.

Mom and Dad stared at each other, silently communicating. Dad's face grew more red. Mom took a step toward me. "So you're saying you'll go to Mississippi College now and not argue?"

"Yes, ma'am." I looked into my dad's flinty eyes, then hers. "I'll go, and I'll make the best of it. I'll live on campus, and I'll do pre-vet classes for two years."

They looked at each other again. "Okay," Mom said. "And in two years, if you still really want to go to Kentucky, we'll support you."

I looked from her to my dad. His face was a definite scarlet shade, but he agreed. "Give MC two years, and if you still want to transfer, you can." I could hear the disbelief in his voice.

I wanted to smile. We had a deal. I wanted to cry. Two years felt like a lifetime. What if in two years I still couldn't make it happen?

"I'm going to my room," I mumbled, rushing past that cursed green envelope on the kitchen counter. Huddling on the bed with my favorite stuffed horse, I cried and begged God to help me. The tug I had felt when I stood in front of Churchill Downs in Louisville was still there. It was like a rope tethering me to a dream, and I clung to it with both hands, praying for help to get to the other end.

In the fall, I arrived at Mississippi College determined to make the best of it. My dorm room was tiny, and I crammed it with three carloads of junk that felt impossible to live without. My roommate's eyes grew when she saw all my stuff, but then she said, "He-Hey Roommate! That's all right! I love stuff!" She was as untamable as her wild, curly hair. We were so different, yet so similar. She wore medical scrubs that she cut off below the knee and usually had a cigarette between her fingers as she traversed the quad of our Baptist college. She was loud and didn't have a filter and I loved her.

She saved me in her phone as "Roommate," and I did the same; it became our nickname for each other. We barely knew each other before freshman year, yet I couldn't imagine sharing a tiny dorm with anyone else.

They announced the upcoming election for student government. I put my name in the hat for class president and dyed my hair blue so no one could miss me. I joined a social tribe, tried out for plays, and spent two days on the softball team before deciding it took too much time away from the barn. I visited Gideon several times a week to rehab an injury he got that summer. All while taking pre-vet courses.

I decided I wouldn't date my first year. Maybe it was my "give it my all because I'll be leaving soon" attitude or maybe it was my complete lack of interest in dating, but for the first time a lot of guys were interested in me. It was cute, weird, and surreal. Whatever it was, I didn't think too much about it because I wouldn't be here long enough to fall in love with a guy.

I did, however, feel myself falling in love with Mississippi College. It was nearly perfect, and I could see why my family pushed so hard for me to get there. There was just one problem: there were still no racetracks nearby.

Chapter 6

Names and faces looped through my mind and I longed to cruise down the highway with my friend Chip, the road our stage as we sang every song on my favorite Broadway soundtrack. I imagined bobbing up and down in Lake Bruin with Lauren in the driver's seat of her family's boat as she pushed the accelerator and lifted me onto a wakeboard. Or maybe sitting on Gideon at Winterview Farm under the hot Mississippi sun, practicing jumps. I'd like to be anywhere, really, aside from where I was.

My bladder pulled me from my daydreams and back to the reality of cords and machines, and the realization that I hadn't used the bathroom since I left my apartment around 6 a.m.

The ER felt sleepy. Faces that were once alive and vibrant were now more creased and their steps dragged. I'd guess it was two in the afternoon–naptime or coffee time.

Simple sounds became offensive: shuffling feet, muffled voices, papers, machine beeps. The hub of activity forgot about me again. I reached up to brush hair out of my face and my fingers grazed crusty dirt.

People hustled past my door. "Excuse me," I called, earning a side glance before they hurried off. "Excuse me!" I tried again a little louder. But my urgency just melded into the rushed atmosphere. "HELLO!" A few eyes glanced up before instantly dismissing me as "not my problem." My bladder demanded relief, but cords connected to machines held me in place.

I did the only thing I knew to do and started peeling stickers off my skin. A machine to my left screamed and two nurses dove through the door.

"Whoa whoa whoa, you can't just unplug yourself!" the one in front exclaimed.

Watch me, I thought, nailing her with a look that challenged her to stop me. I pulled another white sticker off my skin.

"I've been in here for hours and I need to pee!" I seethed, continuing to pull at wires. There was so much more I wasn't saying.

The boar of a lady shifted, joining my fight for freedom as she helped disconnect me. I stood, turning to see small piles of dirt between wrinkles in the sheets. Lifting my chin, I limped along. The nurse followed with my IV bag and guided me to the small bathroom. My mouth felt like it belonged to a monster, and as I swung the bathroom door open, I realized I'd have to look in the mirror.

My stomach twisted and I considered foregoing the whole thing and just not peeing. A throb from my bladder stole that choice. I vowed to keep my eyes down as I shuffled through the door with the IV bag. "I'll wait right out here," the nurse said.

"Thanks." I kept my eyes trained on the doorknob while closing the door. I backed up to the toilet, and as I tried to maneuver my sore body into position, my treacherous eyes swept over and up before I could stop them.

There I was.

Clean lines connected the outside corners of my eyes to the tops of my ears. I realized they were tear tracks. The rest of my face was several shades darker than my barely tan summer complexion. Brown patches looked almost like a beard trying to grow in. I reached up and touched one of them and dirt fell into my lap. *God. They let me lay there for hours looking like this. They glanced in that open doorway, removed me from the board, and attached me to machines without even a thought of letting me wipe my face?* It seemed like such a simple, essential piece of humanity. A clean face. *God, please help me through this. Help me not to hate them.*

I finished my business and washed my hands. The soap and water turned brown before swirling down the drain. I grabbed two paper towels, folded them into a rectangle, and ran them under the water to clean my face.

"Ma'am, are you okay?" I heard through the door.

"Yeah, I'm just..." What was I doing? Cleaning myself? Surveying the damage? Facing reality? "Yeah, I'm coming."

I tried to wipe the rust-looking spot on the side of my mouth. The metal smell of blood had clung to me for hours, my new perfume. My top two front teeth were twisted, tapered to sharp points. A toothless gap extended on the right to a premolar pointing more toward the inside of my mouth than down. One tooth on the bottom broke off at the root. I felt the roof of my mouth with my tongue. It was the one thing I had felt all day. The right side felt bigger, like somehow bone had been pushed in or down.

I stared, realizing I could clearly see where the hoof made contact. Huge welts on my top and bottom lip lined up to tell the story. It was disgusting and painful. But I looked up an inch from the hoof marks. If he'd hit my nose or a couple inches higher on my head, where would I be? *Okay, God. Thank you*, I prayed, gritting my teeth at Him in my mind. *Now can you get me fixed up so we can get over this?*

"I'm done," I mumbled to the nurse, who opened the door and helped me back to the bed. It was paradise compared to looking at my face.

Fresh sheets and kind smiles greeted me, and I breathed a little easier. Another hour passed, an hour more in line with my initial expectation, where people actually checked on me and seemed to care. A dentist in residency showed up, a thin woman with boy-short blond hair, and I remembered the time in ninth grade when I tried a similar haircut. It looked much better on her (and on my inspiration, Meg Ryan) than it ever had on me.

The lady grabbed dental tools and asked me to lie back so she could peer into my mouth. Sitting on a stool, she leaned over with a headlamp that shined into my face. I squinted and opened my mouth. She stared for a moment before moving the instruments around, seeming unsure of what to actually do with them. Then she sat up and faced the wall, taking deep breaths.

Well, this is interesting, I thought as she hovered over me again, waving a mirror and a pointy thing. She sat up and looked at the floor.

"My tooth's in that cup," I said, gesturing toward the little side table. "We only found one of them." I was no expert, but it looked like more were missing.

"Okay."

Her skin seemed lighter than when she arrived. I peered into her face, finding it incredibly intriguing and a bit unnerving that I caused such a reaction in this sharp-looking lady. It would have been funny in nearly any other situation. She shakily declared she needed to call a specialist, wrapped up her tools, and fled.

I had ripped cords from my body, earned the respect of some tough nurses, and scared off an intern. I felt brave, so I ignored the no cell phone signs and responded to my text messages while I waited on this "specialist."

A nurse strode in and my bravery wilted as I scrambled to hide the phone behind my leg. "Don't worry about it!" she chuckled. "I've brought someone to see you."

Macy, my roommate, followed the nurse into my little home for the day, brandishing a bag. Her pasted-on smile was as fake as Dolly Parton's breasts, but I appreciated her effort. Her eyes darted around before finally laser-beaming to my own, an obvious attempt to avoid my mouth.

"I walked Sandi for you! And brought you some clothes."

"Thank you so much. It's been a long day. How's Sandi?"

"She seems good," Macy replied with a softer tone than normal. "I think she misses you."

How can she know my dog misses me? I wondered, but maybe it was true. I definitely missed Sandi.

"I'm going to Bob's tonight, but I'll be home around ten or eleven. Do you have a way to get back to the apartment?"

"Yeah. Craig said he'd pick me up and give me a ride home." I hated being a burden to Macy, and Craig seemed like he wanted to pick me up. I figured he wanted to lay eyes on me after the accident.

"Well, see you later tonight!" she said as she ducked out of the room.

"Bye! Thanks so much!" I called after her. I grabbed my phone to check messages. Craig was asking when I thought I'd be done and telling me he'd come in a couple hours.

"Waiting for specialist. That should work. Thank you!" I sent back. I shot Mom a quick message to let her know I was doing okay, then texted my riding friend Lauren. She had told me racehorses were dangerous and not like the show horses we were used to. *Yep*, I thought as I updated her on my injured status, grateful she kindly withheld the "I told you so" she could say. Last, I texted my boyfriend Joey. He was on the road to his final beach trip with his friends before moving an hour and a half south of Louisville to start grad school at the University of Kentucky.

My two nurses took turns checking in, fluffing my pillow, and offering to get me things. The idea of eating or drinking terrified me, so I politely declined. A few hours after the resident bailed, the specialist showed up. He ordered x-rays and they wheeled me back. I considered telling them I could walk. It seemed ridiculous to ride when my legs worked fine, but it seemed like protocol. Plus, it was kind of fun after being stuck in that cloth box of a room for so long. I stared at the walls and down the halls, trying not to gawk at other patients as I rode by.

Back in my cloth prison, the dentist studied the x-rays for a few seconds. "There may be a bone chip in your lip," he informed me with a heavy accent. "I'll need to lance that lip."

Dixie once had a wound on her face that refused to heal. When the vet flushed it we found out why—bone chips were floating around in there. Imagining Dixie's gnarly face that wouldn't close until all the fragments were out, I simply replied, "okay."

He reclined the bed and scooted up next to my head. He was a man of few words but carried a confidence that demanded the rest of us shut up and let him work. After a quick shot of numbing medicine into the wound, he took a scalpel and lanced my lip open. He squeezed on it to push the possible tooth fragments out, but all I saw was a stream of blood coming from my face. "No bone chip," he declared casually.

I want to punch him, I thought as he moved to the next order of business like he hadn't just ruined my lip and left an even worse gaping wound.

"I'm going to glue this bar onto your front teeth. One is stable, but the other is not. The bar will help anchor the unstable one for now." I stared at the ceiling with my mouth open and instruments moving in and out. *Am I supposed to respond? It can't be any worse than braces, right?* The part of my brain that believed unicorns are real wondered when they were going to wheel me into surgery to fix my face.

The dentist sat up and broke the silence in his abrupt tone. "That's all I can do for right now. You'll need to wait two weeks for things to heal and then you can come back to the dental school."

Um... what?

"Two weeks? I'm supposed to stay like this? Isn't there surgery or something you can do to fix this?" It was a desperate plea.

"No. Two weeks. We can't do anything until your mouth heals from all the teeth moving around."

Are you freaking kidding me? I wanted to scream, cry, or if this was true, stick my head in a hole like an ostrich until it was over. But I was also exhausted with this place and ready to go back to my apartment and Sandi. I recalled the words of Scarlet O'Hara, whose book I never actually finished, *I'll think about it tomorrow.* Then I excused myself to the bathroom.

I flipped on the light and my eyes caught my reflection in the mirror. I definitely looked like I had somersaulted with a thousand-pound animal. My ponytail hung lopsided and limp and lines spread from the inner corners of my eyes to the middle of my cheek. I couldn't feel my lip and was afraid to move my mouth for fear of catching it on the point of one of my teeth and wounding it more. I hoped Red was doing better than me. *God, can you take care of Red?*

I leaned forward, studying the dentist's handiwork in the mirror. This wasn't braces with thin wires and colorful clean brackets. It was a metal bar. Maybe they'd cut half-inch off a nail somewhere? Surely this wasn't a typical dental thing. The glue was tobacco-spit brown. I looked like every kid's nightmare when their mom tells them to brush their teeth or they'll rot out. *God, what is this?* I seethed. *Did the dentist rummage through the toolbox in his car and just grab some scrap metal and Gorilla Glue?* My lip was huge and felt like a rubber tire protruding from my face. *What the heck, dentist guy?* I thought, shaking my head. *Is this even real?* I considered pinching myself to make sure, but my body had enough trauma for the day.

I'll think about it tomorrow. Maybe I can complete my crazy new look with a dress made out of curtains. The ones from the ER would work perfectly.

"You're free to go whenever your ride gets here," my nurse said with a smile as I limped back into the room. "Can I get you anything while you wait?"

"I'm fine, thank you. My friend said he'd be here soon." Actually, Craig said he'd be here at three, which had come and gone a while ago, but my ride choices were slim. I shot him a quick text: "Hey, they said I can go. Where are you?" I needed to update my mom and Joey, but exhaustion pulled me back onto the sterile white sheets. I stared into the fabric hanging from the ceiling until it looked like millions of little particles weaving around each other. Then I eavesdropped on the nurses' station, and when that grew boring, I closed my eyes in an attempt to shut everything out.

Eventually, Craig arrived.

His smiling eyes and devilish grin washed away the top layers of desperation. I'd guess Craig was double my age, but it felt like he was a high school kid playing guardian to my barely-adult self. We filled out paperwork and got my prescriptions and discharge notes.

God pushed the dimmer switch on daylight as we walked into the parking lot. Craig asked about food.

"I don't know," I replied. "I'm sure I need to eat something—I haven't eaten all day. But I don't know what I can get down, or if I even want to."

He bought me a milkshake and some carry-out food that sat in white Styrofoam containers on my lap. While he ran into Walgreens to get my prescription filled, I called my parents and Joey so they could hear my voice and know I was really alive.

"Man," Joey said when he answered the phone. "Man, I'm so sorry. We're so sorry." As he apologized for something he had no control over, my petty satisfaction with putting a damper on his boys trip fizzled out. I had wanted him in Kentucky instead of the beach, with me instead of his guy friends. I could see the insecurity and jealousy for what it was—immaturity. I couldn't hang onto that if I wanted to survive, so I let it go and it drifted out the car window.

"Thanks," I muttered, struggling to talk. Craig emerged from Walgreens, bag in hand. "Hey, Craig's coming back. I gotta go."

"Love you. We're all praying for you," he said as the voices of his friends came through the phone.

"Love you too. I'll call you tomorrow. Bye." I finished the conversation but waited for him to end the call before snapping the phone closed.

I tried to drink my milkshake since there was no audience to see me spit it all over myself. I debated over the spoon but was afraid it would bump my teeth. What if the milkshake hurt? What if it caused an infection? What if drinking from a straw caused issues like it did when you got wisdom teeth out? But eventually I realized I didn't have many choices. I put the straw on the left side of my mouth, which was practically damage free, and tried to ingest some calories as Craig got in the car.

My mind drifted to the tables in the cafeteria at Mississippi College—some long and slim and some round, but all containing friends who smiled, laughed, hugged, stressed over tests, and gushed over parties. I felt life there moving on without me as tangibly as I felt the bar on my broken, pointed teeth. I was ready to get back to my apartment and lay in my own bed with Sandi's warm back pressed up against me.

Craig helped me up to the third floor of my apartment, the wood floors groaning and squeaking beneath us. He walked Sandi for me and then left.

My prayers had significantly simplified.

God.

God?

A plea. A statement. A name. It was all I had.

Depleted, I crawled into bed. Sandi nosed her way under the covers and turned so the entire length of her lean, silky body was pressed against me. Facing the wall with one hand under my pillow and the other wrapped around my dog, I drifted into the darkness that had been calling to me all day.

Chapter 7

Light seeped in through my eyelids and reality sat on me like a weighted blanket. My phone buzzed and I briefly rolled away from Sandi's warmth to see whose call I missed. *God help me*, I prayed before flipping the phone open. A voicemail waited and I pushed the button to listen.

"Hey Sarah, it's Terri. I'm on my way to campus and wanted to check on you. Can I get you some breakfast or something? It's no problem; just give me a call before I get to campus if you can. Bye."

I rolled out of bed, biting back a groan. I needed to check in with my roommate and call Terri back. *God, thank you for Terri*. Bringing me breakfast at home was well beyond the duties of an academic counselor, much less one I'd known only a few weeks.

Even before I opened my bedroom door, I could hear the emptiness of the apartment. Disbelieving my ability to sense "emptiness" or my roommate's ability to leave me alone overnight after yesterday's events, I limped to our tiny kitchen and then our giant living room, Sandi's claws clicking against the hardwood next to me.

"Macy!" I called. Sandi touched my hand with her nose. I peeked into Macy's room to find her cat lounging on the bed, but there was no human. It was hard to wrap my head around this. What if something had happened last night? What if the doctors missed an injury or complication and I needed her? Truly, life or death needed her?

A chasm stretched wide and uncrossable between us without her even there to realize it. I missed Roommate—wild and untamable, yet deeply caring. I missed my people from home who would have been here for me. I pushed a few buttons on my gold flip phone and Terri picked up on the second ring.

"Hey, how are you feeling this morning?"

"I'm a little sore but not terrible considering. I'm just going to lie low for a couple days and try to recover. My teeth are really messed up, though. He kicked me while he was flailing."

"I'm so sorry, Sarah. Hey, I'm driving to U of L now. Can I grab you anything? Some breakfast maybe?"

Her offer lifted some of the weight that had settled on me. "Yeah, that would be great. I don't really know what I can eat, though. My mouth is really messed up." I stared at myself in the bathroom mirror while we talked. Lifting my shirt, I looked at my torso to see if there were bruises. I turned and had to work to contain my gasp so I didn't alarm Terri. A thunderstorm of colors painted my lower back.

"What if I got you some pancakes? They should be soft enough to eat," Terry responded. *She's kind and a genius,* I thought as I continued gaping at myself.

"Yes, that should be perfect. I can douse them with syrup and won't need to chew much," I replied, deciding not to mention my new discovery.

"Okay. I'll be there in a few minutes." She drew the words out with concern. I told her where my apartment was and we ended the call.

Craning my neck to see my entire back, I pulled my shorts down a tad and my shirt up higher to see where the bruise started and ended. Thankfully there was no pain or sensitivity. The realization that the God who allowed a horse to tumble down the track also protected me was more than I knew how to handle. Should I say thank you? Or should I slam my hand on the vanity and yell?

My heart felt an oddly simultaneous lift and drag. That bruise told me I am loved. Protected. And it told me I nearly died. Gratefulness, humility, and a resolution not to be angry at my God filled me. But I wasn't exactly sure what to say to Him. I settled on a weak *thank you*.

A few minutes later, footsteps tapped up the back stairs and an angel with straight brown hair, crow's feet, and a Styrofoam carry-out container stood at my door. I wanted to hug her, but I didn't want to be touched, so instead I reached for the container and muttered "thank you" repetitively like a banged-up CD stuck on one spot. She even took Sandi for a quick walk before heading to campus.

After eating pancakes that were more syrup than bread, I snuggled into the fuzzy overstuffed couch with Sandi and drifted in and out of consciousness. The buzz of my phone pulled me back to awareness every hour or two—people checking in. Mom, Joey, Lauren, Craig. Moving my mouth to talk was painful, but they needed to know I was okay. Mom asked about Sandi and said she was glad I had her. "Me too," I mumbled.

God, please just hold me in your hand, I prayed as I hung up and clung to my dog.

Joey called from the beach house and gave me play-by-plays of his friends' shenanigans the night before. Then he told me his parents were praying for me and that he missed me.

"You too," I said, unable to muster much more. We hung up and my mind drifted to another time and place. Before the accident. Before Kentucky.

The summer between freshman and sophomore years had been nearly perfect. It was windows down, cranking my favorite band and singing at the top of my lungs with the wind whipping my hair. Freedom. I worked at a local barn and at the vet hospital and spent time with Gideon. Most evenings were spent at Buffalo Wild Wings with six medium wings and a trivia board in front of me. On weekends, I slept in a waterbed next to Lauren at her lake house in Louisiana. We woke up with the sun to catch the best water before all the other boaters were out.

But amid the perfection I felt a tug on my heart. God hadn't taken the dream away. Kentucky was calling. It was time to take my parents up on their promise. Two years at MC and then I could spread my wings. When I stepped onto campus at Mississippi College for sophomore year, my body flooded with emotions. This would be my last year with this family. I would miss this place and these people deeply, but I couldn't wait to leave and chase the dream.

As school got underway, loneliness grabbed hold of me. Some friends had graduated and others were busy with sports practices, classes, and work. The pre-veterinary classes were demanding, and the sophomore slump hit hard. It was like standing in a wobbly canoe on a wavy lake while my friends zoomed around on sleek ski boats. I waved and smiled, laughing the fakest laugh I could muster, while trying not to plunge into murky waters. I had an unexplainable understanding that God was at work, and I clung to it to keep from drowning.

A few weeks into the school year, the student government gathered for the annual yearbook picture. As sophomore class president, that included me. Dressed in my only professional outfit, I pasted on a smile and took my place in the group. The photographer arranged us by class and height on the risers and took several pictures amid the back-and-forth joking that happens in a room full of social butterflies. I loved these butterflies in small settings, but they overwhelmed me in large groups.

As the photographer finished, the mass of people broke into chatty clusters and I bent over to gather my backpack and leave. When I stood up, Joey Hickner, the Senior Class President, stood on the step below mine, blocking my exit.

Everyone knew this guy, and everyone on our small campus knew me, but somehow we'd met only once. It was an evening I'd never forget. At the end of freshman year, the four class presidents sat on the floor sorting slips of paper with names on them, determining which friends and classmates won or lost the race for student senate. The spotlight quickly shifted onto this Joey Hickner guy, who regaled us with the story of being selected for a summer internship in Washington, DC. I counted votes in silence.

Here we were on the risers, meeting again. This time, Joey Hickner, center of attention, turned his attention on me. The corner of my mouth tipped up in amusement as I took in his blue eyes, messy brown hair, and reddish goatee.

We were eye to eye, and when he smiled I got a close-up view of how his entire face lit up.

If I were a romantic, I would have fantasized about jumping into his arms, being swung in a circle with centrifugal force pulling my feet out from under me, then walking arm and arm into the sunset.

But I'm a horse girl who'd done a lot of life on her own since school started, so I cocked my eyebrow and allowed some warmth to seep in.

"Hey, I was wondering... d'you wanna go to the Homecoming Dance with me?"

In my head, I became a fish, mouth opening and closing in shock. *Joey Hickner just asked me to Homecoming?* I laughed at the absurdity of it all. Boys I barely knew noticed me, yet I felt so alone. *This is weird, God. This is the opposite of normal life.*

On the outside, I gave a coy smile. I tried to let him down easy. He was a baseball player with more than enough confidence to handle it, but nobody likes rejection. "Thanks so much for asking, but I've already got a date."

"Oh, really?" He said it like he didn't believe me. Like it was some lie I concocted to get out of his offer, as believable as "I'll be washing my hair."

"Yep! Thanks for asking, though. I'm sorry I can't go with you," I said, shocked to realize it was true. But Mom had taught me that you go with the first person who asks or you don't go at all. I felt silly and old-fashioned, but I'd never break it off with one guy to go with another.

"All right, well, I've got to go study in my top-secret study spot." Joey backpedaled from his rejection by throwing out a line. I saw it for what it was and laughed as I took the bait.

"Oh really? Top secret, huh?"

"Yep! But since you're not going to Homecoming with me, I'm not telling you where it is." Electricity zinged through my body as the first genuine smile in recent memory graced my face. *Man, I want to go to Homecoming with this guy.*

"Well, I guess I'll never know. It's fine, anyway. Roommate is almost never in our room this year. She's always with the softball team or something, so it's pretty quiet." Even mentioning it opened the chasm in my chest. She had been one of my closest friends freshman year and now, no matter how late I stayed up, she was rarely home when I finally crashed. If I saw her, I was tiptoeing past her to an 8 a.m. class while she slept. "Have a good study session." I gave Joey a lopsided grin, knowing he wanted me to bite again, to beg to be invited.

We slung our backpacks on our shoulders and walked out together. It filled part of the emptiness to have someone next to me as I exited the room.

I turned to look at Joey, from his curly brown hair to his well-worn Doc Martins. "All right, see ya later," I offered, not sure what else to say.

"See ya! I'm heading to my top-secret study spot! Don't you wish you could come?" Even in the darkness, I could see the sparkle in his eyes. I turned toward my dorm with a wave and yelled over my shoulder, "Good luck with that! Have fun!" and walked through the darkness between buildings.

God, he seems quite interested in me. My insides warmed at the thought and I almost laughed. Of all the guys who were doe-eyed around me at this place, I never expected Joey Hickner to be interested. *Maybe I'll let things play out and see what happens.*

My phone buzzed, bringing me back to the blue couch in Louisville, Kentucky. *I'll check it later.* I allowed the warmth from that night with Joey to seep into my chest. Right now, though, I needed to survive the next two weeks until the dentist could fix me. I wrapped my arm around my dog and we drifted back to sleep.

The door swung open. Sandi and I startled, lifting our heads and blinking. The quick, confident steps were the opposite of the serene girl who shared the two-bedroom apartment with me.

"Hey lady, how are you? Macy told me about the accident. Where is she, anyway?" It was Kat, Macy's best friend.

"Hey," I muttered, letting the condition of my face tell her what she needed to know. "Macy never came home last night. She said she was going to Bob's and would be home late, but I haven't seen her since yesterday."

"What? Honey, I'm so sorry." Annoyance darkened her face. *Same.* "Do you need some food?"

Kat walked Sandi and grabbed lunch for us. We scooped noodles from Chinese takeout boxes with chopsticks while she chatted nonstop, and I nodded every few seconds. *At least my roommate picked a good best friend.*

Kat left as abruptly as she arrived, leaving the space empty in her wake. I switched from the couch to my bed and back, Sandi always at my heels. About the time I decided I was over being pitiful, a message pinged in from Craig.

"Hey, how are you feeling?"

"Okay. Sore. Bored."

"Want to grab dinner? I can pick you up."

My mind bounced with options. *No, I probably shouldn't. I probably can't even eat. I don't need to give Craig ideas. But I may go crazy in this apartment by myself.*

A couple hours later, I sat in a booth that was more like an overfilled exercise ball. My brain signaled to smile, to sit, to tell the waitress my order, to respond to Craig, but it felt like someone else's body, someone else struggling to smile, and sit, and trust. Craig's eyes had roved over me before in ways that made me question his intentions. Surely it was in my head. I didn't want him to expect anything beyond friendship. Even as I thought the words, his gaze lingered.

He pulled the paper off my straw and put it in my drink, dressed my baked potato, and cut my steak into tiny bites so I could eat with minimal chewing. I didn't want to need him. Technically, I didn't. My hands were possibly the only part of my body not hurting, but I didn't object. Feeding myself seemed like so much work. If left to me, I wouldn't have cut the steak. I wouldn't have eaten it either.

Chapter 8

Monday morning I walked into a small dentist's office an hour before the normal opening time.

The front desk stood just five paces from the door and behind it sat a brown-haired, middle-aged woman with a gentle smile. She introduced herself as Judy and said she would let Dr. Vittitow know I had arrived. She disappeared into the back hall and I absorbed the clean scent, stacks of brochures, waiting room with just four chairs, and TV that played a video about gentle aesthetic dentistry on repeat.

My eyes were drawn to pamphlets with before and after photos. I looked considerably worse than any of the before pictures. Whoever made them needed to find a case like mine. That would be a much more exciting makeover.

Judy returned and behind her strolled a tall man with disarming dimples. My childhood dentist had told us about this man. "Back in dental school, Charles really loved the Lord," he'd said. "He could have changed, but he was a really good guy back then." Judging by the fact that he opened his practice early for me, he hadn't changed.

"Hey, Sarah! I'm Charles Vittitow!" He extended his hand and I grasped it, pouring strength into the shake. "Let's get you looked at and see what we can do." Then he started in on a story about he and my childhood dentist in school together. It seemed easier to breathe in this place.

He peered into my mouth, moving instruments around and gently touching things. "They sure did a number on you at the hospital with that bar! Next time something like this happens, come straight to me, okay? Don't go to the emergency room. Come to me."

"Okay, I'll be sure to come straight here next time," I nodded, trying to decide whether I should laugh or cry at the idea. *Dear God, I hope there's never a next time.* It seemed as improbable as being struck by lightning.

Soon I stared into a camera while Judy told me to face forward with a straight face, then smile, then turn to each side. She showed me the photos on a tiny rectangular screen. My sun-bleached ponytail hung to the side and my blue eyes reflected the light like swimming pools while I smiled with brown, jagged teeth. The lip wound battled for attention, still swollen and weeping, like rotted flesh. *It'll heal. This'll pass*, I tried to console myself. *Just get through today. God, help me get through this.*

Dr. Vittitow popped back into the room. "Unfortunately, the ER dentist was correct. We've got to give your mouth time to heal for a bit before we can do anything. That one front tooth ..."

Everything after "give your mouth time" was a blur of medical jargon and things I didn't care to hear. My teeth were messed up. Details weren't important. "Okay," I said in disappointment. "Is there anything we can do now? This bar with the glue is just so embarrassing."

"Well, I've assembled a team for you, Sarah. I've got an orthodontist and a periodontist. We're meeting for lunch today to talk about your case and we're going to get you on the path to recovery. We'll take great care of you and move things along as fast as we can, okay? But for now, you just need to wait a couple weeks to heal. By the way, have you found a church in the area yet?"

Had it really been just over a week ago that I struck out looking for a church? It felt like another lifetime. I had seen a church advertised on TV with an address near my apartment. Weaving through streets of numbers and letters, the building eluded me and I pulled into the next church parking lot I saw. If they believed in Jesus, that was good enough for me. I had watched friend after friend fall away from their faith when they were on their own, and I was determined to hold on even without parents or peers pressuring me.

I hopped down from my truck and took in my surroundings. A black guy about my age approached me with a knowing grin. "Is this your first time visiting?"

"Yeah!" I replied, a bit confused but happy to see a friendly face. "I just moved here and I couldn't find the church I was looking for. I figured I should just pull in somewhere before I missed all the services. Seems like they all started at 10:30."

"Well, you're welcome here! You can sit with me if you want."

I sighed in relief. Even as a Christian who'd grown up around it all, new churches were intimidating. We walked in together and did a sideways shuffle to get into the second pew. Women old enough to be my grandma walked up one after the other in their Sunday hats and best dresses to greet the guy. He smiled, dimpling his caramel-colored cheeks, and I could see a few of them swoon. I couldn't help but grin at the spectacle. A few of the ladies cast disapproving looks my way and I smiled back. Between handshakes and hellos, he leaned over to me. "My dad's the pastor here."

"Ah, that makes sense! My dad's a preacher too. It's kind of a new thing though—just got ordained last year." We shared knowing grins. The older congregants at my dad's church did the same thing every time I visited.

The music began, quieting the conversations, and I took a second to observe my surroundings. Craning my neck, hoping no one noticed me staring, it hit me. *This is how he knew I was a first-time visitor.* A smile stretched across my face as the music started, and I tried to focus on the hymns and not laugh out loud. I was the only white person in the entire building.

I couldn't remember the guy's name. He probably thought I didn't come back for a reason completely different from the truth. I wished I could tell him what happened, meet him for coffee or meander around downtown together as brother and sister in Christ.

My response to Dr. Vittitow was simple. "I visited one before the accident, but I haven't found a church home yet. And right now I'm not getting out much, obviously."

"Well, if you want to give it a try, I really love my church! It's called Southeast Christian. It's right off Blankenbaker Parkway; you can't miss it!" His eyes sparkled as he talked about it.

"Oh yeah! I think I've seen it! Is that the one that looks like a huge basketball stadium?" It was the biggest church I'd ever seen, and that was saying a lot because I grew up at the largest Baptist church in Mississippi. I'd heard so many weird rumors about megachurches I just wasn't sure I wanted to go to one. Plus, wouldn't a church by my apartment be good enough? Once I was a little more healed, I'd try again to find the one I'd seen on TV.

By the time I walked out of the office, my original idea of a quick surgery and putting this all behind me was officially and completely snuffed out. Two weeks of walking around in public with broken, crooked teeth. Two weeks with this bar and brown glue that looked like rot and addiction. Maybe it was an addiction that did this, just a different sort. At least I had Dr. Vittitow and Judy in my corner.

The next morning I trudged across the Louisville campus to my summer history class, black squirrels scampering across my path. Every time I walked through the glass doors of this odd little brick building between crisscrossing sidewalks and grass, I muttered a string of complaints in my head. *How did none of my history classes from Mississippi College count toward my history requirement at U of L?* I would almost have a history minor once I finished my credits, which is absurd considering it's my least favorite subject.

The building was as cold as the bored sea of faces that turned to me when I walked in. My eyes sought the one friendly face in the class. Nearly every morning we happened to walk into class together, smiling and offering casual greetings like we knew each other. She sat in her regular spot, the second row against the furthest wall. It was next to the seat I claimed the day this doldrum of a class started. This morning either everyone was early or I was late. Blood pounded in my ears as gazes followed me across the room. I imagined the assumptions people were making—epic bar fight, abusive boyfriend, car accident.

I zeroed in on the chair and didn't lift my eyes until I was lowering myself into it. Even then I was only brave enough to look at one person. The girl's eyes met mine and she smiled, her face twisted into a look of pity. The sympathy annoyed me. Did I want people to treat me like normal? Not really. Life wasn't normal. But I didn't want to be a victim either. *I just want to pick up the pieces and keep going. God? Can we pick them up and get going? Help me, please.*

I mumbled something to her about an accident on the track. She nodded. People in Louisville seemed to know the dangers that lurk on the dirt ovals that made Kentucky famous. The teacher walked in and lectured. Class ended. I grabbed my backpack and raced across campus to my truck, keeping my head down the whole way. At the apartment, I grabbed Sandi and we set out to see Gideon. I really needed some barn time, and if I was well enough for class I was well enough for the barn.

Craig took me out the next night. Seeing Gid had revived my spirit. The light was returning, starting at my core and coming through my eyes, though it was still dim. As he sat across from me at dinner, Craig said, "I tell you what. What if you move your pony out to the training track while you get better? I can take care of him."

"You mean my horse Gideon? He's not a pony." I managed a small laugh. It felt good, even if it stretched the lip wound and exposed my broken teeth.

"You know what I mean," he said with the same Cheshire grin he'd had the day I met him. A grin that seemed to say *let's go back to my place*. But that must be in my head because he knew about Joey, and who would want to take my busted face back to their place?

He kept going. "I call all the non-racehorses ponies. Anyway, you'll be super busy while you're doing all your dentist appointments and going to class. Let me help you. He can just stay at the training track and I'll take care of him."

"Really?" I exclaimed. "That would be helpful since his barn is an hour away."

I imagined Gideon being on the Kentucky side of the river. *I could save money while I'm not working.* I would breathe easier knowing Gideon was with Craig while I recovered. Maybe he could go on the walker they used for the racehorses. A picture of Gid on the walker popped into my mind—head lifted high with white-rimmed eyes while he decided whether the mechanical arm leading him in circles was trustworthy. Or maybe the grooms would spend a few minutes rubbing him down every day and his summer dapples would shine even more.

"Okay!" *Maybe things will be fine.* "When should I move him?"

This is good, right God? I asked rhetorically. It seemed good. How could it not be? I wasn't sure what to say to God right now, anyway. Thanks for letting a horse crash with me literally seconds after I asked for safety? Because that's how it happened. I had prayed for safety not three minutes before we somersaulted. Yeah, "thanks" didn't ring true.

On Thursday I attended that drudgery of a history class, knowing as soon as it was over I would move Gideon to the training track. In Indiana I loaded Gid into the trailer, my barrel saddle, bridle, and grooming box all piled into the backseat of my pickup. Sandi sat as copilot. Life was moving back into place.

A mental image of Ms. Brenda barking at me not to speed up on turns played in my mind as I turned onto the Indiana highway. I pulled my foot off the gas, slowly coasting southwest toward Louisville, remembering being sixteen with a fresh driver's license and my cousin's old white pickup. Mr. Dale, an older horse friend, had let me borrow his horse trailer. Who knows where I was going or why he was kind enough (or dumb enough) to let a sixteen-year-old borrow his trailer. I turned into Ms. Brenda's driveway and gunned it through the turn to go around the circle, my chest full of pride. *Look at me*! I wanted to say until Ms. Brenda's scowl caught my eye. She waved and I lowered my window. She was yelling before I got it all the way down.

"Don't accelerate through turns when pulling horses! The horses get thrown around and you could flip the trailer!"

"Yes, ma'am," I stuttered, instantly deflated at the idea of hurting what I cared for most.

Her tone was softer as she kept going. "When you're done turnin', pick up speed slowly. If you speed up too fast it throws the horses back. It's hard on 'em."

The trailers I borrowed, as well as their owners, flashed through my mind as I sped down the highway. I imagined the places those trailers had carried Gideon. From English shows where Gid and I always took ribbons against kids several years my junior (which made me feel awkward and a tad guilty), to rodeo pageants where I couldn't even win the spirit award. Rodeo pageants were like slamming my head against a wall, yet I couldn't seem to quit. My competitive spirit drove me toward the shining belt buckles that eluded me. Year after year, girls with big smiles, piles of makeup, and perfectly trained horses all but kicked dirt on my little DIY self and the horse I loved so dearly.

In my last pageant, the coordinator gathered us together in the stands as we waited to perform our horsemanship patterns.

"Okay, y'all! Remember, this pageant is for rodeo queen." She put a strong emphasis on the word rodeo. "This isn't a basic pattern where you want to go slow. Rodeo is fast, like barrel racing. We want to see some speed."

We all nodded, stiff with nerves. *You want fast? You'll get it*, I thought with a smug and somewhat nervous grin. Gid loved speed. He was bred for it from both his momma and his daddy.

Gid and I ready for our horsemanship pattern!

A bit later, Gid and I stood huffing like we had sprinted a lap at the track. The judges glared down at me. "How do you think you did?" a heavy guy in a cowboy hat asked.

They had the expressions of people who'd seen a girl play chicken with an oncoming freight train, which made me a bit uncomfortable about how I'd performed, but I plowed forward.

Still gasping for air, I looked at Gideon, then back at the man before my face stretched into a smile. "That was exhilarating!" I gulped down a couple more lungfuls of oxygen and kept going. "We hit all the marks in the pattern and got our lead changes. We even got our last one right before the stop! I think we did good!"

The judges frowned, turning to notepads and scribbling. "Okay, thank you." A stiff woman with glasses excused us as the heavy guy bore holes into me with his eyes.

Gid and I ambled out of the arena toward his bath and dinner while I reviewed our pattern in my head. We flew like the pageant coordinator recommended and still hit every lead change, including the last one most girls missed. Our transitions were right on cue, and there was a clear size difference and a slight speed difference between our large and small circles. Admittedly the speed difference could have been more pronounced. But I could have sworn we were nearly perfect. The look on the judges' faces said otherwise.

"We'll have to wait and see," I told Gid, pulling his saddle off. He looked at me and nodded, lipping a treat off my palm. "Either way, thank you. You did great!" He responded with slurping noises, the edge of his pink tongue protruding from his lips as he savored the cookie.

That evening, when all the contestants lined up in leather fringe dresses, the girl with the slowest pattern won the horsemanship award and the queen belt buckle. The corners of my lips turned up, but my eyes shot daggers at the pageant coordinator. It seemed the judges missed the memo on speed. *Plus, we hit the last lead change and she* didn't. I seethed as I ducked out to pack up and head home, nodding to my family on the way out.

Along with reminding me I wasn't pageant material, the rodeo pageants lured me back to barrel racing. When Gideon became mine, I swore to myself and Ms. Brenda I was done with that. Gid would be my jumping horse, and I didn't want to spend all my time and money chasing three cans.

But every time I felt Gideon's surging stride, the speed stole oxygen from my lungs. When he tucked his hind end and turned on a dime, the longing churned in my chest. He was the most incredible athlete I'd ever sat on, and he was mine. Maybe I couldn't win a rodeo pageant to save my life, but with talent like this I couldn't help but dream of Vegas and pro rodeos. Craig had even talked about sponsoring us. Once my teeth were all back in place, I could be a racehorse-galloping, barrel race-dominating equine business student. My dreams were right in front of me, a few steps beyond reach. I just needed to keep going.

Chapter 9

I crossed the line between Indiana and Kentucky and the interstates became a maze of crisscrossing lines and bridges. My eyes darted from the Tom-Tom to the road to the mirrors to make sure the trailer carrying Gideon was good. A split was coming and I needed to make sure I went the right way. The highlighted route went left, so I turned on the blinker and checked my left side before moving over.

All was clear, but as I changed lanes the trailer started bumping behind me like one of those waddling duck toys. It wasn't just once or twice but over and over again. I searched the mirrors that pointed behind the truck and tried to keep the trailer between the lines. There it was on the right side—a trailer tire in tatters. Moving over to the shoulder, I pushed the button for my flashers as cars zoomed past.

God help me, I whispered. Even if He was allowing all this mess, He was also the only one who could save me from it. Sandi looked over and her *oh crap* expression matched my own. Cars were flying past us.

I stood behind the trailer, staring at the flat tire that was on the same side as the traffic. Picking up my phone, I called the only person I could think of to help me in this situation.

"Heeeello," Craig answered.

"Hey, Craig. I'm on my way to the barn with Gid in the trailer and had a blowout on the interstate."

"Are y'all okay? Do you think you can change it?" he asked.

"Honestly, I'm not sure if my jack is big enough. And I'm not really sure how," I admitted with shame. What kind of DIY horse girl can't change her own tire? I mentally chastised myself.

"I'll head over," he said, and my insides warmed. It was good to have a friend, even if I hated to burden him more.

"Okay, thanks. I'm in the split to Interstate 71 on the Louisville side of the river."

"I've got a couple things to do at the barn and then I'll head your way."

The call ended and I climbed back into my pickup to wait. The truck rattled with each passing vehicle. Sandi sat tall, pressed against me, and I relished her warmth as I stared through my windshield at the beautiful day. I recalled my old youth pastor telling us about Satan's flaming arrows, and I narrowed my eyes in anger. I felt the need to dive behind a barrier and cover my head with my hands. This seemed too coincidental after the accident. "This isn't funny," I whispered. *God, protect me from these flaming arrows*, I prayed. *What do I do now?*

Was Satan truly after me? Was God giving him permission like with Job in the Bible? I imagined Satan, beautiful and evil, leaning casually against a podium of sorts, staring nonchalantly at his fingernails. He said, "How about that one, God? Sure, she's faithful when things are good, but what if I rough her up a bit? Maybe an arrow to her tire?"

God responded, "Yeah, that's fine, but don't take her life."

My heart was heavy. Everything felt heavy. Why would a God who loved me allow this? Was it all in my head? Dwelling on it was pulling me into a hole I wasn't sure I'd crawl out of, so I pulled out my phone to text Joey.

Craig arrived and tension filled the air between us. The poor guy was probably in the middle of something. I tried not to worry about how much of an inconvenience I had become to the only people I knew in town. He looked at the tire, then at the cars flying past a few feet away.

"This is too dangerous. I'll call Triple-A." I felt validated for not changing the tire myself and also like I stepped deeper into indebtedness.

Roadside assistance arrived and set orange cones along the shoulder to catch drivers' attention. The technician went to his truck and returned with a jack that made mine look like a windup toy.

Craig and I leaned against the Triple-A truck and waited. "Even if you knew how to change a tire, you don't need to be doing it on the same side as traffic on the interstate. Plus, he's got that huge jack. It'll be way easier for him." The tension was gone and we filled the time talking about how the horses did during training that morning.

Within a few minutes, the spare tire was in place and the guy drove away. I asked Craig how much I owed him. "Don't worry about it. You don't owe me anything," he replied coolly and hopped into his car.

Between spending most of my cash on moving here and the accident keeping me from working, my bank account was on the struggle bus. Mom and Dad had sent money and I was definitely grateful, but after rent, food, gas, and textbooks, I was hitting danger level. Even so, the idea of Craig doing one more thing for me tied my stomach in knots. We just met a few weeks ago. He'd paid for a few dinners, offered to take on my horse, and now this. Did he expect more than friendship?

I'd been very clear about Joey, and my face was still an undesirable mess. *He's just being nice*, I told myself. *Thanks for taking care of me, God, and for Craig*, I whispered as I pulled onto the interstate behind Craig's sports car. I followed him down I-71, my stomach doing flips over returning to the place I'd last seen from the back of an ambulance. I forced myself to think of the good times I'd had at the track. It really wasn't hard. Actually, it was bliss.

The first true work day, just three weeks before, was rough. How had it only been three weeks? It felt like a lifetime. A horse I was hot-walking took on the responsibility of orienting me to the world of racehorses. Friends tried to warn me, telling me how different it would be from the show barn I came from. This horse showed me how right they were. The rogue stood on his back legs, pawing the air like the Black Stallion. In a moment of pure shock and denial, I just stood there, jaw unhinged. Craig dove under the fence and rescued me before the horse pawed my skull like he was killing a coyote to protect the herd. Or for sport. Whatever.

My lips twisted into a crooked grin just remembering it. I thought for sure Craig would send me home and tell me to find another dream, but a couple days later he brought out a horse for me to learn to gallop on. It was supposedly "an easy ride" he borrowed from another trainer. He planned for us to ride out together. I'd be on the easy racehorse and he would lead me from the back of the "pony," which was an older horse they used to lead the young ones around the track for training or exercise.

The "easy" ride that was supposed to teach me the ropes spent more time with his front feet in the air next to Craig's head. The trainer's face was several shades lighter than normal as he battled the beast, trying to keep its feet on the ground and moving forward. I would have laughed mid-rear if his face hadn't been so devoid of color. By the time we made it back to the barn, I had proven I could sit a horse.

The next day I strode into the barn with my hand-me-down half-chaps and oversized velvet helmet under my arm, hopeful to ride, expecting to hot-walk some more.

"You're going out in the second set," Craig informed me like it was a normal thing, like the dream borne from reading my favorite Thoroughbred series and a myriad of other horse-racing books wasn't about to finally, actually come true.

I smiled, cool as a cucumber, while my insides did somersaults. *What if I'm terrible? What if I fall off? What if I'm good? What if this is my calling? What if I could be a jockey someday? A top jockey? Okay, calm down Sarah. Just survive this first ride. God, help me do this and help me to be good. Please!*

Craig and his other rider, Jen, were going to ride next to me for my first outing. When the groom led my gleaming chestnut mount out of the stall, Craig gave me a leg up. I tied my reins like he taught me and fixed my stirrups to a comfortable length, slightly shorter than normal, while the groom led us around the barn. When everyone was ready, we rode up onto the track together, my heart pounding. No matter how hard I tried, I couldn't wipe the cheesy grin off my face. As we passed the striped poles that reminded me of the candy park in *Charlie and the Chocolate Factory*, Craig explained what each one was and the distance it marked.

We made our way to the far side of the three-quarter-mile training oval and Craig and Jen pulled their horses to a stop, instructing me to do the same. "We always stop here and have the horses stand for a few minutes." I nodded in eager understanding. "That way they learn to be patient. Otherwise they'd pick up bad habits like spinning and taking off."

"Okay, that makes sense." I scratched the horse's chestnut neck and pressed my heels down, stretching the back of my calves and attempting to orient myself to the slightly shorter stirrups. Two horses galloped by with riders perched over their withers, and I wanted to pinch myself. The early morning air was crisp, but the sun was bright with promise.

"Okay, are you ready?" Craig glanced over at me, for once with no mischievous grin, just work mode.

"I'm ready. Are you ready?" Jen asked over her shoulder.

"Yep! I'll follow y'all's lead!" I said, acting as calm as possible. We nudged our horses away from the rail into the middle of the track, picking up a happy jog. The three of us made eye contact.

"You ready to pick it up a bit?" Craig called over his shoulder. I'd never been more ready for anything. Craig's horse transitioned from a trot into a gently rolling gallop.

I released my horse's reins a quarter inch and hugged him with my calves, telling him it was fine to keep up with his stablemate. The little chestnut moved from the up and down motion of a trot to an easy rocking gallop. Craig and Jen lined up on either side of me. We were three astride as we rounded the first turn.

Coming out of the bend and onto the straightaway, the pounding hooves and heavy breathing created a song, one I realized I'd heard a hundred times. Before that moment I'd heard it when reading *The Black Stallion, King of the Wind,* the Thoroughbred books, and so many others. It was the difference between hearing the song on the radio and being at the live concert. But this was even better. I was on the stage, and I could feel the vibrations of the drumbeat, the danger of the lyrics, the harmony of the horses and riders on either side. This was real.

A smile stretched across my face as I hovered over the withers of the chestnut. My dream was actually happening. I'd persisted and sacrificed, and it was worth it. There were two years left of undergrad and I planned to spend every morning flying without wings. After that, who knew? Maybe I'd become a trainer, maybe a vet, maybe even a jockey, but whatever happened I knew that right here, right now was where I was meant to be.

That moment had been perfect. I had touched Heaven. God had given me that dream, hadn't he? We got there together, didn't we?

At least that's what I told myself a week or so after that perfect ride when I heard a whisper: "quit your job." It must be in my head; my subconscious whispering my greatest fear. Why would God tell me to leave when I had finally made it?

The next morning I pulled my boots on to head to the track with those whispered words and my counter-argument circling through my brain. Why would God ask me to leave when we got here together? The words continued to cycle as I jogged Red around the track to warm up. They only stopped when I took a few seconds to pray for safety before I asked Red to gallop. Before he vanished from beneath me. Before I lay dazed in the middle of the track trying to figure out what went wrong and if we would be okay.

As I pulled the horse trailer into the parking lot of the training farm with my still scabbed and swollen lip, grotesque teeth, and bruised body, I couldn't help but wonder if I had been wrong. Maybe God had told me to quit my job and it wasn't my subconscious after all.

Part of my brain whispered that this was punishment for not listening. Another part reprimanded those thoughts. God doesn't dole out punishments like an angry headmaster. Consequences, yes; punishments no. But what's the difference? Didn't Jesus take the punishment for all my screwups? That's the whole point of the cross. So, I'm good. I wasn't being punished, right?

Punishment or not, the dream I had held in my hand slipped away and it was up to me to chase it back down. Craig waved me toward a spot to park the truck and trailer as my mind grappled with it all.

Chapter 10

The sun was warm on my shoulders, lifting my spirits as I swung onto Gid's back. It was my first time on a horse since the accident, but this wasn't just any horse. It was Gid. This was good—almost normal. Friends, Gideon, sunshine, and Sandi. Class was over for the day, and Craig, Jen, and I were going on a trail ride.

We laughed at one of Craig's dumb jokes as we followed his lead out the front gate of the farm to the other side of the road. Sandi was a blur of joyful motion. She shook off the dust of apartment life, bursting from a fence post to a tree until she couldn't contain herself and sprinted circles around us. Her body unfolded, nearly inverting her back before she brought it back together, her front and back legs crossing to form an x like pictures I'd seen of cheetahs in the wild. She was free, and her joy was contagious. Gideon arched his neck and lifted his tail. My heart swelled. Craig and Jen were seeing the two things I was most proud of: my little family.

We rode along the side of the road in a horse community. To our right was a black four-board fence, and to our left was a steep, grassy slope that went down to the road. From my place in the saddle, it looked like nearly a ten-foot drop to the blacktop, and I made a mental note to stay up by the fence. I touched Gid's side with my left leg to push him away from the hill and preened when he responded immediately, sidestepping a couple feet.

Birds fluttered from branch to branch in the pine trees overhead and I inhaled deeply. Normally I didn't notice the smell of pines. They were everywhere back home. But today their fresh woodsy scent combined with newly cut grass was aromatherapy at its finest. Smelling the grass tuned me into the buzzing of a lawnmower in the distance. My right hand held the rope I used as reins and my left rested on the high back of my western barrel-racing saddle, a smile tugging at the corners of my mouth. It hurt to smile but it was impossible to refrain on this beautiful day.

Craig turned in his saddle to face Jen and me while telling a story. He was in front and she rode in back, leaving me between them. I leaned forward a tad, trying to catch what he was saying. Sandi darted by on my right and birds chirped loudly as I strained to hear. Before I felt anything, Craig's eyes widened and his brows lifted. His mouth turned to an "o" shape I could have tossed a golf ball into.

I rose several inches as my horse launched into the air, followed by a jolting lurch when his back heels kicked up. He took off and we moved as a single unit, a waterfall flowing over a ledge. My hand still rested on the back of the saddle, and from habit alone I shifted my weight back to keep my balance as Gid bolted down the hill in a single ground-eating stride.

A solid, steady rhythm beat in my chest—a stubborn determination not to panic amid chaos. My eyes zeroed in on what was ahead. We would land on soft grass. It was perfect, nearly bluish-green, and would easily absorb his flying hooves and hold them in place. But the next inevitable stride would give us the unstoppable momentum of a 1000-pound horse moving from grass to pavement.

The road sparkled and my jaw nearly dropped. It would be like oil under Gid's metal shoes, and his body would be out of balance. I sucked in half a breath, eyes wide, as his hooves hit the spongy grass. His back legs propelled us forward like springs toward what might be our doom. *I can't believe I might die on my own horse*! The lawnmower roared in the distance and the birds fluttered overhead like everything was normal. Like in this moment everything wasn't changing.

As Gid's feet hit the pavement, they struggled for traction. I heard the scraping and sliding of metal horseshoes grasping for purchase. My body melded to Gid. We tilted and I saw the asphalt coming closer and closer to my already mangled face. *This may be it,* I thought, in resignation that bordered on anger. The image of Satan leaning against a podium, smiling a devilish smile, flashed through my mind again.

The happiness that had started to return like a fresh-budding flower wilted. *I just need to survive*. But I also knew, and hated, that some things are beyond my control.

I was inches from the gray-black flecks of asphalt when I squeezed my eyes shut and accepted my fate, with more anger than fear.

When I opened my eyes again, the sunlight flooded in, nearly blinding me. Gideon moved forward, balanced and upright, and I was still on his back. I pulled on the rope reins, needing just a feather-touch of contact, and he took one prancing step before he was calm. The mower and birds never stopped.

I inhaled shakily. Craig and Jen gaped as if they had seen my face hitting the asphalt as clearly as I had. Jen's mouth hung open and her eyes darkened. Was she judging me? Or was she scared for me? When Craig recovered enough to talk, he declared, "The horse spooked at your dog!"

"No, he didn't," I bit back, offended both at the accusation and that he didn't even say Gideon's name. "I felt it happen and it wasn't because of the dog. He knows my dog. He's used to her running around and he's never spooked at her."

I held onto my anger because it was easier than admitting what was happening in my chest. My skin prickled. *What is this?* I asked myself. *Fear,* my subconscious whispered back.

My eyes widened a tad at the realization; I scrambled to shut that door. Fear kept people from chasing adventure. It made riding difficult horses nearly impossible. I didn't have time or space for that. I scrambled to fix it, purging this thing that had leaked in. I yelled at my subconscious, conscious, heart, whatever needed to hear it—*I am not afraid*. Noticing a tremble that lingered in my hands, I screamed louder in my mind. And then changed the subject to finding answers.

If I could figure out what just happened, the fear would be gone. I could reason it away. *What was it?* Gideon was his own brand of crazy. According to Ms. Brenda, one of his previous owners had been really rough with him. When he got scared he lost his mind. It was a downward spiral of anxiety until he hardly knew what was going on and I needed to step off and be done for the day. But spooking like this, instant, big, and then regrouped and calm within seconds, wasn't something he had ever done before.

Craig and Jen chatted like everything was normal. I rode silently between them, trying to grapple with what happened.

However awful my accident was, it hadn't surprised me. The track was dangerous. Everyone knew it and freely told me so. Even the heroes from my favorite books nearly died chasing their racehorse dreams. I had fully expected at least one ambulance ride in my two years in Kentucky. I thought a horse would buck or spook and I'd land wrong on my arm or leg. I didn't expect a rotational fall. If I fell off a horse, that was my problem. That meant I couldn't stick well enough. But when the horse fell, it wasn't my riding skills. I tried to brush my unease under the rug. *That was on the track*, I told myself. *Those were racehorses.*

But this was Gideon. My Gideon.

It was like experiencing an earthquake for the first time. The one thing in the world that's supposed to be safe and stable, that we build our homes and barns and lives on, is anything but.

We rode into the woods and the canopy of leaves blocked out the sun. With each step away from the warmth I felt my insides grow colder.

I was broken. I was a house whose foundation had cracked—a tiny little hairline fissure making its way across the very thing that held me up. Gideon felt like home just a few minutes ago, and now the thing I loved most in the world seemed determined to undo me.

Craig and Jen joked and chatted, carrying on while I held myself together in silence. I racked my brain for anything that could have caused Gid's behavior—anything strange or sudden in the fence line, trees, or road. There was nothing.

My mind drifted to Balaam's donkey in the Bible. The story had always seemed strange. Balaam was trying to go somewhere, but an angel of the Lord stood in his path. Balaam couldn't see the angel, but the donkey could and refused to go forward. The poor steed took several beatings over his disobedience, until God gave it the gift of speech and he pleaded his case before his owner. Eventually the angel showed himself to Balaam as well and he understood.

What if Gid could see more than I could? The image of a mighty angel, or more likely a messenger from Satan, standing on the hill by the fence was the only thing my mind could muster to explain what had happened. I was also pretty confident a guardian angel had held Gideon up as we careened toward the pavement, protecting us just like my back had been protected when Red rolled over it. The bruise on my back was morphing from blues and purples to greens and yellows.

We rode over logs, across ditches, and ducked under limbs of pine trees with prickly needles. Again, I thought about Job in the Bible. I couldn't seem to get him out of my mind. The description of Job said, "blameless and upright...he feared God and shunned evil." God allowed Satan to take everything but Job's life. Even when Job begged for death, he never cursed his maker. And in the end, God restored his health and wealth and even blessed him with more kids.

It wasn't exactly an empowering story. Job tried hard, he trusted God, and he lost it all because Satan said, "Let's see if he'll stay faithful." And God, my loving, faithful God said, "Okay." It's like the payment for being faithful was suffering. My high-achieving, people-pleasing self, who strove to make people happy and reap the rewards, felt betrayed to the core by this story. It upended my theory on how to have a good life—try hard, do good, believe big, be kind, and get everything you want.

As my mind grasped for an explanation of what was happening, why I felt like I was hanging from a ledge, I kept returning to that mental image of Satan asking God, "Hey, what about Sarah? Sure, she trusts you, but she's got everything she wants. Try taking it away." And God said, "Okay." He set some stipulations like "don't kill her." And here I was with a marred face and so much internal baggage I was running out of strength to carry it.

My feelings warred between betrayed, determined not to curse my Creator, and needing Him for my very next step. Either way, as we returned to the farm along the same road that had almost become one with my face, I imagined a battle between angels and demons raging all around us. My eyes jolted from right to left, ahead of us between Gid's ears, and up on the hill. I could almost hear the clang of swords and sank deeper into my saddle for safety. *God? What's really going on?*

Chapter 11

The oak trees at the University of Louisville towered overhead as people rushed by, glancing at their watches and phones. It was a far cry from walking to class at Mississippi College, where I'd see a friend across the quad and take off at a jog. The momentum only slowed when we collided with open arms. It was ridiculous in the most beautiful way, full of warmth, love, and safety. The students at Louisville didn't see me beyond a casual glance and dismissal. It was fine. It was better to be alone right now, to trudge through this murky swamp in the aftermath of the accident without pulling other people down too. I could handle it. Anonymity was my friend. Just one foot in front of the other.

As I trudged across campus, I thought about all the dentist and orthodontist appointments I'd have this week. Dr. Vittitow and his colleague Dr. Tran said braces were necessary to straighten things back out. I just wanted my teeth covered. Maybe if people saw metal wires instead of broken and twisted teeth, I'd feel less judged.

Either way, if my junior high self, who hated every day of her two years with braces, knew how excited I was for them now, she'd be...well, I'm not sure what she'd think. It's a good thing I couldn't go back and warn myself. This felt like a story I needed to live. If I'd known about the accident beforehand, I might have stayed home.

The thing I most looked forward to—I was driving to Lexington to visit Joey on Friday! He was moving close to the University of Kentucky to start grad school. It was a little over an hour away, according to MapQuest.

The busy week left no time for Gideon. When guilt or anxiety started to spiral in my gut, I reminded myself he was with Craig and being cared for. After history, I swung by the equine department offices to see Terri and tell her the good news—soon I'd have braces! Then I rescued Sandi from the confines of the apartment and we meandered around downtown.

She prowled toward squirrels and birds, her eyes morphing into golden orbs. Passersby stopped to watch her frozen form. With one front paw lifted and her long tail straight out, a slight tremor passed through her body from the thrill of the hunt. When she sprung forward, we laughed and my heart filled with joy. Every time she looked at me I felt needed. She was God's gift to me and I knew it with every fiber of my being.

I left Sandi, rushing to the dentist for root canals or to get more impressions of my teeth. Always the impressions. I hated them. When they pressed the plastic thing full of cold, squishy material over my teeth, the extra crept down the back of my throat, sending panic signals to my brain. I needed to throw up or spit it out and run or something to save myself. But I sat there, trying to be brave and strong as tears streamed down my face and I told myself to breathe, relax, and do whatever I could not to panic or vomit on myself and the other person.

Friday morning I walked into a beautiful reception area with a welcome desk shaped like a wooden wave. A woman with a bright, warm smile sat ready to welcome me. Tears pressed against the back of my eyes, knowing this lady rearranged her day and woke up early to help me. I pressed my finger to the scanner pad to check in, marveling at the technology. The place was a kid's dream with a mini movie theater, walls of fish tanks, and splashes of bright colors all around. The main room had gleaming wood floors and a row of orthodontist chairs across the center. I stared at them, wondering which one was for me.

"I'm ready for you!" a cheerful voice said from behind. The owner of the voice was soon past me, showing me to my recliner.

"Thank you so much!" I gushed. "I am so ready to get this bar off my teeth. It's embarrassing."

A shadow crossed her face. "That bar is awful. We'll do what we can. There's a chance you won't be healed enough or it'll be too painful, but we won't know until we get started."

"I can handle the pain," I said, knowing I would endure whatever it took to get the metal piece with its brown glue off my teeth.

Dr. Tran popped in to give guidance, but for most of the appointment the lady worked on my teeth while I watched a screen, absorbed in the story of a saber-toothed tiger, woolly mammoth, sloth, and a little squirrel thing saving a human baby and themselves from the ice age.

An hour later I ran my tongue along rough brackets and smooth wires, and my heart rejoiced. Who would have thought braces could make my life so much better? They raved about how tough I was, and for a fraction of a second I saw Dr. Tran's smile dip and his eyes darken. I wondered if he imagined his own kid going through such a disaster. The moment passed and the light returned to his eyes. I knew it was no accident that I was standing here in this building with these people. God may have allowed the accident, but He orchestrated this—people who barely knew me, yet loved me like one of their own.

Craig offered to keep Sandi while I was in Lexington. We weren't sure if Joey's new apartment allowed dogs and there would be a lot of in and out with unloading and unpacking. After dropping Sandi off, I hit the interstate to Lexington. My memories of the college town included touring Keeneland racetrack, the beautiful horses at Kentucky Horse Park, and sitting in an admission adviser's office when the lady told me I needed a 31 on the ACT to get a full out-of-state scholarship.

My parents and I had started the tour of colleges in Kentucky to see which one I would go to. I had good grades, a résumé packed full of versatility and leadership, and after five attempts, a 30 on the ACT. Thirty seemed like a good, solid number—a score few of my classmates had met or exceeded, even if their GPAs were higher than mine.

I remembered sitting in a black cloth-covered chair across from a faux wood desk while the adviser smiled and told me freshmen weren't allowed to bring cars to campus. "Well, how will I be able to drive to the racetrack?" I asked, and she gave me a vague non-answer about being a busy freshman. She kept chatting as my parents stood behind me since there wasn't room for everyone to sit. She read down my transcript, saying, "Oh, I see you were the lead in your school play and that you're in student government! And I see you have strong grades in advanced classes. That's wonderful! Oh, and you have a 30 on your ACT! That's wonderful! Did you know if you have a 31, you'll be eligible for a full out-of-state scholarship?"

Red crept up my face as my dad nervously chuckled. "Well, we sure are proud of Sarah's 30 on the ACT!" My heart warmed at Dad's support.

I took a deep, calming breath, swallowed my frustration and declared with a shaky smile, "Well, I've taken it five times to get the 30! But sure! I can try again! I'm sure I can get a 31!" I said it with a fake laugh. My insides cringed at the idea of sitting in a freezing classroom and taking that stupid test again. But if it's what I had to do, I would go home, take it again, and try my hardest to get a 31.

I took it two more times after that trip and got a 29 and another 30. At least I proved the first 30 wasn't a fluke.

God's hand was on it, though, I reminded myself. I loved Mississippi College, and I met Joey there. It was still surreal. It had been less than a year since I kindly rejected Joey's invite to the Homecoming Dance. Thinking about it made me laugh. The next time I ran into him was another night I'd never forget.

Sophomore year at Mississippi College was barely underway and classes were already intense. I needed to crack down on my study time if I had any hope of making it into vet school. My backpack hung on my shoulders, filled with ridiculously large and heavy books, while I shuffled across the dark quad to a startlingly empty building.

The door to a vacant classroom stood open and I slipped inside. I had studied in here with my friend Pat the year before. The thud of my backpack hitting the table filled the room and my shoulders sang in relief. But the emptiness of the space gave me pause. Until he wasn't there, I didn't realize how much I loved and depended on my friend's presence. I grabbed a dry erase marker and wrote notes on the whiteboard in an attempt to help my brain absorb information. As the seconds ticked by, my heart rate picked up and my imagination spun with the things that could happen to a girl alone in a classroom on a college campus.

I read from the textbook and wrote definitions of words I needed to know on the board, but nothing was soaking in. Giving up, I wiped the board clean and headed one building over to the library. I set my textbook, notebook, and pen on the table and tried to focus. I read the same line over and over, but all my brain heard was the conversation at a nearby table.

When my eyes lifted, I refused to look at the people talking. Instead, I surveyed the aisles full of books. *Were these novels? Or study aids? There are so many. Do they all get read? Have some of them been sitting in the same spot untouched since they were first shelved? Does someone dust these? Wait, focus!* I chastised myself, forcing my eyes back to the page.

Staring at the words and demanding my brain to zone in on the textbook, movement outside the window caught my eye. Students laughed on the other side of the wall of glass. *I wonder what they're laughing about. What's Roommate doing? How's Gid?* My mind drifted until I slammed my book shut and left. Studying here wasn't working.

A few nights later, one of my classes required a trip to the library, so I figured I'd try again. Bag heavy with books, I headed across campus to talk to the librarian about my project. Once that task was complete, I waffled with the decision to stay. Scanning the large main level, I saw students clumped together at tables. A weight rested on my chest. *What an unexpectedly lonely year*, I thought. *Talk about a sophomore slump.*

As my eyes scanned the room, there was Joey Hickner sitting at a table near the atrium. He smiled. I squinted as my cheeks lifted and the left side of my mouth turned up. He nodded toward the vacant seat across the table. I broke into a full-on grin. There was something about this guy. I swaggered over to the big wooden chair with mauve padding and took a seat.

"What happened to your secret study spot?" I couldn't resist the good-humored jab.

"Someone was in there tonight." I watched his annoyance melt away at my presence and my chest warmed.

"That's lame. It must not be that big of a secret!"

"You don't know where it is," he challenged, and his piercing eyes made me gulp. "Do you always study here?"

"Actually, I normally just study in my room. I had to come to the library for a project and wasn't sure if I'd stay. I tried studying here a couple nights ago and couldn't focus."

"So you're staying for me?" he quipped with a smile that was supposed to look confident, but I could see the hope in his eyes.

I shrugged as I pulled out my textbook. "I'll give it a try."

We sat in companionable silence. I needed to learn more about cell biology, but as my eyes scanned the text, my brain spun out of control over the guy sitting across from me.

"What are you studying?" He broke my nonexistent focus and I relished the opportunity to ignore my book and focus on who I really wanted to study.

The library faded into the background while Joey and I talked. He made me laugh and the weight of loneliness slipped away. The librarians glared and shushed us. We both jumped at the scolding, looking down at the table to gain composure. But when I looked back into his eyes we simultaneously exploded with laughter.

Something buzzed on the table next to my open book. I glanced over to see "MOM" on the tiny screen of my flip phone. Excusing myself, I scrambled out of the library to answer it. Once the call was over, I gazed into the heavens for a quick and necessary conversation.

Really, God?! This feels so right! It's time for Kentucky and now this guy is here?! Are you making me choose or something?!

I tried to swallow my grin as I returned to the table, but it was impossible. His eyebrows furrowed in question as the light sparkled in his blue eyes.

"Was that your boyfriend?"

"Ha! No." An entire family of butterflies took flight in my stomach. "It was my mom."

His face stretched into a relieved smile, gorgeous brown curls looping around the edge of a ratty ball cap. *Why do guys get the good hair*? I wondered. But then something caught my attention. His white ball cap said U of K in blue block letters. It couldn't mean anything, could it? I mean, it could be Kansas, right? Plus, even if it was a University of Kentucky hat, southern boys wear caps from just about any school. But I was so curious.

"Is that a University of Kentucky hat?"

His lip quirked up when he replied. "Yeah, I applied there for grad school. I may be going in the fall."

My heart did an unsolicited leap. *Really God? Really?!* Shock, confusion, and excitement warred within me as the butterflies morphed into birds. This seemed wild, impossible, too good to be true.

"Oh really? I'm going to the University of Louisville in the fall." Saying it out loud gave life to the plan. My body buzzed with the possibilities of it all.

He mentioned his other options—law school at Mississippi College and two other out-of-state programs—reducing UK to a 25 percent chance for next year's landing spot. But I was 75 percent sure those other schools weren't actually options because I had a delightful little niggling in my belly. I was 75 percent sure this Joey Hickner was it for me, and I was 100 percent sure God was in the details.

My chest warmed at the memory while I cruised down the interstate. It was such an unassuming evening, but I had known in my gut that nothing would be the same after that.

Signs on the interstate said Versailles, Kentucky. The landscape was changing from rocks that looked cut out of a mountain to the seemingly endless farms of bluegrass and four-board fences that had drawn me to this state. Before I could accidentally veer off the road from drooling over the horses and properties, I conferred with my TomTom and focused on my route. Joey was growing closer by the minute and my joy was morphing into nerves.

A few blocks from his apartment, I considered whipping a u-ey and heading back where I came from. Was I ready for him to see me like this? Even with braces, I was a mess, just a mess with wires. But I was ready to see Joey and his parents.

I pulled my truck up to a long two-story apartment complex. Joey's dad was in the parking lot with a moving box in his arms. When he saw me, he smiled and walked over. His brows furrowed in sadness and concern while he told me where to park and ran in to get me a parking pass.

I took a shaky, fortifying breath and backed into a spot across from Joey's new home. His mom met me with a hug and managed a smile when she told me how worried they'd been and that they'd been praying for me.

Joey rushed from the apartment and wrapped me in his arms, cocooning me in a hug. It felt strange to be touched. Since moving to Louisville, the only hugs I'd received were from Sandi and Gideon. But it was good. It would be okay.

The deep sound of a horn carried into the parking lot and we all made eye contact and chuckled. "Apparently, one of the neighbors plays the tuba," Joey's dad said.

"That'll be a fun neighbor to have," I joked, trying to sound normal. My heart beat against my chest like it was clambering to escape. We finished greeting each other and I ducked off to the bathroom under the guise of needing to pee. The truth was, when I lifted my arms to hug Joey, an odor like nothing I'd experienced hit me. I grabbed a washcloth and some hand soap and tried to scrub the putrid smell from my armpits. "You've got to be kidding me," I whispered to the mirror. It was wretched. *Where did this even come from?*

Rivulets of water made their way down my shirt and onto the edge of my bra. My cheeks heated as I stared at myself and fought back tears. *Perfect. Just add it to the pile of issues. How can Joey even stand to be in the same room with me at this point? These people are freaking saints. God, can you please make this go away?* I just wanted to feel normal for a minute.

I took a second to glance at the fading bruise on my back. It was slowly turning a sullen yellow. Every time I looked at it I remembered that God had protected me. I tried to be grateful that I walked away from the fall, but it was hard with broken teeth pressing against my lips. *I'll think about it later,* I told myself as I tossed the rag into the clothes hamper.

That evening I got my first view of his family's utter devotion to Papa John's pizza with their two pepperoncini and garlic sauce in every box. Joey found a fork and knife and I cut mine into bite-sized pieces while laughing half-heartedly at Seinfeld reruns. They snuck glances my way, eyebrows angled with so much concern it looked painful. The scab on my lip just barely perched over the wound, threatening to fall off any second. I felt like a mouth-breathing monster and couldn't bring myself to make eye contact with anyone. When they tried, I glanced to the side or the floor. Joey reached out and grabbed my hand, threading his fingers through mine, and my breaths came a little easier.

Chapter 12

Louisville demanded my return, so on Sunday evening I drove back to my dog, the last week of summer school, and always more dentist appointments. I didn't have time to visit Gideon, but Craig said it was fine. He'd put Gid on the walker for me so he could get some exercise. There was a lot to do before Joey arrived for his first visit to Louisville over the weekend. Every time I thought about him my stomach did somersaults. I couldn't wait.

Friday morning, I nearly skipped out of my history final, shaking off the dregs of my least favorite subject. I had an hour to kill before settling into Dr. Vittitow's dental chair. Taking the exit off the interstate, I steered toward Krispy Kreme. My mouth watered at the mere idea of a chocolate-covered custard-filled éclair. There was a Barnes & Noble nearby as well, and I loved meandering through bookstores. I could have a doughnut book party to celebrate the end of summer school.

I walked into Krispy Kreme with its retro barstools, immediately mesmerized by the circles of raw dough that floated through hot oil in rows like a little army. The doughnuts rose on a conveyor belt, beautifully golden brown, and marched forward through a waterfall of milky white glaze.

"Miss? Miss?"

"Oh! Sorry!" I replied to the girl behind the register, scratching my neck. *How awkward*. When I opened my mouth, red crept up my face. "One chocolate-covered custard-filled éclair and a small coffee," I muttered, handing over my bank card and swallowing down guilt for not smiling and chatting. Even with the braces, it was all I could do not to cover my mouth with my hand. I glanced down at my card, the register, anything to avoid eye contact before grabbing my doughnut and coffee and ducking out the door.

Sitting in my truck, I took a bite of the éclair, savoring the indulgence as my eyes fluttered closed. The chocolate icing, custard filling, and fried dough neared perfection, a taste of Heaven. It only left me wanting because no matter how slowly I ate and how small my bites were, it was gone in under two minutes. My first sip of black coffee, a perfect complement to the éclair, left scald bumps on my tongue. The doughnut was gone and my coffee needed to cool, so I left it in the cupholder and strode into the bookstore.

In high school and over the summers, my parents and I occasionally visited Barnes and Noble after dinner. My brothers had moved out of the house, so it was just the three of us. I turned down trips to get ice cream or frozen yogurt, but never the opportunity to walk along rows and rows of books.

Just walking in, the smell of paper and glue, of stories, filled me with a longing I never understood. I could have sung my way down the aisles, sweeping my fingers along the spines like Belle in the beast's magnificent library.

For years, I went to the magazine section first to pore over the horse magazines, soaking up anything I could about the horse-racing industry that seemed so foreign in Jackson, Mississippi. Then I'd go to the horse section and see if there were any books I hadn't read yet. I flipped through breed books, making a mental list of all the types of horses I hoped to own one day. Once I got to college and began studying biology and chemistry, I added the science section to my routine.

The Louisville Barnes & Noble seemed older than the one in Jackson. It was aged bourbon barrels, old books, and polaroids.

No one approached as I walked through the double doors. I scanned the store, expecting a worker to appear from behind a bookshelf to welcome me and offer help. No one noticed my presence, and I sighed in relief.

I took a deep breath, inhaling the scent of one of my favorite places, but even that couldn't chase away the unease clinging to my insides. I skipped the horse-racing magazines since the racetrack was no longer a faraway dream and zig-zagged through the clearance aisles. Nothing caught my eye, so I steered toward the section labeled with a green "horse" sign.

My eyes skimmed the book spines expecting, hoping for, the usual inspiration. It didn't come. Instead of the call to touch a book, open it, and dream, my stomach soured. I felt betrayed. *They're just books,* I reminded myself.

A fog settled over me and I tried to shake it off, blaming it on the lack of new material. My legs dragged and the world blurred as if I were walking through water. My mind was adrift, and the ticking of my heart increased in the confusion. Hopefully the biology and chemistry books would bring me back to the surface.

Standing in front of the rows of material, I scanned titles and authors, leaning in, needing something from it. What *it* was I didn't know. Maybe I was hoping for a sense of warmth and belonging, of hope for the future. But my insides shriveled even more as it dawned on me: I wasn't a science nerd studying biology and chemistry anymore. I'm a business major. My identity was changing.

Nothing in the store spoke to me. It was paper covered with words nestled between cardstock. Rows and rows of paper, words, and cardstock inside a big store with lights and shelves and pretty floors.

None of this matters, my swirling mind said as I paused to try to understand what was happening. The bookstore began to spin. Or was I spinning? Or was I being pulled into a different realm? Did I walk through a wardrobe or portal? I blinked. Everything was the same.

Nothing was the same.

The horse books that had meant so much to me and had shaped who I was were just words on paper. I wanted to love them, to hear their whisper, to close my eyes and dream of horses, but the line that drew us together was cut. Things were changing. I didn't even know *what* was changing, but it was.

I inhaled, clueless to what this whole unraveling was about. But as I exhaled, the curtain lifted and scales fell from my eyes. Realization dawned, and I wanted to shrink back into ignorance.

A question had been swimming in my subconscious since the day my tire blew. Before it could drown and disappear again, it exploded to the surface. *Is God punishing me?*

It ricocheted around my insides, making my skin buzz with the realization, the fear. The God of the universe, who gives and takes away, who is love, Abba Father, the Beginning and the End, is also the God who kept Moses from the Promised

Land because of one screwup. He took the life of King David's kid after David committed sexual sin and murder. He allowed Job's kids to be killed in storms and his farm and livestock to be swept away over nothing, really. Job wasn't even being punished, just ruined on a whim from Satan. This God I believed in wasn't always warm hugs and breathtaking sunrises, and maybe I had screwed up too much. Maybe I was receiving divine correction.

I rushed from the bookstore. The familiar sensation of running through a battlefield had me turning my head to check for flaming arrows. The rows of bookshelves provided cover as tears streamed down my face.

But He also promised to never leave or forsake his people, I reminded myself. I'd sung in choir about how deep the love of Christ was. The Bible talks about it. We can't hide from it. Nothing can separate us from His love.

I dove into the truck, my haven from the world, leaned against the steering wheel, and cried.

Why do I feel so separated from His love right now? Does a God who loves like that also punish? It's not like I killed somebody. I defended my actions in my mind, but a memory niggled in my brain. It was one I had tried to forget.

A night or two before the accident, there was a small incident, almost silly and nonexistent, except now it felt like my entire world hinged on that moment. I had been getting ready for bed, pulling off my jeans and boots and rubbing Sandi's belly, when I heard a whisper in my mind: *close the window*.

Strange, I thought, unsure if it was God's voice. I had only heard something like that a time or two. *Was that real?* I wondered. But there didn't seem to be a reason not to close the window. The sun was down and my room would cool off whether or not the window was up, so I strode over, grabbed the pane, and slid it closed. My lips stretched into a smile at the oddity of the moment as I wondered if it was indeed God's still small voice.

Then I heard the whisper again, but this command was vastly different. "Quit your job."

Quit my job? I railed back, blinking profusely. *That can't be right. God? Is that right? It can't be. We worked together to get here. This is my dream job. That wasn't a command from God. That had to be my own mind whispering my worst fear,* I told myself.

As I drifted to sleep that night, I prayed, *God, if you want me to quit my job, I need you to make it completely clear.*

The next morning, the early rays of sun peaked through my closed window. I walked over to slide it open and allow a breeze into my oppressively hot bedroom. The city outside was drenched from unexpected overnight storms. *If I hadn't obeyed that voice, it would have rained into my room. But that doesn't mean it was a message from God,* I told myself as I laced up my boots and hurried out to the training track. *God, you've got to be clearer than that.*

The memory was a weight dragging me down into water and holding me there. *Oh God,* I muttered.

I had fooled myself, but I couldn't fool God.

For years, I had told myself and the world that my life was built on my faith and that everything else was a distant second or third. God was all that truly mattered. I prayed and worshipped and believed. I loved God. It's just that I loved horses, and this dream, more.

If I truly trusted God, I would have quit my job as nonchalantly as I closed that window.

God asked me to close the window to protect me from a storm. Did He ask me to quit my job because He could see this storm coming?

If I had quit, I wouldn't have been on Red when he tumbled down the track. I wouldn't be so broken. I would have dodged a major storm. Was this punishment or protection? Or perhaps a little of both?

"Oh God," I moaned between hiccups. "I'm sorry! Help me, please," I cried. "I'm sorry. I'm so sorry."

I knew God loved me with every fiber of my being. But I also knew that like any good parent, He gives, takes away, and allows bad stuff to happen, and it hurts. I hurt.

That afternoon I returned to my apartment. Joey would arrive soon, but first I wanted to do a little research. I couldn't stop thinking about Job, so I grabbed the hunter green Bible my granny and granddad gave me for Christmas a few years before. Running my finger over the gold foil letters of my name, I imagined Granny in Heaven, cheering me on, and Granddad in his greenhouse in Jackson, Mississippi, praying for me while tending his plants. With a fortifying breath, I opened my Bible and flipped the pages until the book of Job stared up at me. I huddled on the floor against my bed and pored over the verses. There had to be something in here for me.

It started off strong in Job 1:1, "There once was a man named Job who lived in the land of Uz. He was blameless—a man of complete integrity. He feared God and stayed away from evil."

The story kept going with Satan showing up in Heaven. God bragged on Job, but Satan said, "Sure, he's loyal to you because he prospers in everything and hasn't had any real challenges. Try taking it away and see where his heart truly lies."

Verse 12 said, "'All right, you may test him,' the LORD said to Satan. 'Do whatever you want with everything he possesses, but don't harm him physically.'" So Satan left.

I was breathing like I had walked up all four flights of stairs to my apartment. "All right, you may test him..."

Was this a test? Or was it punishment? Either way, I didn't appreciate it. *I don't deserve this!* I wanted to scream into Heaven. But my heart stirred. A voice of reason countered my rant. Why didn't I deserve it? Was I blameless? Not even close. I screwed up. I didn't listen. I put horses before God. Creation before the Creator. The gift before the Giver of gifts.

I kept reading, and the book went on and on with more bad stuff happening. Job's friends and wife visited and told him to curse God and he refused. *Same*, I thought.

I was worn out, confused, and unable to follow all the dialogue. My eyelids drooped and I considered stopping to take a nap. *This is a lot, and it's helping less than I expected*. But as I neared the end of the book, it took a hard turn. At the beginning of chapter 38, the Lord answered Job, and my wandering mind snapped to attention:

2 "Who is this that questions my wisdom with such ignorant words?"

My eyes widened. *Oh, snap. Have I done that? Have I questioned God with ignorant words? Probably.*

4 "Where were you when I laid the foundations of the earth? Tell me, if you know so much. **5** Who determined its dimensions and stretched out the surveying line? **6** What supports its foundations, and who laid its cornerstone **7** as the morning stars sang together and all the angels shouted for joy?"

I felt at once scolded and loved. My heart inflated, knowing that even if I was being punished, it was because the Creator of the universe loved me.

It kept getting better in chapter 39.

19 "Have you given the horse its strength or clothed its neck with a flowing mane? **20** Did you give it the ability to leap like a locust? Its majestic snorting is terrifying! **21** It paws the Earth and rejoices in its strength when it charges out to battle."

A wave of awe washed over me. This love of horses that was so ingrained in me was divine. The words were also a solid reminder that God gave the horse its strength. God came first. *Okay God, I hear you.*

Closing my eyes, I meditated on those words, this new revelation. *God forgive me,* I prayed again, *and help me keep you first. Protect me from the flaming arrows. Hold me in your hands.*

The phone buzzed on the floor by my leg before I was done. Joey was almost here and needed help finding the parking lot.

Chapter 13

Joey stepped through the door of the apartment building and wrapped his arms around me. I leaned in and pressed my head to his chest, savoring the human connection, his warmth, and scent. He was in Louisville! He pulled back first, looking into my eyes for a moment before I impatiently grabbed his hand and dragged him up to the third floor.

My lip was healed enough that I could smile, and I couldn't wipe the cheesy grin off my face. Joey was here! He strolled into my apartment behind me and we stood there together, hand in hand. I sighed in contentment. This apartment was a restoration hardware dream with original wood floors and dark stained beams and doorways. My roommate's cats peeked at us from behind my dad's hand-me-down leather chair. I took it all in, imagining Joey doing the same. His silence stretched until I had to break it.

"What do you think?" I blurted, ready for him to gush over the floors or the cool vibe. Sandi was wriggling in front of us, slapping my leg with her tail in excitement.

"Hey, do y'all have a broom or something? This place is a mess!" he replied.

Joey relegated Sandi and I to the couch as he became a Tasmanian devil in reverse. In an hour he swept, mopped, and even wiped the bathroom down while I tried to ignore the tiny twinge of guilt. *Who is this guy? Oh yeah, the same guy who cleaned my truck on our first date.* I chuckled to myself at the memory.

That night in the library had been a turning point in both our lives. I could now see how the painful loneliness during sophomore year was used for good. It was like God cleared my schedule and emptied my heart to fill it with something better. It reminded me of Romans 8:28, where God promised to use everything for our good if we love and trust him.

Okay, God, I hear you, everything for good, I whispered, slipping back into the memory of that night at Mississippi College.

Sitting at the old blocky library table, unable to withhold our laughter, Joey apparently found it the perfect time to call me out on rejecting his offer to the Homecoming Dance. It was a stab to the heart. I hated rejecting people and this guy seemed really great. So I countered with an offer I had mulled over for a few minutes, "Hey, the Sadie Hawkins Dance is coming up! Want to come with me?"

His face stretched into a wide grin. "Naw, I've already got a date!"

My jaw dropped before I could stop myself, but I leaned forward with a lift of my eyebrows. "I guess we're even then," I quipped.

The light hit his smiling eyes and my stomach did a flip. This was no longer about soothing his ego or being nice. Now I truly wanted him to be my date. There was one other event coming, the biggest of the year—my social club's annual formal gala. We'd travel to Fairhope, Alabama, dine on fine china, dance the night away, and pile as many exhausted, blissful college students as possible into the resort rooms.

My face heated a tad. Asking a guy to formal was a big deal, but I seized the moment. Completely nonchalant, as if I didn't care one way or the other, I popped the question. "Okay, if you can't come to Sadie Hawkins, will you be my date to formal?"

His eyes glimmered with mirth, but the corners of his smile dipped a bit when he said, "I've already been asked to that too."

My recovery was quicker this time. "Well then, it looks like I need to book you a year out if I want to take you anywhere." I laughed to cover the sting.

"Hey, it's payback for Homecoming!" he chuckled.

"Come on! I already have a date!" But I wished more and more every second that I could trade the other guy in for Joey Hickner.

Later that week, Joey dropped by my dorm. Our private Christian college didn't allow boys into the girls' dormitory, so I grabbed my key card before running out to the parking lot. He had two Starbucks cups and held one out to me. "I got you a vanilla latte," he said with a grin that was quickly becoming my favorite.

My stomach was doing somersaults and I looked away, pretending to care who was coming out the door behind us. Taking deep, calming breaths, I tried to keep my face from stretching into an embarrassingly huge grin. *Act normal*, I told myself, bringing the latte to my mouth to cover the smile.

We leaned against the concrete half-wall. I waited for my coffee to cool while he told me about baseball practice and his dad being in town. I told him about my organic chemistry lab and a test I was nervous about. Several minutes later, as he backed out of his parking spot to head to his dorm, I tried to appear calm. I strode, confident and cool, to the door and scanned my card. It took three tries before my shaking hand could get the doors to unlock. Joey's car was out of sight, so I sprinted around the bend down the hall to my room. Roommate was gone, so I crossed through the shared bathroom to Suitemate's room and shook her awake.

"Whaaaat?" she said in a droll voice, not amused at being woken from a deep slumber when she had softball practice before the sun rose. I only felt the tiniest twinge of guilt.

"Suitemate! Joey Hickner brought me coffee!" What I didn't say because it felt dumb and way too soon was *I think he's the one. I think we're getting married someday.*

This boy I barely knew, who had applied to grad school in Kentucky and was still weighing his options, was changing everything.

"You woke me up because Joey Hickner brought you coffee? Suitemate I love you, but you're crazy. Goodnight." And she rolled over and went back to sleep.

Joey and I did the dance of occasionally studying together, meeting at the intramural fields to cheer on our friends, a quick phone call or two over Thanksgiving break, and finally, we went on a date. It was the night before formal and we planned dinner and a movie. As we pulled out of the parking lot, my favorite band was blaring on the radio. "Oh my gosh, I love No Doubt!" I exclaimed.

"Oh yeah? I like them too!" he said casually.

"Are you kidding? They're my favorite! We went to see them at VooDoo Fest a few months ago. It was insane."

"Really? I was there too!"

The entire way to the restaurant, we talked about VooDoo Music Fest and our favorite No Doubt deep cuts. We went over formal plans and realized we should probably skip the movie to finish packing. As we made our way back to campus, I mentioned I needed to clean out my truck for the drive to Alabama the next day.

"Really? I can help. I detail cars in the summer to make money," he said with pride.

"Um, Okay, but it's really messy," I tried to warn him.

"No, it's fine!" he declared with confidence.

A few minutes later, we pulled up next to my truck. He took one look and his eyes grew. "Wow."

I practically lived out of my truck and it showed. Jackets for every type of weather, fast-food trash, horse gear, books, shoes for different occasions, backup outfits in case I needed to go somewhere after the barn and not look like I rolled in dirt, and so much more.

I laughed nervously. "Told you! It's kind of normal for horse people. It's just, I need to be prepared."

He dove in and I hovered just behind him. "Let me help!"

"No, I've got it," he said in a way that brokered no argument.

"Okay, well I'll go get a bag to put all my stuff in." I ran to the dorm. As I bounded up the stairs, I bumped into a friend. She was giddy when she blurted, "So how's the date going?!" We squealed in the stairwell together, and I wondered what girly phenomenon had taken over my body.

"It's great! He's helping me clean my truck for tomorrow!" Then I ran up to get the bags and back out to the parking lot to observe Joey cleaning my truck from top to bottom. Apparently, cleanliness was a thing for him. I rarely noticed or cared about mess.

Now months later, Joey was speed-cleaning my apartment just like he tackled my truck on our first date. Once my place met his approval, we moved on with the day.

"Get your leash!" I told Sandi. She darted around the living room until she found it. Her tail whipped back and forth as she brought it to me, lashing Joey's leg.

"Ow!" Joey yelled, and we both laughed.

"Okay, sit!" Her little German Shorthair brows furrowed as she tried to sit while I clipped on the leash, but she couldn't stop her excited body from wriggling. She popped off the ground like a pogo stick.

With the leash finally attached to my dog, Joey and I explored downtown Louisville, hand in hand. We walked three blocks down Fourth Street to City Park, where Sandi barked at the lion statues. I initially fretted over disturbing the peace, but when I looked around, park-goers were cracking up. The evening ended with Chinese takeout and a movie on the blue couch.

The next day I showed him the McAlister's Deli closest to my apartment. The restaurant was a staple back home, the go-to place for every group outing, which meant I had never wanted to eat there. But now I could get chicken tortilla soup with a side of chips or eat a grilled ham and cheese sandwich off the kids menu for under five dollars, all while feeling closer to the people who dragged me to this restaurant for years. Plus they had the best sweet tea. It was a staple lunch spot.

We drove around campus and parked at the baseball stadium to marvel at the pristine field. I remembered the time I drove past this exact place when I came to Kentucky to visit colleges and Churchill Downs. Back then, trash tumbled across the infield.

"Are you sure you don't want to visit U of L?" my parents asked as we cruised past the University of Louisville silos on Interstate 65.

"Definitely not." I had assumed it was an inner-city college and not up to some invisible, undefined, yet nearly impossible standard I had set. The paper drifting across the infield affirmed my suspicion, and I didn't even consider it.

Those two years at Mississippi College felt like torture in the beginning, but now, standing next to Joey, I could see God's hand on it. There must have been a veil over my eyes to keep me from seeing U of L as a viable option until the time was right. The University of Louisville campus was beautiful, and I was proud to be a student there.

Hands intertwined, we drove the city block around Churchill Downs and pulled up in front of the main entrance. The famous racetrack was just three miles from my apartment. I stared at the spot by the gift shop where a few years prior, I had sworn not to give up on my dream. The points of my teeth and the brackets from my braces pushed my lips out awkwardly, and I nodded to my younger self, promising to hold on, to dig in, to not give up.

Chapter 14

On Sunday morning we tried out the church I had seen on TV. Everyone seemed to know each other and was quite aware we were new. When my eyes strayed from the pulpit I'd catch people staring. Their faces stretched into excited grins. I missed my church back home, but I was committed to giving this one a chance.

Afterward, Joey and I stood in my tiny kitchen discussing lunch options when my phone buzzed. It was Craig. Anytime the person in charge of my horse's care called, anxiety hit the pit of my stomach. Worst-case scenarios raced through my mind. Normally it was something simple like, "The vet's coming out, do you need anything?" Or "Hey, I'm going on a trail ride later. Want to come?" A million concerns and reminders that *everything is probably fine* flashed through my mind as I pried my phone apart and put it to my ear.

"Sarah, did you move your horse last night?" Craig demanded in a low, urgent voice.

"Um, no," I responded in confusion. *Why in the world would he be asking?*

"Oh God, Sarah, tell me you moved him," he nearly wailed. I stared at the surface of the Formica table in my kitchen, trying to process what was happening. The little black dots moved in and out of focus, making the table look off-white one moment and like it was crawling with ants the next.

Joey dipped his head in front of me and whispered, "What's going on?" I ignored him, focusing on the phone call and trying to figure that out myself. *Why would Craig ask if I moved my horse?*

"No, I've been with Joey all weekend. This was his weekend to visit, remember?" He should have remembered because he had asked if I wanted to eat with him and I'd said, "Nope. Joey's coming to town!"

"Well, he's not here." I could picture Craig running his hand through his hair as he spoke. "I came out this morning and your horse is not here."

Horses don't just disappear, I thought, refusing to panic. *He's got to be around somewhere.*

"Look, Craig, he's got to be around. He probably just escaped from a groom, or someone left a gate open," I offered, trying to calm everyone. Anger was rolling off Joey in waves. "Horses can't just disappear," I reiterated.

"Sarah, I'm telling you, your horse isn't here." It sounded like his voice shook a little. My eyes widened into shocked orbs and a weight sat high in my chest. *Horses don't just disappear. God, where is he? He's a thousand-pound animal. He can't just disappear.*

"Okay. We were planning to eat lunch and then head out there this afternoon, but we'll head on over," I uttered. "See you soon."

I snapped my phone shut. *I will not panic.* Years of Gideon's near-death experiences had taught me to remain calm and I mastered the rhythm of my heart. If anything it slowed, yet with each beat, it said *Gideon. Is. Missing*. So I responded with *I. Will. Find. Him.*

Joey appeared in my face. "What? Your horse is just gone? This guy *Craig* lost your horse?" Joey demanded.

My nostrils widened as I tried to inhale, steady and calm, but there was a slight tremor I couldn't stop. "I don't know. That's what he said. But Gid's a horse. I mean, he can't just disappear into thin air." The corners of my mouth drew down.

He couldn't, truly. I was a science major and this was elementary stuff. Matter cannot be created or destroyed. Gid was at the most high-end and secure farm I had ever set foot on, with a ton of horses worth six figures or more, so he would be fine. He had to be, right? *God? Where's Gid? This is weird.*

"Something's not right here," Joey said. "I don't trust this Craig guy."

I understood why Joey didn't trust Craig. Even over the phone he oozed mischief. But *I* trusted him. I had to. Aside from Terri and my animals, Craig had been my only friend these last couple weeks. Sure, he wasn't perfect. Sometimes he looked at me like he was appreciating my entire body, which was a bit inappropriate. And I'd driven him and his car home from dinner the other night because he'd drunk too much. But he had also been there for me and taken care of me when I needed it most. I didn't blame my family or Joey for not being there. I was the one who moved away. But Craig *had* been there.

We climbed into Joey's car and sped out to the farm a few hours earlier than originally planned and with a lot more urgency.

We walked in and went straight to Gideon's stall. It was indeed empty: clean straw bedding, a bulging hay net waiting to be eaten, and his happy yellow halter looking like a fraud hanging on the hook. *Where would Gid be without his halter?* If anyone were to take him somewhere surely they'd need that. The idea of using any other of the hundred halters at the barn never crossed my mind. *He must have gotten loose somehow.*

I decided to explore the property, Joey at my back whispering, "This isn't right. Something smells fishy." I all but ignored him. *No one would steal Gid. Not at this farm with so many horses way more valuable than him. Sure, Gid is invaluable to me, but he's all but worthless to racehorse people.*

We walked around the barn and peeked in all the stalls, then headed toward the training oval, checking all the paddocks along the way. *Surely someone just put him in the wrong place.*

Craig found us on the path up to the track. He explained that they had turned Gideon out in a paddock with his pony last night, but this morning the pony was there and Gideon wasn't. The few people at the training farm gawked as they walked by, leaning toward each other and whispering.

The manager of the facility came out to help. He had been on the track with Robert and Craig after my accident. His brows furrowed every time he looked at my face, but I didn't have the bandwidth for pity. I was there to find my horse.

We made Craig tell us what happened over and over. Joey hurled questions while I stood stunned, racking my brain for every scenario that could lead to my horse not being in his paddock and his halter still on the stall door.

"What about the cameras?" Joey asked, pointing to the ones overlooking all the barns.

"They're not actually turned on right now," the manager replied, casting his eyes down.

"Wasn't anyone around? I mean, there are really expensive horses here. Surely people were here. Grooms live on the property," I asked with calm resolve.

"We've asked around and so far no one saw anything." The farm manager's voice was full of remorse.

"Tell me what happened again?" Joey demanded.

Around and around we went. Joey's instant reaction was to explode and accuse. Mine was to pull back, think, and observe. I needed to search. If Gid had been in the paddock with the pony and the pony was still there, someone had to take Gid out. I'd had this horse for years and he'd never jumped a fence. And these fences were higher and more substantial than most farms he'd lived on. Craig swore they scoured the property and he was nowhere to be seen. But horses don't just disappear. He had to be around.

Joey and I turned and walked away as my brain grappled with the strange fact that Gideon was missing. Not only was he lost, but he was lost from a training track crawling with workers.

With some distance between us and Craig, Joey spat, "It was him. I can tell. Something's not right about him. I can feel it." I had sensed that energy too—the day we met, when he picked me up at the hospital, when he cut my food the day after the accident, and when he took me to dinner so I didn't waste away in my apartment. But did weird energy make him a candidate for horse theft? He reminded me of my mischievous guy friends back home. They might say something inappropriate or pull a practical joke, but they'd never truly hurt someone. At least not on purpose.

This had to be some kind of accident and the person was afraid to fess up. I could see it clearly in my mind. Maybe a track worker wanted to go for a ride. It must be torture to work around horses all day every day and never get to ride. Racehorses were strictly forbidden and hardly rideable outside the track. Gideon was a riding horse that was trained and pretty well-behaved. The person would think *what damage would it do to ride this horse around?* So, maybe they went for a ride early in the morning before the bosses were awake, or late in the afternoon once everyone had gone home.

Gideon had recently become head-shy. He'd run backward when I dropped the halter to put on his bridle. Maybe something was wrong with his teeth and he needed a visit from the horse dentist, but I'd been too overwhelmed after my accident to deal with it. Someone probably thought they could ride him, but when they took off his halter to put on a bridle, he ran backward and got away. That would explain the halter without a horse.

The best plan I could think of was to go door to door asking people if they had seen my horse. The farm was in the back of a neighborhood where many residents had their own horses and barns, or at a minimum large yards. Gid was striking. Not only was he hard to miss, but anyone would notice a loose horse, especially in an equestrian neighborhood.

We got into Joey's black Camry and he drove from one house to the next. At each stop, I climbed out, walked across the front yard, and rang the doorbell. People opened their doors to a young stranger with a mangled mouth standing on their stoop. "Hi, I'm just coming by to see if you've seen a horse? He got away from the training center at some point last night or this morning."

Their faces molded into an expression you might make during a gruesome scene in a horror movie. "No, I haven't seen him. What does he look like?" The conversations were all the same. I described Gid. They said they'd be on the lookout. Occasionally as I turned to leave, someone would say, "Are you that poor girl who had the accident on the track?" Apparently, word got around the community, but my horse hadn't. I was now the poor girl who had the accident and who also lost her horse. By the third house my cheeks were red with embarrassment, but we kept going.

After I knocked on every door on the street and called Terri, we swung by the track one last time. Cops would be there soon. They would let me know if they heard anything. Maybe someone would speak up.

The drive back to my apartment was mostly silent. Joey was determined Craig stole my horse. I couldn't wrap my mind around the fact Gideon was gone, much less that someone had purposely taken him. Who would want him besides me? He was a little nutty, and his farrier in Mississippi suspected he had a degenerative foot disease called navicular. All I knew was I would keep searching until we were together again.

As a kid, Ms. Brenda took us to horse sales so we could purchase horses people were ready to get rid of. We would take them back to the barn, train them up a bit, and resell them for profit. The meat buyers were at the same sales, buying the cheapest horses. What if Gideon was taken to one of those sales? What if no one at the sale wanted him? I couldn't let myself go there.

Joey needed to get back to Lexington for class. "Go," I told him. "I'll be fine. I'll keep looking." He searched my eyes, but I had stepped into my *figure it out, get it fixed* mode. I had nearly perfected this thanks to Gid's consistent attempts at death. From a fractured leg to a poisonous snake bite to a sudden allergic reaction to penicillin, there was not a single incident where panicking or melting down was helpful.

Sandi stood by my side as we watched Joey pull out of the parking lot. Then I did the only thing I could think to do—turn on the computer and start searching.

God, what's going on here? Where is my horse? Help me, please.

Chapter 15

Realization moved in like a slow-moving storm—calm, almost peaceful when the lightning is a flash on the horizon and the rain is a gray cloud muting out the sun.

When Gideon had been away from his stall from sunup to sundown with no one reporting a loose or found horse, there seemed to be only one possibility. The hours ticked by as I moved from shock to denial to acceptance.

Gideon was gone. The change in air pressure made it difficult to breathe. *Gone.* Was this the *Wizard of Oz?* Did the same storm that smothered me carry him to a faraway, magical land?

How could someone just load him on a trailer without being noticed? And why? Why, out of all those expensive racehorses, would someone take Gid?

It had to be someone at the training track, someone no one would question when they loaded a horse onto a trailer and drove away.

Why? Why? Why? raced through my mind in a continual loop, threatening to pull me into a black abyss. But my heart demanded *Where? Where? Where? Find him! Now!* So I stepped away from the darkness to find my Gideon.

Maybe the thief took him to a horse sale to get rid of him. Gid could be in a kill pen somewhere, awaiting a fate I couldn't save him from.

Maybe someone wanted a show horse. He was undeniably, shockingly handsome. Everywhere we went, appreciative murmurs followed. His muscular Quarter Horse genes had blended with his lean Thoroughbred ancestry to create a masterpiece if it weren't for the suspected navicular disease in his front feet and the loose screw in his head.

Who wouldn't want him in their barn? I could see a girl in a cowboy hat and western boots pulling him off a trailer at a horse show, excited to try her new horse and clueless he belonged to someone else.

Or maybe he was deposited in a field somewhere in the thousands of acres of bluegrass around here. He'd graze and occasionally lift his head, looking over the fence, waiting for me to find him. A needle in a haystack.

The Bible said God is good.

The Bible said all good and perfect gifts are from above.

But this. This life I was living—it wasn't lining up.

I could see that image of Satan bargaining over my future. "Sure, she didn't reject you when I caused the accident, when her tire blew out, or when her and Gideon nearly fell, but what about if I take her horse?" he must have said.

I wanted to shake my fist at him and scream, unhinged and guttural, to throw things against the wall and see them shatter. I wanted to lie on the floor, a broken heap of flesh, and be done.

My eyes sought the hardwood of my apartment with its swirling wood grain and dark mahogany coloring. I could see myself melting like an ice cube, the water absorbing into the cracks between the planks and into the wood itself, disappearing from the world.

I wanted that.

I wanted to disappear.

But if I did, who would save Gideon?

There was a whisper in my mind. *Jesus intercedes for us when we can't pray.* I didn't know what verse or chapter in the Bible it came from, but I knew it was in there. I hoped it was right because the storm had stolen my ability to breathe, much less speak.

Jesus.

God.

Hold me.

Two years before, I thought I'd lose Gideon. It was the first day of summer. High School was officially over. I hopped out of bed, grabbed a five-pound bag of carrots, and drove to the barn way too fast. *Freedom!*

I wasn't going to Kentucky in the fall, but at least I'd have Gid nearby. *We have each other,* I thought as I pressed the accelerator, careening around the curves on the two-lane country road to Winterview Farm. The blacktop changed to gray and it was time to slow down. Gravel crunched under my tires as I parked. Grabbing the carrots, I slammed the truck door, announcing my arrival.

Walking through the doorway in the center of the barn, I greeted the old guys, Festus and Bacardi, with a smile and turned to see Gid next door. I peeked in, ripping a hole in the carrot bag, but his stall was empty. Fresh pine shavings and a pile of hay, still in its square shape from being pulled off the bale, awaited an occupant.

Gideon must not have come up this morning. I made my way out to the pasture, but no horses waited in the field. The roar of a lawnmower drew my attention. The wide-brimmed hat draped with mosquito netting could only be one person. Ms. Patti hummed along, taking out every buttercup in her path from atop the green mower. I traipsed out to see if she knew where my horse was, and she powered down the engine when she saw me coming.

"Hey, I can't find Gideon. Do you know where he is?" I asked. If anyone knew where he was, it would be her.

"Yeah." She peered up at me from beneath her wide-brimmed hat. It was an odd style, but smart with the intense Mississippi sun and excessive bugs. "Nicole was doing chores this morning and said he came up with a big cut on his leg. She stuck him in the wash stall until I could take a look."

"Okay, thanks. I'll go check it out!" I smiled and turned to bebop my way to the other barn where the wash stalls were. Injuries and horses go hand in hand. I was a little bummed I probably wouldn't be riding today, but we had all summer for that.

Gideon stood patiently waiting for something, anything, to happen. His bright eyes said, "Hey Mom! What's going on? I want breakfast!" When the plastic bag crinkled, he nodded and swiveled his ears toward me. I held a piece of carrot and Gid's lips grazed my flat palm as he lipped it. He crunched and dipped his head so I could rub the spot between his white-rimmed eyes and up to his forelock, causing a snowfall of tiny white hairs that tickled my nose.

He finished the carrot and sucked his tongue to savor the juices while I rubbed my hand along his body, on my way to the slightly puffy right rear leg. I crouched next to him, gaping at a bloody open wound about six inches down from his hock. Patti arrived and dismounted the mower to survey the damage with me. "Well, Sarah, it doesn't look that bad, but since it's right there on his leg, we should give the vet a call." She had the vet's number pulled up on her phone before she even finished speaking.

Disappointment weighed me down, but I refused to give in. *This is part of owning horses,* I reminded myself. "Okay, let's call him." I leaned into Gid and she meandered off, phone against her ear.

I pulled up a chair and sat with my horse to wait and savor this time together without the burden of school or sports practice. He seemed content as he bonked me with his nose to beg for carrots and chased my arm, trying to touch it with his sticky pink tongue. My friends arrived and tied their horses in the hallway. We chatted while they groomed and tacked up. The rumble of a heavy truck told us the vet was here, so I jogged out to greet him.

A lady stepped out of the truck. "Hi! I'm Dr. Smith! Dr. Vice is out of town and I'm his intern. I'm filling in for him while he's gone."

"Hi, I'm Sarah!" I stuck out my hand and gave her a firm shake. "Gideon's right in here." We walked to the barn where he waited. "He doesn't seem to be in much pain, but it's in a bad spot on the back of his leg, so we wanted to have it looked at."

She crouched by his hind leg while my horse looked to me for reassurance. I rubbed his forehead to distract us both. She appeared by his head in just a few seconds with a somber expression. *Shouldn't this take longer? Does she want to maybe clean the wound or something?* As the vet popped her rubber gloves off, Patti appeared by my side. In my periphery, I saw my friends pause next to their horses to listen. The vet's gaze met mine and her voice cracked when she told me, "I feel bone chips. We need to get him to the clinic to take x-rays right away."

My boots were cinder blocks. My brain was a mess of firing pinballs, thoughts I couldn't seem to grasp as they moved too fast. *What if we're out of plays? Doesn't a broken leg on a horse mean game over?* Gideon looked so normal.

Patti and the vet walked through the long barn, making plans while horses peered out of their stalls to see what was happening. My friends descended on me. My carefree summer smile was still partially pasted on, a denial of the truth as they muttered condolences and encouragement. Everything was hazy. The vet's words settled around me like a thick fog. *I feel bone chips*. Gideon might die. My Gideon. Might die. He looked fine. He wasn't.

All the things that had mattered when I pulled up to the barn—freedom, fun, and graduating from high school—swirled down the drain. Gideon had to live.

God, Gideon has to live. A fear like I had never known pushed into my heart. I pleaded with God, a plea that would consume every waking moment of the next week. *Please save Gid.*

A memory from when I was twelve years old stayed in the back of my mind that week. My best friend's stepdad was dying of cancer. Ms. Brenda not only taught me about horses but also about prayer. She quoted from the Bible, "I tell you that if two of you on earth agree about anything they ask for, it will be done for them by my Father in heaven." My friend and I held hands and prayed. I believed with my whole heart. One night a couple weeks later her stepdad died. *But we agreed*, I thought desperately when my mom gave me the news.

What if God lets Gideon die? What did I do wrong then so I can do it right this time? Was my faith not big enough? I thought I only needed the faith of a mustard seed. I can't lose Gideon.

I helped Patti load Gid into the horse trailer and she took him to the clinic for x-rays. I was told to go home. Dr. Vice would be home from his trip in three days and would look at the images and decide what to do. Surgery or "humanely euthanizing" were the two options.

God, please save Gideon. Please make him be okay.

I begged and pleaded, worried His answer for Gideon would be the same as the answer for my friend's stepdad. Wasn't Gideon a gift? Why would God take Gideon—the thing I cared most about in the entire world—away from me?

A tiny whisper broke through the cacophony of rage and grief. *Put me first.* It didn't make sense, and I ignored it.

For three days, I teetered on a ledge. If I fell off, if Gid didn't survive, I wasn't sure I would either. I clung to a tiny thread of hope that he could have surgery and everything would be okay. The possibility that he wouldn't was a gaping canyon ready to swallow me.

The night before Dr. Vice returned, I dreamed I was riding Gideon through a park. As we walked over a bridge, he lost his footing and fell over the edge. My body became a specter, looking down at my broken horse, who surely wouldn't make it. I woke with a lead weight in my stomach.

At 10 a.m., I climbed into my truck to drive to the clinic. Gideon's Frosted Flakes sat in the passenger seat, and I backed down the hill of our driveway onto the road.

Put me first, I heard again.

I clenched my jaw. *My horse may not make it today,* I shot back. I reached for the gearshift to put the truck in drive.

Put me first.

Everything roiling inside of me exploded. Tears streamed down my face and I gasped for air. *God, please fix this! God, please make this okay! Oh, God.* I leaned my head on the steering wheel and my shoulders shook.

God.

I finally understood.

God.

God, I am so sorry for putting Gideon first. I'm so sorry. The prayer poured from me. *He's a gift from you and I love him so much. I'm so sorry I put him first. How dumb that I put the gift before the One who gave him to me. But I did. Please forgive me, God. Please. And take care of him, please. Please don't take Gid away. But even if you do, I love you and I'm sorry.* My knuckles were white on the steering wheel and hiccups made breathing nearly impossible.

A vision played out in my mind. A farmhouse with a wraparound porch, kids swinging on a tire swing, and an older me, probably in my forties, carefree and laughing with my hand resting on the chestnut coat of an old swaybacked Gideon.

At that moment I wasn't quite sure if it was a figment of my imagination or if God had really given me a vision. My gut told me it was the latter.

Taking a deep breath, I whispered, "Thank you." Then I put the pickup in drive. Peace and hope settled over me.

I pulled up at the clinic and saw Patti's beautiful pearl white dually out front. I had been prepared to face this alone but was grateful for the support. Gid feasted on Frosted Flakes in his clinic stall and I gawked at the fresh bandage on his leg. It looked more like a huge pole than a bony horse's leg. Dr. Vice called us back.

Patti stood behind me as he looked me in the eye, then turned to point at the bone on the images. "It looks like the splint bone is crushed right here," he gestured to the x-ray and spoke in a no-nonsense tone. "But we do have a couple of options. I think the break is low enough that we can take out the bone from the fracture down. As long as we have this large piece here at the top, all the tendons and ligaments here will get stronger and be able to do the job of the splint bone." He looked at me, eyebrow cocked as I tried to withhold my excitement and match his professional tone.

They looked so serious. Surely, I missed something. "Okay, so we can take the bone out and the tendons and ligaments will just take over?" I asked both for clarity and to hear again that it would be okay.

"Yep," he said. "There is a chance we go in there and there's not enough of the splint bone left. But judging by the x-rays, we have enough bone and can do the surgery. When this happens, he should be able to make a full recovery and be rideable again. Or if you don't want the risk or expense, you can euthanize him. Which option do you want to do?" He looked at me without cracking even a hint of a smile. I peered into his eyes, trying to figure out if he was that businesslike or if he was trying to hold back his own joy. He didn't crack, but I did.

A grin stretched across my face as I exclaimed, "Let's do the surgery!"

It took months of leg wrapping and spoiling my horse with Frosted Flakes, and a summer of cleaning stalls at the clinic to work off the bill, but well into my freshman year of college, Gideon was good as new. The scar on his white stocking always reminded me of the time I thought I would lose him.

Now that Gid was missing, that scar was crucial. It was the identifying mark I would put on all the fliers. There were plenty of chestnut horses with four white stockings and a blaze, but not many with a nearly twelve-inch scar on one leg.

As sleep slowly overtook me, I clung to my dog and the vision of an old Gideon and my future self and family. It couldn't happen if he was gone forever. I had to find him.

CHAPTER 16

I WALKED INTO THE first day of Equine 101 a couple minutes before class started. The hum of conversation reduced to a whisper. Eyes followed me to the closest vacant seat I could find. It was in the center of the room in the second row. Heads dipped together, hands covered mouths, and brows furrowed.

Word was getting around fast considering the semester just started. Not only was I the girl who'd crashed on the track, but now I was the one whose horse was missing. I laid my notebook on the table, pen in hand, and tried to pay attention to the professor as he took the podium.

"Do horses have rights?" he asked. Students raised their hands, giving their two cents. By the third answer, my mind was elsewhere.

Where is Gideon? What can I do to find him? Terri's having fliers made today. I'll drive them to different sale barns after class.

I studied the odd swirls and lightning bolt shapes on the classroom's carpet to try to distract myself. It reminded me of late 1980s sitcoms. Whoever chose it must have felt so on trend. I wondered if they thought it was "timeless."

When I dipped into macroeconomics, I was merely a face in a large crowd. From there I had another equine department class, where the students and the professor watched me with a mix of curiosity and pity. I gazed back, lifting my eyebrow a tad, daring them to say something. Begging. *Tell me where he is. Someone somewhere has to know*. But their sympathy couldn't fix my face or give me any clues as to Gid's whereabouts.

After my final class, I crossed to the business administration offices. Terri was waiting with a stack of beautiful full-color fliers that would have cost me a fortune to print.

"Sarah, I really think he's at a racetrack as a pony," she said.

I laughed, empty and desperate. "He would never make a good pony. There's no way."

A "pony" at the track was a horse used to lead nervous racehorses. Images flashed through my mind of Gideon, white-rimming his panicked eyes and defying physics as he ran backward down the track before smashing into the rail or another horse. Or, if he didn't lose his mind in fear, he would crow-hop the entire way around the track, demanding to release his speed before the rider gave up and took him back to the barn. No. He'd never make a good racetrack pony. Someone probably took him to a sale or sold him to a show barn.

"Okay well, I'm going to take some fliers to the trainers who have our horses, just in case," she replied.

"Thank you!" I was 100 percent sincere, even if it was a waste of her time and paper. I was grateful to have someone helping me.

I ducked into the small computer lab reserved for equine business program students and pulled up AskJeeves.com.

"What Horse Sales are in Louisville, KY?"

"What Horse Shows are in Louisville. KY"

"Stolen Horse"

"Found Horse Louisville, Kentucky"

"How do I find my horse?"

"What do I do if my horse is stolen?"

I jotted down all the horse sales I could find in the area and saw that Louisville was hosting the second-largest Quarter Horse show in the world. Maybe he'd be there. They would need registration papers to show him at an official Quarter Horse show, but he could pass hands.

Grabbing the fliers from Terri's office, I hastily thanked her and made my way to the truck. The weekend was approaching. I couldn't be at every horse sale, but I could get fliers up at the sale barns now.

The office door at the first auction house was ajar. I tapped my knuckles on the dirty blue door, heart pounding in my ears. "Come on in," sang through the crack. The lady on the other side looked at me, forehead crinkled in expectation.

"Hi," I said, realizing I hadn't planned what I would say. There was a lot to tell. My face heated, but I pushed through. "My horse. He's missing. We think he was stolen."

Her face froze in a mixture of confusion, shock, and pity, and I paused to breathe. Pressure built behind my eyes and refused to be released. "Anyway, could I leave some of these fliers here? I thought maybe whoever took him would be at a horse sale this weekend trying to make some quick money." The unreleased pressure was making my face hotter.

"Sure, honey!" Her yellow hair didn't budge as she nodded, and her thick accent was shocking even to my Mississippi girl ears. "Where'd he go missin' from?"

"I had him at a training track outside of town. Do you know of any other places I should check out?"

"Well, you know, there's a slaughter sale that happens right close to that track. It's once a month. In fact, it was last Saturday. What day did you say he went missin'?" she asked matter-of-factly.

My mind spun out of control with calculations. We didn't really know when he disappeared. Craig had called Sunday morning to tell me he was missing. But what if Joey was right and Craig was the thief? He could have loaded Gid into a trailer, sent him to that sale, and waited 'til Sunday to tell me he was missing. "Hopefully he didn't end up there." I couldn't dwell on that possibility. Plus, the vision of me and old swaybacked Gid couldn't happen if he ended up there.

"Here's the fliers. I'll tape a couple up out by the corrals, if you don't mind."

"That'll be just fine, shuga. I hope you find yer horse."

"Me too." I nodded and smiled as I walked out to tape up the fliers.

Slaughter sale. Slaughter sale. God, help.

I taped a flier to a metal wall and stepped back to look. A full-color photo of my Gideon stared back. At the top it said, "Missing Horse," and the bottom gave details, including the scar on his leg and a phone number. I couldn't recall ever seeing a missing horse sign before. When I said I wanted to be a trailblazer, this wasn't what I had in mind.

Hopping into the truck, I turned for one last glance at the bright white flier in the middle of an ominous gray wall. It would be hard to miss. *God, please.* I refused to give in to a mental picture of my Gid being tagged and piled into an overcrowded two-level livestock truck. That was a figment of my imagination. It wasn't the truth.

I sat on the floor that night, keyboard in my lap, sipping McAlister's sweet tea. It left a ring of water on the floor that I wiped away with my hand. A desk would be helpful.

A stolen horse is newsworthy. I found every TV station and newspaper website in the Louisville area and emailed my story.

"I'm new in town. I had an accident on the track. Two weeks later, my horse disappeared, probably stolen." It was a story for the ages. Or, at least it was the most impactful story to happen in my life. Surely if I could get some news coverage, someone would come forward.

A video played in my mind: Gideon being kept in someone's backyard pasture with overgrown grass and a shoddy fence. Their neighbor sees my story on the news. Gid's picture fills the screen while I plead for help. She realizes that's the horse the crazy person next door has been keeping! She lunges for the corded phone on the wall, dialing the number at the bottom of the screen while staring at Gid with wide eyes through a curtained window.

I found an organization called Netposse that was dedicated to finding stolen horses. Reading story after story, I realized most horses were still missing. With each unresolved case, my chest grew heavier. I vowed to find my horse.

The next morning, no news stations or papers had responded, but an email from "stolen horse international" was sitting in my inbox. Her words were kind, hopeful, and determined to make my story a successful one. She promised to get the word out to her network. They would all keep an eye out for a flashy chestnut with four white stockings, a blaze down his face, and a scar on his back right leg where a splint bone should be. With more than just Terri in my corner, a little hope crept in.

"I'm coming to get my gear," I texted Craig after class. All the new gear I had purchased for galloping was still at the training track. It was time to retrieve my things and be done with that place.

"Your helmet's in the office, but your vest disappeared. Someone must have taken it," Craig replied.

Anger roiled through me. Someone took my brand new safety vest? I didn't have an extra $250 lying around to buy a new one. Plus, too many things of mine conveniently disappeared under Craig's care.

"I'm coming out anyway. I'm going to look around," I texted back.

"Okay, well it's not here. I looked."

My nostrils flared. Since Gid disappeared, I'd hardly heard from Craig. There had been two texts asking, "Did you find your horse yet?" They felt obligatory. I wanted my gear, but I also hoped someone would be willing to talk. Pulling into that bluestone parking lot was a punch to the gut. How had things turned so bad so fast? This place of dreams was now my nightmare.

The manager intercepted me before I was even out of the truck. "Have you heard anything?" I asked, taking in his gray hair and matching mustache.

"Well, the cops came. No one seems to know anything..." and then I stared into the mouth of Charlie Brown's teacher. "Wah wah wah wah wah wah wah" His face contorted in remorse and pity, neither of which would help me find Gid.

My jaw tensed. I couldn't even clench my teeth together. I nodded and thanked him. "We'll let you know if we hear anything," he said as I strode away.

I walked into the third barn to find Craig in the center of the aisle looking for all the world like I was the last person he wanted to see. The camaraderie of those nights eating together with him cutting my food had morphed into the head scratches and stutters happening in front of me.

"Hey Craig, I need my vest," I stated matter-of-factly. If he knew anything about Gideon, he was either hiding it or would have called to tell me. He hadn't called.

Following him into the office, he shoved things around, as if a vest the size of my torso was hiding under a pile of papers. He repeated what he said in his text. "Yeah, Sarah, I don't know. I mean, I brought it back from the track after you left in the ambulance, but it disappeared. Your helmet's there."

I grabbed my brand new skullcap off a hook on the wall, tucking it under my arm. Rage was becoming a rock in my belly. Craig slipped out, saying he needed to do something somewhere else. I looked around the office, but there were only so many places a safety vest would be. Exiting, I hooked right to take a peek in the stables. Maybe, somehow, all this time, Gid was just in another stall.

I crossed from Craig's side of the barn to the other end, which was run by a different trainer. I checked each horse, hoping someone would grab me and tell me they knew where Gideon was and how I could find him. When the trainer for the other side, years older than Craig, emerged from around a corner and pulled me to the side, I was speechless.

The tall man bent over to meet me at eye level, and I became a toddler in a nursery with a scary grownup wagging a finger in my face. "Let me tell you, sweetie," he said as he pushed his glasses up on his nose and sweat trickled from his sideburns. "I know you want that horse back, but you ain't never gonna see him again. I'm sorry to be the one to tell you this. I don't know what happened, but I can tell you he's gone and you best move on with your life."

I stared at his flushed complexion. Spittle flew when he talked, a combination of anger mixed with—care?—in his eyes. My belly churned with rage. "I'm sorry to be the one to tell you this, I really am." I knew he was because I'd heard he had a daughter my age. He was trying to be kind in his own hardened, hopeless way. But if I opened my mouth, I might erupt.

My nostrils flared as I sucked in air in an attempt to soothe the fire in my body. Nodding, I whispered, "Thank you," parting my lips just enough for the words to escape before I walked away, peeking into the last few stalls as I passed, rushing to the parking lot.

Leaping inside my truck, I slammed the door to block out any more evil. How had I loved this place so much? It felt like it was crawling with demons, a place of despair. I gripped the steering wheel, pressing my forehead against it, shaking with anger.

How dare he? Maybe he was trying to be kind, but he doesn't know me or Gideon. He doesn't know that we're a force to be reckoned with, a match made by God. Soulmates. How! Dare! He! He obviously doesn't know us. God, he doesn't know us.

The anger was like nothing I had felt before, and as I sucked in deep breaths, a few determined tears escaped. I imagined this unholy anger releasing little by little with each breath and tear. *God*, I begged. *Hold me.* I imagined a gigantic hand carrying me, my head resting on His palm like a pillow. And then I pulled out of the parking lot, flinging gravel in my wake, to get some food and figure out my next step.

Chapter 17

The Quarter Horse show arrived at the fairgrounds in Louisville, just minutes from my apartment.

I'd competed at some of these shows in Mississippi, where people drove from two states away to compete. There were always horses for sale. Someone would ride over while we waited our turn to compete and say, "Hey, you gotta watch this one go. We just decided to sell her."

Or a person would sidle up to Ms. Brenda, eyeing her best and favorite horse, and ask, "Is that one for sale?" Brenda would get a look in her eye that made my heart sink. For the right price, nearly every horse was for sale. I hated seeing the good ones go.

I could only imagine how much of that would happen at the second-largest Quarter Horse show in the world. This wouldn't be a Mississippi show with people driving from Louisiana or Tennessee. Competitors and trainers would haul horses from across the country to compete this week.

A reel played in my head: A trainer awaiting his turn in the arena would ride up to an acquaintance he only sees at these big shows. They live on opposite sides of the country, so this is his only chance. With a casual air, like everything was on the up and up, he'd flick his head and say, "Hey, I just got my hands on this gorgeous chestnut barrel horse. We don't have papers on him so he can't show here at the registered shows, but man would he dominate on the barrel-racing circuit."

There were plenty of barrel races where you could win a lot of money, and it didn't matter whether your horse had the finest breeding record in the registry, or if a mystery stallion got loose and visited your mare in the night.

I had to get to that show. Gathering up the stack of "Missing Horse" fliers, I drove to the fairgrounds with Sandi in the passenger seat. We slowly looped through the parking lots that surrounded the complex. The show office seemed like a smart place to start.

A barn of temporary metal stalls stretched from the central building to the edge of the expansive blacktop. Parking spaces had become bathing areas with bottles of shampoo, relaxed horses, and water splattering on everything within a ten-foot radius. Horses with glistening coats and hooves coated in polish were being led from the stabling area into a wide doorway in the main building.

I spotted a small structure with people milling in and out, papers in hand. That had to be the show office.

My stomach twisted as I parked and grabbed Sandi's leash, stepping down from the truck. This wasn't Jackson, Mississippi. There was no Ms. Brenda or Ms. Patti to introduce me to people. There would be no giddy moments with my barn friends, gushing over the fanciest horses or joking behind the alleyway to cover our nerves as we waited our turn to run. It had been a while since those moments, anyway.

Since I got my driver's license, I'd stopped depending on friends and trainers when I wanted to go to horse shows. I'd load Gid in the trailer, my saddle in the back seat of the pickup, and hit the road. Sometimes friends or family would tag along, but if no one was free it was just me and Gideon. The hot knife of realization hit. I was walking up to a horse show without my horse.

What if I don't find him? God? I whispered. Tears pressed into the back of my eyes, but I refused to allow them. Tears were a waste of time. They wouldn't bring Gideon back.

An older gentleman in a golf cart met my eyes from several parking spots away, the corner of his lip turning up in a welcoming grin as he zoomed over to me. "Can I help you, ma'am?" His voice was gruff with a thick southern accent, and his belly nearly touched the steering wheel. I smiled, remembering all the big-bellied men at the Quarter Horse shows back home, who flirted with Ms. Brenda and smiled at us barn rats who flocked to her.

"Well, actually, I'm here looking for my horse." I juggled with Sandi's leash and the stack of fliers as I pulled one out of the pile. "He disappeared over the weekend and I thought maybe he could have ended up here?"

"Wowee! I haven't seen anything that looks like this horse. He sure is a looker. I'm sorry to hear about your horse goin' missin' though." His words rolled out from beneath a bushy white mustache.

"That's okay." My eyes glistened with the lie and I swallowed. "I was thinking I'd put some fliers up in the show office. Do you know where it is?"

He pointed me in the right direction. "Mind if I keep this?" he asked. His white brows tilted up and the corners of his mouth tilted down, pulling the mustache with it.

"Yeah, that'd be great!" I said with a weak smile.

Papers covered the glass door of the office, making it nearly impossible to see through—reminders of required forms, legal notices, horses for sale. The door swung toward me as I reached for the handle. Two chatty women emerged, glancing at me before moving on. I felt judged by their roving eyes and ducked into the room before fear could stop me. Inside, people were scattered about, filling out show entries.

"Hi, can I help you?" drawled a woman from behind a cinder block half-wall. These people didn't sound like they were from Louisville. Folks in the city didn't add extra syllables to their words.

"Hi, yeah." Sandi jerked at the leash. Gripping it tighter, I jerked back and she returned to my side. Heart in my throat, I pulled out a flier. "Um, my horse went missing." If the people scattered around the room were pretending not to listen before, now they all unabashedly watched. "I was thinking whoever took him could have brought him here to sell. Can I leave some of these around, and maybe put some up?"

"Just leave some here. I'll put them around," the lady said matter-of-factly. I handed her several fliers, and with a weak thanks, turned to leave.

None of the gawkers smiled. No one said, "Oh sweetie." They were probably worried or sad for me. Maybe they imagined a horse thief on the loose who might take their best friend or biggest investment in the dark of night. I felt my resolve crumble under the weight of the silent stares.

One person stepped forward. “Can I have one of those?”

Those simple words knit me back together enough to keep going. “Yeah, of course.” I handed him the flier with a quick thank you before ducking out the door. It slammed shut behind me, and I wondered if the beautiful photo of Gideon was being tossed in the trash as I strode away. *This is hard, God.*

Normally, walking up to a stranger to ask a question set my heart into a frenzy. I did it when I needed to, but I’d rather not. Now, it was the only thing I could think to do if I wanted to get my horse back. It was embarrassing. My lip looked like I was on the losing end of a bar fight over the weekend. But it was a vast improvement over the swollen, weeping wound that had struggled to scab over. The braces were comforting, but my teeth underneath were still broken, twisted, and pointy.

Dr. Tran had attached a fake tooth to the wire. It was definitely better, but I had a long way to go. I reminded myself it didn’t matter how I looked. No one but me cared if I was pretty or had perfect teeth. Well, Joey might care, but he didn’t seem like the type to leave me over busted teeth.

On top of all of it, fear gnawed at my insides. *What if he’s not here? What next?*

The stable area was arranged in long rows that stretched on forever. Starting at the very front of the barn, the first stall on the furthest left row, I peeked in to see what waited inside. It was a shiny Quarter Horse, shorter than Gid, with sleepy eyes and his tail in a bag. Maybe, just maybe, if I looked in every single stall, I’d find Gideon waiting on me with wide eyes, wondering who these new people were and why I wasn’t there.

Every few stalls, people sat in monogrammed director chairs chatting with one another. Heart pounding, I’d barge into the conversation. Their heads would turn politely, eyebrows raised as they appraised me. Maybe they expected me to ask for money, try to sell them something, maybe ask a show-related question like, “Do you know how many entries are in the open division?” or hand them a gospel tract.

Instead, I asked if they’d seen my missing horse and handed them a flier. A couple people asked questions like, “How long has he been gone?” or “Where did he go missing from?" Most dismissed me fairly quickly with a pitying look, saying, "I'm so sorry but I'm not from here," or "No, I haven't seen him, but good luck."

One pair, voices dripping with annoyance, declared they hadn't seen him and turned their backs dismissively to continue talking. I glared, lifting my chin and an eyebrow. If they deigned to look they would not see the pain from their sting.

From stall to stall, I peered in at happy, big-bottomed Quarter Horses. I made my way to the end of the first row at the edge of the parking lot and turned to come down the center aisle. I looked at every horse and asked every person. Occasionally I taped a flier to the wall and walked away quickly, Sandi tugging on her leash.

Each horse that wasn't Gideon was a rejection. Every person who hadn't seen him made my goal seem more impossible. As I walked the last row of stalls, peeking in each one, my hope dwindled. Unless he was in one of these, he wasn't here. *Where is he? How will I find him? God?*

The third horse from the end was a fat chestnut, lighter and shorter than Gideon. He turned his head to me, wood shavings clinging to his forelock, and munched his hay. I wanted to lean into his warm body and feel hope. But he wasn't Gideon, so I kept going.

There was one more group of people clustered nearby. I warred with myself. *It's just another no.* My body quivered, and I glanced at my hands to see if they appeared steady. *But what if they've seen him? What if they can help?*

"Hey y'all." My voice was barely above a mutter.

"Hi!" they chorused, curious smiles lighting their faces. A blonde woman in a loose blouse leaned forward, ready to hang on my every word.

Taking a breath, I said it one last time. "My horse disappeared last week. He's part Quarter Horse, so I thought maybe he ended up here. Someone could be trying to sell him or something." Each member of the group reacted with wide eyes and mouths turned to o's. It was definitely the biggest reaction of the day.

"Oh, no!" the blonde declared. My body felt a zing of energy, like when I didn't get enough sleep and drank too much coffee. I could tell by their expressions that they hadn't seen him. I wanted to walk away then, but I refused to be rude to a group who actually seemed to care.

"We haven't seen him! But we'll take a few fliers and pass them around." She and the others nodded to each other.

They seemed sincere. Still, I felt like a joke—like a little kid being catered to with polite, overzealous words and actions. Handing them a stack of fliers and attempting to match their enthusiasm, I replied with "Thank you," while my insides shriveled.

I cut across the parking lot, making a beeline for the truck. The pressure behind my eyes was mounting. I imagined everyone I had just talked to watching me leave. The rude people, the kind people, and everyone else, sitting in their director chairs and saying things like, "poor girl," or "that's wild," or maybe even, "she's never going to find that horse." To break down in front of them would be to admit defeat. If they saw me cry, maybe it meant I didn't really believe I'd find him.

I wrenched open the truck door, nearly throwing Sandi in ahead of me before I dove into my metal cocoon. I gasped for air as my phone buzzed in my hand. The little window lit up—Dad. He rarely called, so I quickly flipped it open, as if somehow my dad in Mississippi knew something about my horse and could help. "Hello?"

"Sarah?" He almost sang my name.

"Hey, Dad!" My voice exuded fake cheer lined with clear desperation.

"We miss you, and we're worried about you." He paused long enough for me to take three breaths. "We're real sorry about your horse."

I could tell he was. I knew he was. He was my dad, and unlike some truly unfortunate people in the world, I knew my parents cared.

"Thanks." I shoved a thousand different meanings he probably couldn't hear into one word. *Truly, thank you. You saying this shows you love me. I love you, too. I feel really far away from y'all right now. I know you don't understand my love for horses, but I know you love me and that means you care that he's gone. I'm doing everything I can to find him. I know you're praying for me and I'm grateful. Thanks for being my parents and caring.*

"What if you came home this weekend?" he delicately proposed. "Just come for the weekend and see your momma and me. We really miss you."

I imagined going home, walking into my parent's kitchen with Sandi by my side. Mom would look up from where she stood over the stove preparing a special dinner for me, probably fried deer steak, rice, and black-eyed peas. She would leave the gravy, setting the wooden spoon on the edge of the pan, because coming to hug me—a long, warm embrace that is safety and love—was more important than gravy.

Two of their three dogs would sniff noses and butts with Sandi while the boldest little Westie, Bama Jr., would ignore her and come to me for a belly rub. Before I crouched down to rub his soft white hair, dad would come into the kitchen and wrap his arms around me. With red eyes and wet faces, the three of us would let our embrace say what none of us know how to say, and eventually the smoke alarm, smell of burned gravy, or an attention-seeking dog would force us apart.

I knew in the deepest part of my gut that if I went home over the weekend I'd never return to Louisville. Mississippi College would let me back in, reinstating my scholarship. Sandi would live with my parents while I stayed in the dorm, and I'd abandon this dream. At this moment it wasn't even about the dream. I couldn't leave my horse. Going home would be the ultimate white flag and my dear Gid would be lost to the wilds of Kentucky.

Leaning my head against the steering wheel, Sandi sat in the passenger seat staring at me. I took a shaky deep breath and closed my eyes. "I'm sorry, Dad, but I can't. I would love to see y'all, but I've got to find Gideon."

What I didn't say was *I miss you. I'd like nothing more right now than to sit at the kitchen table, you singing dumb songs and making me laugh while mom stands over the stove stirring gravy to go with the fried deer steak. Then we'll sit together and I'll gorge myself on my favorite meal that can make my mouth water just thinking about it.*

The dogs would sit at our feet hoping for scraps and Gideon would be in his stall at Winterview as if none of this happened. As if I hadn't chased a dream that was ripping my life apart. But it did happen. I'm here now. And I can't come home because I can't leave Gid.

"Okay. Well, we love you," he said in the whipped puppy voice he uses when he's not getting his way.

"I love y'all, too. Bye."

The line disconnected. I looked at my phone. Sandi looked into my eyes, leaning toward me as if she could see my soul shredding piece by piece and didn't know how to put it back together. Grasping the steering wheel, my storm of emotions exploded to the surface.

Gideon was gone. I was drowning, gasping for air, unable to form a word or a thought beyond *Gideon is gone*.

My mind was a movie reel of my worst fear. Gideon packed into an overstocked livestock trailer—dirty, nervous, and resigned. Gideon in a narrow corral in Mexico, like a dirty horse-sized version of an airport security line, except instead of waiting for an adventure, he was waiting to have a rod shot into his brain. Irreversible. Gone. Me in an ocean, being pulled under while reaching toward Heaven for help. Flailing. Crying. Hopeless. Overwhelmed. Unable to fill my lungs. Slowly losing the will to fight.

He's gone.

Sandi's cold nose touched my arm and my hand found her soft head.

God! I cried.

Fissures spread through my body. I was breaking and soon there would be nothing left. The image of Job on a pile of rubble scraping his sores returned to my mind. It could be worse. I could lose more. My parents, my brothers, Joey. Though losing more seemed unfathomable.

The scene in my head changed, moving from a devastated Job to a backyard. There was a tire swing and the sound of laughing kids. A beautiful old farmhouse stood to the side and left of center was swaybacked old Gideon. My hand was on his back, fingers threaded through a stringy coat of chestnut hair. It was his spring coat—the one he has when the long, insulating hairs of winter lose their luster and begin slowly shedding off. His eye sparkled and his right ear swiveled toward me as I laughed, the corners of my eyes crinkled. There was joy, hope, love, and a hint of sadness from knowing Gid wouldn't last forever.

I remembered the first time I'd had that vision—sitting in this same seat. I thought for sure Gideon wouldn't survive the broken leg. It felt like a message from God then, and I wondered if just maybe God was giving me another one.

The sobs and heaves turned to hiccups as a seed of hope was planted. How could that vision ever happen if I didn't get him back? It couldn't. I had a choice:

I could let the fear and what-ifs pull me down into a tunnel I may never return from, or I could lean into faith and the vision.

Chapter 18

While he visited over the weekend, Joey chauffeured me from one small town to the next, lending me his wheels and warm presence while I checked out livestock auctions. It was easier not to drown in despair with our fingers threaded together.

He pulled up to the first auction. Similar to the horse sales Ms. Brenda took us to, there was a covered, open-sided corral divided into a hundred or more small enclosures. "Just stop here," I directed. "If any trucks or trailers pull up, just get out of their way and I'll find you." I climbed out of his black Camry and scanned the animals. Tongues darted out to lick wet noses and liquid brown eyes stared back at me. My heart sank as cows peered inside my soul. They stepped closer, and part of me longed to climb through the slats of the corral and lean against their warm, stable bodies. Instead, I saw a sign that said "office" and jogged to it.

I rushed among strangers in boots and faded jeans. My face felt like a Salvador Dali painting. All of me, really, was like those melting clocks I had adored in high school. It was one of the few paintings that had ever made me feel something, and now I was living the vibe that piece of art radiated. On the outside, I probably looked thin and fit. Food didn't hold the same value it had a few weeks ago, and I was down to the tightest hole on my favorite belt. People couldn't see the droop of my cheeks in the downturn of my mouth, the dripping of my heart, the drag of my feet.

My heart rate picked up when, two steps from the office door, I realized I'd have to say it all again and watch their reactions. Someone exited the office and smiled, holding the door for me. "Thanks," I said with a small nod, that tiny act of kindness buoying me. A lady stood on the other side of a desk. "What can I do you for?" she said with a wide grin. My heart calmed a tad.

"Hi. My horse disappeared a week or so ago. I'm trying to get fliers to all the sale barns this week in case someone brings him through trying to sell him." Everyone around the office turned toward me, horror on their faces. They leaned in to catch every word of this equine Amber Alert. Bolstered by the attention, I kept going. "He's a chestnut with four stockings and a blaze, and a big scar on his back leg from breaking his splint bone."

"Oh, no!" People gasped at the double misfortune of our fairy tale.

"Yeah," I huffed.

"Sure sweetie." The lady was all business. "Hand me some fliers and be sure to put some around the barn. We'll keep our eye out. I hope you find him." Heads nodded and women crossed the office to look at Gid's picture.

"Me too. Thanks," I said with a sad smile before turning to leave, tears prickling my eyes. *Why does kindness make me want to cry more than anything else?* I wondered as I taped up a couple fliers before hopping back into Joey's car. Grabbing his hand, I swallowed my emotion and discussed our next destination.

By the last stop of the day, people were tired and responded with fewer words and pleasantries. I taped three signs around the sale barn and paused to stare at the last one. *Is this real? My Gideon on a missing horse sign*. The weight of my heart and bones told me it was very real. *God*, I whispered. I turned to head back to the car. It waited in the middle of a vast nothingness of red, hopeless dirt. The door stood open, an invitation to return to a place where I was safe and loved.

We attended a church downtown on Sunday, had lunch, and Joey went back to Lexington. Monday morning started another week of classes, dentist appointments, and continuing the search in whatever way I could.

Dr. Vittitow rolled over to me in the wheelie chair, face lit with his disarming dimpled grin. The anxiety over losing Gideon lessened a tad here.

He grabbed his instruments to peer at my teeth, little dental glasses perched on his nose, and said, "So Sarah, what do you think God is trying to teach you in all of this?"

I couldn't breathe. My brain felt like a hamster wheel with a bored rodent on it, spinning, then slowing, then picking up the pace again, but getting nowhere.

What is God trying to teach me? I repeated in my mind, disbelief and rage fighting for space. The oxygen level of the room dropped, but I sucked in air anyway, trying to find some footing.

"Well…" I said, trying to fill the space.

His smile slipped, looking forced.

"I just…"

I wanted to spit and punch. To melt into the floor and disappear from life and this question. And I thought, for a second, maybe I wanted to go head-to-head with God over what He was trying to teach me, but I had enough sense to know that was a losing battle.

I tried to hide all those thoughts and look sane, like I was okay. Like I wasn't a melting clock, I wasn't mad at my Creator, and life was as happy as those stupid felt boards my Sunday School teachers used when I was a kid. I knew all the Sunday School answers, but this was no Sunday School question. I mean, yeah, you can sit in a circle and ask things like, "What do we do when life is hard?" and everyone stares at each other until a brave person pipes up, "Rely on God! He's always good." But He didn't *feel* good right now.

Or I could pick another standard—"God is love." But this didn't *feel* like love.

I resorted to my meager and unsuccessful pageant training and repeated the question. "What is he trying to teach me?" I smiled, maybe even chuckled—fake. Fake. Fake. Fake. Dr. V's eyes shadowed.

I was running on ice, scrambling for purchase that wasn't coming, legs flying in all directions like a cartoon. I was wiping out.

I knew God used hard stuff to teach things. I grew up in Sunday School every week. My parents were so consistent about getting us to church that when something happened, like my brother vomiting his maple doughnut (three-fourths intact because he didn't chew his food back then) into a clear plastic newspaper bag on the way to church, we just kept going. They dismissed it as the new maple flavor not agreeing with him, while I sat wide-eyed in the back seat of the van in my Sunday dress and stockings that squeezed red indentations into my waist.

One winter Sunday when I was in junior high, we woke up to six inches of white fluffy snow coating the world. In my entire life, I had never seen anything like it except when we went to Lake Tahoe for my aunt and uncle's wedding, and vacation snow doesn't count. Our new puppy leaped like a bunny rabbit from one spot to the next, leaving little puppy-sized prints as he went. Central Mississippi was in awe of this gift from winter. After a thirty-second debate, mom and dad decided even a once-in-a-lifetime snow shouldn't keep us from church, even if it would all melt away while we were there. Only four of us showed up for my class, and we spent the hour with our noses pressed to the window, searching for the fluffiness that had disappeared into the parking lots and roads of downtown Jackson.

As I sat in that chair in Dr. Vittitow's office, red creeping into my face, I didn't want to think about what God was teaching me. I wanted to survive, find my horse, and get my face back to normal. Then I'd talk to God about it.

I eventually stuttered out a Sunday School answer that God was teaching me to depend on Him. It was clear in Dr. Vittitow's eyes that he didn't believe me. I didn't believe me either.

The rest of the appointment was quiet as he worked, and I stewed over the question I wanted to forget. Somehow it had seeped into my every cell and wouldn't shut up.

What is God teaching me?

What is God teaching me?

I wanted to stomp my feet like a toddler, shake my fists at the sky, and scream, "I DON'T CARE! I DON'T WANT TO LEARN RIGHT NOW!"

Instead, I closed my eyes while Dr. Vittitow scraped the nerves from inside a damaged tooth, and I breathed in the question over and over. *What is God teaching me?*

Okay, God, I relented. *What are you trying to teach me? Let me learn it and get it over with.*

I was so tired of trying to duck flaming arrows, slowly turning myself to stone so it wouldn't hurt when they hit their mark. The question put a chink in that stone. Like taking a hammer and chisel to a statue, every time that question replayed the stone crumbled a little. I was scared.

Chapter 19

The question drummed in the back of my mind. Impossible to escape. Leaving the dentist, I tried to act normal. I called my parents, talked to Joey, grabbed some food, and walked Sandi. I was cordial to my roommate and feigned interest in a housewarming party she was throwing for us. All the while *what is God trying to teach you?* played on repeat.

What was God trying to teach me? Part of me didn't care to know. I had no interest in learning at this moment. I'd be happy to survive and find my horse. But a lesson seemed inevitable. More than that, with the way the question refused to go away, God must have something to tell me.

Sandi followed me, my little shadow, as I escaped to my steaming hot bedroom and closed the door. *The next time Joey's in town, we've got to get a window unit or something*, I told myself as my scalp went damp with sweat. Growing up in Mississippi, I loved the sticky heat of summer, but not in my bedroom. Sinking down on the floor next to the bed, I begrudgingly grabbed my Bible and whispered a prayer. *God, what do you want to teach me?*

I ran my finger over the gold embossed letters of "Sarah Ruth Bullock." Granny and Granddad gave me this Bible. They loved unconditionally. Their love wrapped around you, sticking to your skin like the humidity that envelopes you on a Mississippi summer day. I imagined Granny being part of the "great cloud of witnesses" the Bible talks about in Hebrews 12. At once I felt uplifted to have her cheering for me, yet empty at her absence. When Granny passed unexpectedly in the winter of my freshman year at Mississippi College, it ripped a hole in my heart, throwing me into a lifetime of hugging my loved ones with an edge of desperation. *What if something happens to one of us and this is our last embrace?*

Granny and Granddad had been taking a morning stroll around their neighborhood. When a car approached, Granny stepped back to get out of the road, tripped on the edge of the curb, and landed hard on her tailbone, causing a compression fracture in one of her vertebrae. It wasn't supposed to be a big deal. They did minor surgery to glue it back together. She was scheduled to go home in a couple days. The grandkids were told we were welcome to visit, but that it wasn't really necessary.

Joel visited her in the hospital a couple of times, but Nathan and I planned to see her when she got home. But when the entire town Nathan lived and worked in unexpectedly lost power he found himself with an open schedule. He used the time to make the hour trek to see Granny in the hospital.

I made watch bands out of old blue jeans and sold them at a store in downtown Jackson. While studying with Roommate, the store called and said one of the bands was missing a buttonhole. That was impossible. I tried on every single one before delivering them to the store. My mind grappled with this. *How in the world could a band I had fastened onto my wrist just a few days ago suddenly not have a buttonhole?* Whatever the answer was, I needed to get to the store to fix it. It was on the same street as the hospital, so I decided to visit Granny while I was downtown.

After remedying the watchband issue, Roommate and I found our way to the hospital. We weaved through the maze of floors, halls, intimidating doors we weren't sure we were allowed through, and nurses' stations until we were in Granny's room. Her skin, usually flushed with life, was a pasty pale beige, like she was wearing the wrong shade of foundation. The joyful spark in her eyes was absent. Her voice was raspy and pained, but she tried to cover it with a meek version of her trademark cheer. My face flushed and my heart sagged. *She's going home tomorrow*, I told myself. *She'll be fine. This is probably just from pain meds.*

I leaned over the hospital bed, eyeing all the cords and beeping machines, and tried to focus on the moment and this very important person. Wrapping my arms around her neck, I thoughtlessly, silently prayed, *if this is her future, if all that's left for Granny is pain and sad attempts at covering it up to make us feel better, just please take her.*

The next day Granny was supposed to return to her olive green home. She would ride past the magnolia tree, which had smooth patches on the branches from the years of being climbed, and see her award-winning gardens humming with bees and vibrant colors. She would return to the man she had loved for over fifty years. But when she swung her legs around the side of the hospital bed to go for a walk, a blood clot went to her lungs and she went to a different home. Less than a week later, her body rested in the ground.

We were dumbfounded. We now saw those random incidents that got Nathan and me to the hospital for what they were–miracles from God so we could say goodbye. Even so, it felt like life was supposed to go on like normal, but the hole in my chest would have hurt less if it were put there with a shotgun. I stared at my sociology notebook, baring down with my pen as I took notes, and told myself that grandparents were supposed to die. This was the circle of life. But if this was the circle, why did it feel so wrong?

We weren't ready. She had been so healthy and full of life. She and Granddad took care of people younger than them, ran the Jackson Garden Club, and taught Sunday School. Granny was a staple in the church choir and often cooked Sunday lunch for our entire family.

A few days later I walked into the free lunch the Baptist Student Union was providing. A line of brown folding tables stretched from one end of the gym to the other, covered with stacks of pizza boxes, plates, and napkins. I shuffled along like an inmate, imprisoned by loss, by expectations I had of myself, that others had of me, to be happy, to move on because death is part of life.

I grabbed a Styrofoam plate and lifted pizza box tops, searching for food. Instead I found my brother Joel, and then I found his arms. We spent the entire hour of the BSU lunch huddled together against the gym wall, sobbing while people—our friends—tried not to stare.

A couple months later, I was sure I had walked from that chasm of grief. Dad's little church asked me to sing. I'm not a brilliant singer, but years in the choir taught me how to carry a tune, and I knew the perfect song.

There was an old hymn written by a guy who lost his young son to illness and much of his fortune in the Chicago fire. Soon after, he sent his wife and four daughters on a ship bound for England, planning to follow in a few days. The boat his family was on collided with another vessel and sank. His wife survived, but they lost their four daughters to the ocean. When he sailed past the site where his daughters died, he was inspired to write the song "It Is Well with My Soul."

Now I was inspired to sing it.

Mom met me before service to practice. Then I sat on the second pew and waited as Dad welcomed everybody. He asked the congregation to stand and sing from the hymnal. In this tiny church, I could hear each person, their voices shaky with age. When they looked at me their eyes squinted into a smile, and I could see their excitement at my presence. I smiled back, uncertain of what else to do.

Mom nodded from the piano, and I walked sideways between the pews while Dad introduced me and the song. He told everyone how I missed my granny, but this was my declaration to the world. Mom began playing the intro. I refused to believe I was nervous in front of the crowd, but my smile wobbled, perilously close to falling.

I never realized how much I depended on my peers in the choir until I stood alone by the piano, trying to figure out when to start singing. I looked at Mom; her eyes grew frantic before softening. I had missed my spot. She nodded reassuringly and circled back, playing the intro again as if it were all on purpose. She exaggerated her hands and widened her eyes, and I knew this was her way of saying *it's time*. Taking a deep breath, I sent it into my diaphragm like all the music teachers taught, then funneled the air through my vocal cords and sang my prayer.

"When peace, like a river, attendeth my way,"

I pushed through the nerves. This was my prayer, and I was excited and kind of grateful to share it.

"When sorrows like sea billows roll;"

Sorrows like Gid almost dying from a broken leg, not going to Kentucky for school, and now the biggest of them all, losing Granny.

"Whatever my lot,"

Granny's gone.

"Thou hast taught me to say,"

Oh God, oh God, oh God; she's gone and I think my insides are cracking open.

"It is well, it is well, with my soul."

Hot tears streamed down my face in front of the entire congregation, and I could see that they could see, and I couldn't stop them. The corners of my mouth turned down. My voice quivered, and I fought for control.

Suddenly it was the part where people are supposed to echo. I had imagined I'd confidently hold the words out, ignoring the echo portion. But this was nothing like I'd imagined. I tumbled forward anyway.

"It is weeeeeell,"

My mind was like tennis balls in the dryer, tumbling and knocking around, yet never getting anywhere. How could I do this?

And then to my surprise, Joel's voice echoed back to me.

"It is well,"

I was hit with a violent wave, the kind that comes out of nowhere and sends you tumbling into the ocean, searching for the way up. For air. Like when you're struggling to hold yourself together and someone comes along and says something nice. *Why is it kindness that breaks me?*

"With my soul" came out broken in the middle. More of a cry than a song.

Joel and Dad's voices rang out together, repeating the line.

"With my soul."

My song was lost to gasping and tears. The little girl inside me, who watched *Wild Hearts Can't Be Broken* on repeat and swore to never cry, screamed in humiliation and rage. Not only was I a blubbering mess, but it happened in front of the entire congregation and my big brothers. I looked to Mom for an answer to some unknown question, but instead I saw a girl who didn't have a mom anymore. She nodded and tilted her head toward the door, giving me permission to flee. And I did.

I exploded through the door to the right of the stage. Part of me wondered what it looked like to everyone, what they thought. Were they worried, confused, or annoyed? Would they finish the song without me? Would they stop and stare at each other in shock or just keep going as if nothing happened? Would they talk about it over lunch or hold it inside and think about it all day? Or maybe, blessedly, they'd forget about it.

I took a left, stumbling across the soft blue carpet until I could get into the tiny bathroom behind the sanctuary. I turned the lock and crumpled on the floor. Emotions and thoughts I didn't know I had erupted from me.

God, I'm so sorry. God, it really is well with my soul. Or at least I thought it was. I swear it is, but why doesn't it feel like it.

As I prayed, I released the emotions that had been building for months. I was tired of holding it in. Tired of pretending I was fine. Tired of trying to keep my pain silent and hidden. *Does this mean it isn't well with my soul? Does this mean I'm lying to myself and God? Am I a liar? How do I make it well with my soul?*

A gentle tap sounded on the door, and I heard my mom through the crack in the door, "Sarah, are you okay?"

"Ye-es" I said with a hiccup.

"Okay. Do you want to come out or stay there?"

"I'll stay here."

"Okay, I'll see you after church," she said. Her feet padded against the carpet until I heard the gentle click of the door as she slipped back into the sanctuary.

Gathering my knees underneath me, hands to the ground with my face pressed into them, I began to earnestly pray. Since Granny died, I had avoided this conversation. But now I realized that, in a way, I blamed her death on my Creator. After all, God gives, but He also takes away.

I also worried it was my fault. What if my prayer was what did it? *If this is what she'll be like just take her home*, I had prayed, and I wanted to curse myself. I reminded myself that Granny was in Heaven, which is better than here. Apparently, it's so much better we can't even fathom it, which is why we cling to our lives here and to our loved ones who go.

I shared my fears and pain with God. I asked for forgiveness for distancing myself and blaming Him. I asked Him to carry Mom and Granddad as they grappled with the loss of Granny. And then I asked a hundred times for Him to help make it well with my soul. I wanted it to be. I wanted to trust Him with everything, even the hard things.

With a sad smile, I asked Him to say hello to Granny for me, and then I remembered that verse about the saints cheering us on. The picture in my mind was like a crowd on the side of the road cheering for marathon runners, except the curb was replaced by fluffy clouds, and they were up high looking down at the people they loved on Earth. Granny was on the front edge, leaning forward with her arms in the air, cheering with the twinkle back in her blue eyes.

When church ended, I emerged from the bathroom, red-faced but at peace. Maybe it wasn't completely well with my soul. Or maybe it was for now, but would it be in the morning when I woke up to a new day with new emotions? I supposed it was kind of like forgiveness because sometimes you have to forgive over and over again—seventy times seven the Bible says. So tomorrow, I would ask again for God to help me make it well with my soul.

I realized then that something being "well with my soul" didn't mean I'd be happy about it. While there might be a deep-seated peace that God's hand was on it, I'd still have moments when life would be hard and things wouldn't feel good.

Sandi's tail thumped on the bed, bringing me back to the present. I reached up and scratched her velvety head. Sitting on the floor in Louisville, things certainly weren't feeling good. *God is sovereign and God is good*, I reminded myself. *God, please help this all to be well with my soul*, I prayed. Opening my Bible to the back pages, I found a list of verses about God's love. My heart and mind needed this reminder.

I flipped to the book of Romans, chapter 8, and read:

38 And I am convinced that nothing can ever separate us from God's love. Neither death nor life, neither angels nor demons, neither our fears for today nor our worries about tomorrow—not even the powers of hell can separate us from God's love.

39 No power in the sky above or in the earth below—indeed, nothing in all creation will ever be able to separate us from the love of God that is revealed in Christ Jesus our Lord.

I read it three times. Nothing could separate us from God's love.

And then I found this one in Ephesians 3:

17 Then Christ will make his home in your hearts as you trust in him. Your roots will grow down into God's love and keep you strong.

18 And may you have the power to understand, as all God's people should, how wide, how long, how high, and how deep his love is.

I read the words again. And another time after that. *God, I need this strength and this understanding*, I prayed. *God, Jesus, thank you for this love.*

I didn't know what tomorrow would hold, but I could trust God, the author and perfecter of my faith. For the next few days, even with Gideon missing, I moved forward with peace that could only come from above. Gideon was somewhere. God was everywhere.

Chapter 20

Gideon had been missing for sixteen days. My stomach felt like a clothes dryer, turning over and over. I whispered a quick prayer, *God, help me find Gid. Be in this please*. I handed the anxiety off, choosing to trust.

My phone rested on the narrow edge of the pedestal sink while I brushed my teeth. I stepped away from the mirror and studied the white subway tiles with nearly black grout. Sandi stood at the door watching me. The smell of mint filled my nostrils.

I will never take my teeth for granted again, I thought as I carefully maneuvered the bristles around the brace brackets. My brain rolled through what I needed to do today—class, followed by a dentist appointment. The sink buzzed and an electronic jingle filled the room. With a mouth full of toothpaste, I considered letting it go to voicemail. I could call whoever it was back when I didn't have white foam dripping down my chin. Curiosity lured me in, and I rushed to glance at the screen, expecting Joey or my mom. It was an unknown number with a Lexington, Kentucky area code. If I didn't know them, I really didn't want to answer. I moved to put the phone back down.

Just before my hand touched the sink, something clicked in my head. *That's a Lexington, Kentucky area code. The only people I know here are already saved on my phone.* The world stopped as I realized it could be someone with info about Gideon.

Spitting the toothpaste into the sink, I flipped the device open. I blurted, "Hello?" as if it was a normal phone call, as if my heart hadn't paused and sped up again, hammering against my chest. The possibility of finding Gideon pulled my mouth into a smile. The realization that it could be nothing special, another disappointment, dragged the corners right back down, leaving my face with a morbidly hopeful expression.

"Hey there, sweetie. I think I've got your horse," a man said.

"Um...okay!" I responded with forced calm. *He has Gideon! It may not be real. He could have some other horse. But what other horse looks like him with that scar?*

He rolled into an explanation before I had time to respond. "Yeah, you see, I'm down here at the Lexington Training Center, and I've been gone racing all weekend. When I got here this morning, I saw a sign about a missing horse, and I realized that picture there is the new pony I got! It's him. He's been here a couple weeks and I knew he must be some girl's horse. He was too nice to be an old racetrack pony."

"Thank you!" My hands trembled. *God, what do I do? Is this real? Does he really have Gid?* "You say you're at the Lexington Training Center? I've heard of it. I've got to go get my trailer from the farm and then I'll head your way." My body was buzzing. *I think I'm going to pick up Gideon*!

"Okay, sounds good. We've got mostly walkers going out today. We'll finish up training around 9 and we'll wait around for ya 'til you get here."

We hung up and I fired off text messages and made phone calls. First was Joey. "Someone just called and said they have Gid! He said he's at the Lexington Training Center."

We worked out details to meet there before I called to postpone my dentist appointment and reached out to Terri. By the time I called Mom and Dad, I was already through the back door, keys in hand to hopefully, surely, pick up my horse.

There's a chance it isn't him, I tried to tell myself. But I knew it was. That brilliant full-color photo on the fliers Terri printed, and Gideon's unique coloring and scar made it nearly impossible to mistake him. I was going to get Gideon.

"Thank you," I whispered to God.

Careening into the parking lot of the training center Gid had disappeared from, I scanned the area for my trailer, borderline shocked it was where I left it. As I backed up to connect the hitch, I marveled at how different things were from my first visit to this place. I had been so full of excitement and hope. It was the place where my dreams started coming true. It became the place where my dreams not only slipped through my fingers, but got run over, chopped to pieces, and scattered to the wind.

Good thing my God is bigger and was there to catch me.

As I pulled the trailer out of its parking spot, ready to hightail it to Lexington, Ryan/Bryan walked out of the first barn with a saddle over his arm and his exercise helmet still perched on his head. His face lit up and he rushed over with a hopeful gleam in his eye. "Hey, did you find your pony?"

This guy was the first one on the scene when everything began falling apart. Now he was here when things were maybe coming back together. I wanted to hug-tackle him, but we were both a little too reserved for such antics. Instead, I laughed the kind of carefree laugh that happens in summer, windows down, a '90s dance song on the radio. I gushed, "I just got a call. Someone says they have him at the Lexington Training Center!"

"Really?" he exclaimed, his face lighting up like he hit a trifecta at Churchill Downs. My heart swelled as I filled him in. It was a moment between two horse-obsessed kids who would never grow out of our love, no matter how wrinkled and weather-beaten our skin got. Then he returned to the barn to work and I headed southeast to pick up Gid.

When I pulled into the parking lot of the Lexington Training Center, all I could think was how huge it was. The barns stretched on forever—black, concrete, ugly, and full of racehorses.

Joey stood in the parking lot waiting for me, a beacon guiding me to the correct barn. His arms were crossed over a blue polo and his mouth was set in a grim line. The lush curls of what I jokingly called his Greg Brady hair made him almost hard to take seriously. Almost. He was my personal law enforcement, there to protect me and get to the bottom of this mystery while I got my horse.

The trainer appeared at the door. He looked older than my parents by a couple years, with sweat dripping down the side of his face. Every few seconds he readjusted his hat, giving away frayed nerves. He didn't stop talking as he led us through the dark barn reminiscent of a YMCA built for horses.

"I don't want no trouble now," he said, holding his hands up in a display of innocence. "I just came home from a weekend of racing and saw these signs everywhere. Someone gave us this horse a couple weeks ago to be a pony." I chuckled. Terri was right. I was never more glad to be wrong.

"We tried ponying with him, but man, that boy just wanted to run! My girlfriend's been having a good time on him though. She's been taking him out and riding him some. Boy, is he fast!" I grinned with pride as Joey and I made eye contact. Terri and I were both right, I guess. Gideon was given away to be a pony, but he definitely wasn't cut out to lead racehorses when all he wanted to do was run himself.

"We got his teeth floated and did his feet when he got here," the man said as we turned the corner. Joey asked how he got the horse, and the trainer repeated, "I don't want no trouble now." He adjusted his hat again. "But the guy I got him from, he's already in jail actually. Something about a domestic dispute or something."

The conversation faded into the background because I looked through the door of the third stall of the row, and there was a gleaming chestnut with four stockings. One of his hind legs was cocked in a relaxed position, his face pointing to the back corner of the stall, nearly hidden. I didn't need to see it to know there was a white blaze that stretched from above his eyes down to his bottom lip. I knew if I blew in his nose he would blow back, then inhale my scent like I was another horse on the range. If I put my hand on his forehead between his eyes, he would start bobbing his head up and down until a snowfall of tiny white hairs floated in the air and his itch was sufficiently scratched.

I burst into the stall.

"That him?" the trainer asked.

"Yep!" Joey and I said in unison. Then I tuned them back out.

Stepping toward his gleaming red shoulder, I reached my hand out and touched him, a gentle stroke of his satiny summer coat. He kept his nose to the corner, but I saw the white rim around his eye, which made him look perpetually worried. His ear swiveled toward me. Another step and my hand was under his mane, one of his favorite places for me to rub since it got hot and itchy and he couldn't reach it unless he balanced on three legs and used a back hoof to scratch like a dog. Another step and I was next to his face, my shoulder to his large cheek.

I tilted my head toward his, convincing myself this was real. He was fine. We were together. I tried to soak it in, his rich horse smell, the thing that made him him and us us. But my hands trembled and my brain pinged around. The whiskers around his eyes tickled my chin, grounding me to the present. God was good.

Gid dipped his nose into his halter and I gently slid the crown piece over his ears. I wanted to rub my hands all over him and press my face into his warm neck, but the quicker he was in my trailer, the quicker I would know that he really was still my Gid and we really would keep going, together. My mind whispered incessant *thank you*'s to God as I led him out of the stall, down the dark corridor of the barn, and into the sunlight, Joey and the trainer following. Gideon was back.

Chapter 21

For days my mind cycled two words: he's back! I pondered them while getting dressed, brushing my teeth, and driving to class. I circled campus looking for a parking spot, walked to class, and sat in my seat attempting to pay attention while *Gid's back* chanted through my head. When class ended, I rushed to my apartment to get Sandi and then to the barn in Indiana. *He's back. Gid's back. God, he's back. Gid's back.* It all felt so much bigger than me.

Gideon didn't go to that slaughter sale in LaGrange or to some other person's farm in another state. He wasn't grazing in a random pasture in rural Kentucky. He was right where Terri thought he would be—on a racetrack.

We tried to follow the trail to figure out who took my horse. No one would talk to the cops when they visited the training center Gid disappeared from. The guy who returned him wouldn't give any names. No one was talking. Joey, his parents, my parents, and everyone who cared about me was angry. They wanted to get to the bottom of it, pelting me with questions and demanding that the police do more. It seemed simple enough to track the hands he passed through. But honestly, my horse was back and that's all I really cared about.

I had ideas. I had been naive to think Gid could live at a training track, and I probably overstayed my welcome. Recreational horses just don't belong at a high-end racehorse training facility. Or maybe Joey's arrival in town was proof to a certain trainer that a relationship between us would never be, so he got rid of me the quickest way he knew how.

There were surely other possibilities, but frankly I didn't care. My horse was back, safe and happy, and I refused to hold on to bitterness over his disappearance. There was enough emotional baggage on my shoulders without that piled on top.

Sitting in my truck at the barn, I glanced at the remaining fliers and took a deep, calming breath. Closing my eyes, I said it again. *He's back. Thank you, God, for bringing him back.*

Should I throw the stack of papers away because I never want to revisit this again? Or should I keep them as a kind of souvenir? My horse was stolen and now he's back. Gid's back. He's back. It's fine. I grabbed the Frosted Flakes and headed to Gid's stall, Sandi matching me step for step.

I thought the weight of it all would lift the second I saw him, but it was a slow-rising fog. I stepped carefully, glancing from side to side as if I could see the next arrow before it hit its mark.

Now that Gid was back and my face was healing, I began settling into life in Louisville. One morning, a girl stood in front of my Equine 101 class and announced she was starting a polo team. If we were interested, we could sign the sheet being passed around. I'd never in my life imagined playing polo. It was an entirely different realm from barrel racing or jumping or even galloping racehorses. But hadn't I come to Kentucky to try things with horses that I couldn't experience back home? I put my name and email on the list.

Several other cars were parked along the edge of the road when I pulled up to the polo barn two weeks later. An old silo full of grain that reeked like swamp rot sat next to a barn covered in flaking white paint. We followed each other through a gate and down to the barn aisle, where we met Coach and took turns riding for our "try out." While we waited, the other students whispered to each other, throwing glances at me. I chatted with a girl named Haley from Kansas.

"You show Arabians?" I asked, both confused and a tad awed.

She tried to explain their showmanship competition—the thing she excelled at most. "They pick their knees up really high, almost like gaited horses. And their tails can be twice as long as their bodies," she explained.

"What?" I asked, so shocked I nearly forgot about the peanut gallery of gawkers. "But Arabians move like normal horses, like a Quarter Horse or Thoroughbred," I argued, choosing to not even mention the tail length. *Impossible,*

I thought. *She must be exaggerating*. She made them sound like Barbie horses. I'd ridden an Arabian at Ms. Brenda's and it wasn't much different from the Quarter Horses, just thinner with a proud tail.

"Yeah, it's kind of hard to explain because they move like normal, but the showmanship horses lift their legs really high." I cocked an eyebrow. I had never heard of such a thing. "Nationals is in Louisville this year and my barn is bringing my horse from Kansas so I can show. You should come!"

A voice cut into our conversation. "So, you had an accident riding a racehorse?"

I looked up to see a girl walking toward me, a small crew of curious onlookers behind her.

"Yep," I replied, trying to be polite.

A chorus of voices started up. "Oh my gosh!"

"What's riding on the track like?"

"I want to ride on the track!"

My eyes pinged back and forth, trying to keep up. I would never discourage anyone from their own dream, but I had just watched a couple of these girls struggle to trot and steer the horse at the same time. The track probably wasn't a good fit for them, at least not yet.

"And your horse was stolen?" the first girl asked. Concern, shock, and confusion all passed over her face like an easy-to-read book. While she seemed authentic, I felt the shift as I became the horrific car accident everyone gawks at on the interstate, secretly entertained by the gruesomeness of it.

"Oh my gosh!"

"Your horse was stolen?"

"Who would steal a horse?"

"Yeah." I sucked in a slow breath. "He was stolen."

"Why would someone do that?" The gaggle of girls kept pressing, stepping closer with every question.

"No idea." I was trying hard to remain polite, but I was slipping, my face losing color with each probing question.

Amid the onslaught of inquiries, Haley stepped in.

"Hey, let's drop it. Focus on polo tryouts," she demanded. Everyone looked at the thin, pretty girl, ducking their heads and turning toward the back of the barn, where people took turns riding the polo ponies.

Gideon is sitting in a stall in Indiana, safe, I reminded myself. Talking about it picked at a scab that was still healing.

It was nearly dark when I watched Haley swing onto the polo pony, controlling her momentum and gently settling into the tack. We were the last two to try out. I mounted a spirited gray horse whose feet danced in place as I arranged the reins in just my left hand like Coach showed us. A twinge of nerves made my heart beat faster than normal. *I'm a good rider. I can do this,* I reminded myself.

Coach asked us to trot. With the slightest movement of the reins, my mount flowed into a trot. Haley trotted parallel to us, balanced and in control. "Okay, turn them to the left," Coach said. I put my right leg on and moved my hands over an inch and the horse did a beautiful U-turn. Haley's ride was going just as well. Coach's eyebrows lifted, causing a river of wrinkles in his forehead, and he started asking questions about our riding experiences. Haley had a ton more show experience, but it was clear—we both *lived* horses. And speaking of horses, this little gray was a lot of fun. When I touched his sides with both legs, he moved into a beautiful, powerful canter. My nerves faded, and for the first time that evening, I smiled.

Within a couple weeks we started practices, and the polo team, especially Haley, were fast becoming my people.

Chapter 22

Some weekends Joey came to Louisville; on others I went to Lexington. When we had responsibilities or my bank account was so low I couldn't afford the gas to visit, we talked on the phone. This was a solo weekend.

I rolled up to the barn in Indiana and instead of the normal three or four cars in the parking lot, there were trailers and horses everywhere. As I meandered to Gid's stall, the owner walked down the barn aisle. He stopped when he saw me. "How are you doing?" he asked.

"I'm fine." The lie was written all over my face, but I was trying so hard to make it true.

"Are you scared?" It should have been a random question. It should have confused me, but it didn't. Anger rushed through my body before I could rein it in. *How dare he think I'm afraid?* I thought, while my subconscious whispered, *how can he tell?* Fear could ruin a horseman's career. It could stop it before it got traction.

"No, I'm fine," I repeated, hoping the more I told myself I was fine, the more true it would be. Then I changed the subject with a question I knew the answer to. "So, is this a horse show going on?"

"Yeah! It's just a little fun show. Why don't you hop into a couple of classes?" he offered.

"Okay, I'll think about it." *I'll think about how I really don't feel like being around people and hadn't planned on showing when I got dressed in a T-shirt to come to the barn.*

All my gear was still in the back seat of my truck, so I slipped Gid's halter on and led him out of the barn to the trailer to tack up. When I opened the truck door, Sandi nearly leaped over my shoulder to escape and see what was going on. Grabbing her before she could run loose and spook horses, I looped the wrist strap of her leash over a bar on the horse trailer.

Gideon put his nose to my face and I gently blew, letting him smell my breath and then inhaling his. We were wild horses, saying hello. I offered a handful of Frosted Flakes and he lipped them from my open palm, then swiped his large sticky tongue over my hand to get the last dregs of sugar. The tip of his pink tongue stuck out as he sucked on the sugary juices in his mouth.

I reached up to groom him by the ears and he turned his head, pressing his tongue against my bare arm. "Ewe! Gid!" I laughed. "That's disgusting!" His eye sparkled.

Sandi pressed against the end of her leash, whipping her body back and forth for attention, and I curried Gid from his head to his rear, working the rubber brush in circles to lift all the dirt and loose hair to the surface. My right arm grew tired, so I switched to the left. All the while, the sounds of people cheering and laughing emanated from the arena.

Pulling out my stiff-bristled brush, I flicked the dirt and hair off until the sunlight bounced off his coat like a new penny. *Maybe I'll just see what classes they have left*, I thought, the sounds of a crowd pulling me in.

I threw on Gid's saddle, bridle, and protective boots and walked him to where I had seen a table, leaving Sandi tied to the trailer safe and out of the way. My heart pounded as I talked to the check-in lady and registered for a few classes. I was nervous to be around people, but my adrenaline was also kicking up. I loved showing Gid and dreamed of competing at the highest levels with him.

Within a few minutes, I was trotting and cantering circles behind the show ring to warm up Gid's muscles, the sound of Sandi's lonely cries piercing the air.

"Western Pleasure competitors, please enter the arena." *Here goes nothing*, I told myself, taking a deep breath before pointing Gid to the gate.

I entered the ring, turning right. The horses would be judged for how leisurely they appeared to go around the ring at a walk, trot, and canter. Sandi sounded like a kid being tortured and I tried my hardest to ignore her. Her cries distracted me from any niggling fear of being on my horse. *Heels down, sit up tall, deep breaths. Sandi, please chill out and be quiet. I'll come to you as soon as the class is over.*

I whispered, "God, please help Sandi relax. Keep us safe."

I focused on remaining calm. Gideon could get really worked up, which wouldn't be good for a class judged on calmness. I demanded my heart to keep a steady rhythm, taking deep breaths. The speaker system crackled before the announcer said, "Trot your horses." Gid and I were so in tune, I only had to think the word and his pace increased.

Nerves were building, but we blended together so much I wasn't sure which were his and which were mine. Either way, we fed off each other. "Canter your horses," the loudspeaker said. This was our weakness. We'd lost many pleasure classes because Gid preferred to gallop like a wild stallion free in the desert.

I pushed my hand forward a half-inch and touched my inside leg just in front of the girth and my outside leg just behind it so we would get the correct lead. He rolled into a lovely canter that built speed with every stride. I leaned back, pressing my weight into my heels, and touched the reins a hair.

We were approaching another rider and I used it as an excuse to circle. It would be rude of me to pass the other rider, and a circle would help collect my horse. As we finished the circle the announcer said, "Walk your horses." It couldn't have come at a better time.

I leaned back with a "whoa" and gently pulled the reins. Gid got in a couple of trot steps before walking, but I don't think the judge was looking at us. The ideal would have been to go smoothly from a canter to a walk. It was something we did all the time outside the show ring, but things were always different with a judge watching.

Sandi yowled like a stuck pig, and I chuckled as we turned and did everything again in the other direction. "Please line up your horses in the center of the ring facing the judge," the announcer said. The loudspeaker popped from putting the microphone down before turning it off.

There were eight other riders in the class, and the judge walked to the rider furthest from me. I was too far away to hear, but I saw the judge look up at the rider, who gave a slight nod before picking up the reins and asking her horse to back up a few steps.

My horse could back a mile at the slightest lift of the reins on a normal day, but at shows I tugged the reins like I was backing a stubborn mule or a horse accustomed to little kids dragging on its mouth all day. I was the epitome of chill on the outside, but I could no longer demand my heart to slow down. It was off on a race, and Gideon could feel it. His raced to catch up, and he danced around until I let him walk in a circle.

The judge meandered down the line, and riders nodded and then asked their horses to back up. Some were lovely; others lifted their head straight in the air, ears pinned and tail swishing, and refused their rider's request.

The horse next to us was perfection. The rider lifted his hand, and the horse's head didn't even move as it took three perfect, amicable steps back. The judge's smile was so wide her glasses lifted, and the rider nodded back. That was so good I couldn't decide whether I wanted to punch the kid or high-five him.

The polo-clad judge strode over to us, offering a kind nod and a simple request, "Please back your horse."

I nodded, smiling with faux confidence. As I lifted the reins, Gid stepped forward in anticipation, a false read of what was happening. I tried not to panic or jerk the reins. "NO!" I wanted to scream. But instead I smiled like it was the best day of my life and pulled back gently on the reins. Gid gave a little irritated nose push and took three crooked steps backward. *Well, it could have been worse, I guess*. I reached down to pat his neck as the judge moved on to the last horse in line.

The decider of our fates, along with her helper, stood facing us, making marks on a clipboard and glancing back at different horses.

As we waited, I silently begged the fidgety Gid to stand still. A murmur started among the spectators. I glanced around, trying to figure out what was going on before I heard, "Dog! dog!" And there, bounding up to the arena, was indeed a dog. Sandi. The announcer's voice came over the loudspeaker, "It seems we have a loose dog. Whose dog is this?"

Sandi zoned in on me, squirmed through the gate, and darted toward Gid, but the judge's helper grabbed her. My dog stood there, tongue hanging out the side of her mouth, whipping her body from side to side. She was so proud and excited to have found me. I sat on Gid, sweat threatening to pour down my face, and pretended I had no idea who this dog was.

Laughter and panic were bubbling up when someone yelled, "Do you know whose dog that is?" I shrugged slightly with a bemused half-grin. I loved Sandi, but there was no way I was going to claim her with a ribbon on the line! Not while she was safe at least.

The helper handed her off to a group of kids and the judge called us out in order of our placings. Gid and I were the third pair to exit the arena, holding a yellow and white ribbon. I found the kids and Sandi bounding up a huge dirt pile together, and had to laugh at the disappointment on their faces when I informed them she was mine, and no, they couldn't take her home.

Next up was a trail class, where obstacles you supposedly might come across on a real-life trail ride are scattered around the arena. One at a time, competitors enter the ring and complete the obstacles while being judged. Ms. Brenda taught us that the best-trained horses could win any class at one of these small shows, even if their primary job was something completely different like barrel racing or roping. I knew Gid and I could do this. I handed Sandi's leash off to someone in the crowd before swinging up on my horse and waiting our turn.

"Sarah Bullock on Gideon, you may enter the ring," the announcer called. I grinned at the gate person as Gid pranced through the opening. With a centering breath, I sat deep into the saddle and pulled the reins a hair to ask him to relax. *We've got this Gid*. I patted him in front of the saddle. He rounded his neck and perked his ears. His back lifted as he raised his tail an inch.

We backed through the L shape with ease, opened and closed a "gate" made of rope and got only a little tangled, trotted some poles, and made our way to the mailbox to grab a piece of mail. The small crowd watched with rapt attention. Gideon was dominating this class and my chest swelled with pride. Just a couple obstacles left.

The mailbox was just an arm's length away, which was close enough. I leaned over to open it and retrieve the envelope and Gid started jigging in place. I straightened in the saddle, regrouped, and pressed my leg against his side. It was a simple request to move sideways to get me closer to the mailbox that sat on top of a black metal barrel. But he danced the other direction.

Gideon's breath became a loud whoosh in tempo with his hopping feet. Victory was slipping through my grasp as I circled Gid and tried to come from a different angle. His front hooves popped off the ground, and a rock formed in my belly. I tried to laugh. I tried to focus on the goal. I would not let fear get to me.

And apparently, I also wouldn't get my horse within ten feet of the dang barrel and mailbox.

"Look at that barrel horse!" A man with a beer belly yelled.

"Woop! You ain't gettin' that barrel horse close to a barrel unless you're runnin' 'em!" his neighbor shouted. Everyone around laughed.

I chuckled with them as I gritted my teeth and attempted to leg yield, back up, whatever it took to retrieve the envelope from the mailbox and finish the course.

The crowd roared with laughter and cheered as Gideon ran sideways away from the barrel. Someone yelled, "You can't take the barrel out of the barrel horse!" and slapped his knee while members of the crowd whistled. With a grin and a wave to our new fans, I conceded and pointed my crow-hopping horse toward the gate to leave. Once Gid worked himself into a frenzy, we were done.

Outside the gate, I didn't even try to stop my nervous horse before leaping to the ground. Gid's eyes bulged while he jigged next to me. We went back to the trailer to pull off his tack and give him some Frosted Flakes.

After retrieving Sandi, I put Gid in his stall for the night, checking his water and hay and grooming off sweat marks. I lingered, relishing the togetherness of my little family and listening to the announcer call out placings, our names absent from the list.

I couldn't help but dream of a bigger competition with three barrels, speed so intense I had to rely on pure reaction, and our names being called in the final placings. I had told Ms. Brenda I'd take this horse away from that world, but on days like today it was obvious—I couldn't take the barrel out of the barrel horse—and I didn't want to either. It called to me as much as it did to him.

CHAPTER 23

"I REALLY NEED TO get a computer desk," I told my dog.

She thumped her tail against the bed and looked down at me as I sat on the floor booting up my computer. I pulled out my phone and started a text to Joey while I waited.

"Will you help me get a computer desk this weekend?"

Within a few seconds, he sent back a "yes!" My insides warmed just thinking about him visiting.

The computer fully awakened and I clicked into my Yahoo account. Sitting at the top of my inbox was an email from the *Courier Journal*, Louisville's newspaper. It was one of the many I had queried when begging anyone and everyone for help finding Gideon. *Nice of them to answer now*, I smirked.

Opening the email and scanning it, my heart warmed. A guy named Byron Crawford said someone had forwarded my message to him. He had a weekly human-interest column and would love to write about my missing horse and help find him. I was grateful for the support, even if I didn't need the help anymore.

I typed up a quick reply, thanking him and informing him with a lot of exclamation points that my horse had been found! Then I shut my computer down and went about my day.

The next morning, I glanced at my inbox before heading to class. There was a response from Crawford waiting on me. My heart did a little leap. Yes, my horse was back, he said, but I still had quite the story and he thought his readers would love to "meet me." I couldn't help but smile. I wasn't sure my story was really that exciting, but if he wanted to tell it I was game.

Within a few days, I drove to the barn in Indiana to meet the newspaper reporter and introduce him to Gideon. Crawford got out of his car with a notepad and a digital camera that fit in his palm. He was around my parents' age, with short brown hair and a kind smile.

"Gettin' Lucky in Kentucky!" he exclaimed, reading my shirt.

"Yeah," I blushed. "I got this before I moved here when Kentucky was just a dream. It used to be my favorite shirt because I wanted to move here so badly. Now I just, I don't know, hope if I wear it it'll come true," I explained with a sheepish chuckle. The truth: I clung to that shirt. It reminded me of the hope I had before I got here, and when I wore it I felt that same hope. Maybe things would still come together.

"I like it!" he said, scribbling onto his pad. "We'll see if we can make it happen—lucky in Kentucky."

I quirked an eyebrow, unsure how he could have much to do with it. Sandi sprinted circles around us. "Um, I'll go get Gideon," I said and left him standing in the parking lot. My hands shook as I slid the halter onto Gid's head. He followed me out of the barn, nose to my elbow. Crawford watched us walk up. "This is Gideon!" I said proudly, with a half-smile because a full one would have shown my broken teeth.

"How about we go over here," Crawford said, walking to the grass behind the parking lot. Gid and I followed, his ears drooped to the sides as we walked. "Okay, so you can just stand over there next to Gideon and I'll take your picture."

"Like this?" I questioned.

"Yep! That's great." He held the camera up in front of him, glasses perched on the tip of his nose, and took our picture. "Here, come look at it and see what you think!"

I stared at myself on the tiny screen. Weeks after the accident my lip still had a lump on it. The smile was awkward, my mouth glued shut to hide broken teeth. I had pulled down my ponytail at the last minute, brushing my fingers through it. "It's fine!" I replied, trying not to lie. I knew that at this point in my life, there was no picture of myself I would like. Sometimes that's just how things are.

He asked me questions, scribbling on his little pad. In a few minutes he declared he had all he needed. "Email me if you have any questions or want to tell me anything else," he said with a gentle smile, like a wrong look could break me.

God, is that all I should tell him? I prayed. Of all the words that whirled through my mind and heart, a precious few had made it to my mouth. *Does he even have enough to tell a decent story?* I wondered. But standing in front of him, the only words I could muster were, "That's all I can think of."

I wasn't prepared. I had never cracked open a *Courier Journal*. Reading the paper was the kind of thing my dad did. Every morning he disappeared behind the black and white newsprint, with sections of the *Clarion Ledger* folded and tossed onto the table. Only a peak of his dark brown morning hair showed.

Crawford emailed me when the piece went live, and I scrambled to get a copy from the corner store. There we were in a slightly blurred photo—Gid and me with haunted, hopeful eyes.

Dad called, "I read the article that nice man wrote about you, Sarah. Your mom pulled it up on the computer. That was real nice of him."

"I know, Dad! He said some nice things, didn't he?" My stomach did flips as realization hit—*people across Louisville are reading my story today!*

"You make sure you thank him real big," Dad reminded me before ending the call.

That's where I thought it would end—a souvenir from Kentucky—a newspaper clipping folded carefully and put into an envelope, then hidden away in a drawer. When I was older I'd pull it out to remember those crazy days in Kentucky.

But when I opened my email the next day, there was another message from Byron Crawford.

Sarah,

I've received numerous calls and emails from people who would like to help you get back on your feet. One person even offered to cover your dental bills if you switch to his dentist! How about I tell you about them and forward them to you if you want to reply? It seems like your story really struck a chord!

Byron Crawford

A local barn reached out offering affordable board twenty minutes from my apartment, promising to keep Gideon's location a secret. I visited the barn, and anxious to have my horse closer, moved him from Indiana to Louisville within a few days.

Churchill Downs sent me a special invitation to tour the frontside of the track where the offices are. When I arrived, women dressed in professional skirts with summery tops and office sweaters greeted me. With my t-shirt and dirt-crusted boots, I felt every bit on the wrong side of the track.

They paraded me from office to office, introducing me to important people I don't remember and filling my arms with swag at each stop—pencils and pens, a beanie horse named Derby, a one-shoulder backpack that said Churchill Downs, and a fancy watch with the logo on the face, which would always be too fragile for my horse-girl lifestyle.

My tour guide introduced me as "the girl from the article," and a knowing smile would stretch across the person's face as they took a break from typing. *Did they send out a company memo?* I wondered. The person on the other side of the desk would say, "wow you're so brave!" to which I mumbled awkwardly. If I had been given the choice, I would have avoided riding a somersaulting horse with a hoof that smashed my face. That didn't feel very brave.

There was also the typical, "I can't believe someone stole your horse!" and "riding racehorses is so dangerous." I could practically hear *you're one of those weird horse girls without a lick of sense* through their shiny white smiles.

Maybe they're right, I thought. But when they offered for me to apply for internships in the offices of Churchill Downs, smiling wide and winking as if to guarantee I'd get anything I applied for, I politely declined. I didn't move to Kentucky to wear business-casual clothes and make photocopies, even if I could have done it at the world-renowned Churchill Downs.

As I walked to the parking lot with all my swag, I called my parents to tell them all about it. Dad piped up in the background, "Sarah, you should see what kind of job they'll offer you!"

"No thanks, Dad. I came here to ride racehorses! Love you though," I replied with a gentle smile. Some people would never get it.

In the article, Crawford mentioned my new safety vest being stolen. A female exercise rider invited me to the backside of Churchill Downs to loan me an old vest. She led me through the maze of barns as effortlessly as I had walked through Winterview Farm back in Mississippi, like this huge place with thousands of horses was her barn home. I guess it was.

I followed her to a barn bordering the road. She opened a tack trunk and dug to the bottom, withdrawing a dusty black vest. She reminded me of the lady I met the first time I came to Churchill Downs, the fairy godmother mayor who gave me a Cinderella experience. I was tongue-tied by her confidence and my lack of it, by this maze of buildings and lithe horses, by this place I dreamed of riding at but right now could hardly walk through. I think the fairy's name was Trish, and I think they were one and the same.

A trainer at Churchill Downs had emailed, mentioning I could come by to see about an exercise riding job. After asking a few of my more knowledgeable friends at school, I gathered he wasn't the warmest guy. But I left Trish and followed the numbers on the barns, weaving in and out, trying to stay out of the way and not look too out of place. Eventually, I found his little piece of Churchill. He had barricaded the space in front of his barn, and I walked onto the edge of the fenced-off area feeling like a trespasser. A man in blue jeans and a black jacket with a grim face stood up from crouching over a bucket. "Can I help you?" he huffed.

"Um, I'm here for Mick," I stammered, wondering if this was him. "He told me to meet him about maybe riding."

"Yeah hi, I'm Mick." He stretched out his hand. I grabbed it, determined to give a strong, firm handshake that would make my big brothers proud, but he crushed my hand like a limp squid. "I heard about your accident," he said as he peered into my eyes. I wondered if he was trying to see if I would squirm.

Pulling my shoulders back, I lifted my eyes to his, refusing to cower. "Yeah, the horse fell with me."

"Well, what I heard was the martingale was too long. That's not the horse's fault," he declared.

I sucked in a breath. For a moment the earth was stripped of everything and everyone but us, standing on this huge expanse of nothing. Him, me, and the truth.

I was humiliated. Everyone was making a big deal out of this accident like I was the victim. I *felt* like a victim. But he was right. In the murkiness of my pride being hit, in my trying to regain confidence like scrambling up a muddy hill, it felt a little good to have a horseman say the truth. Even if the truth sucked and ultimately pointed the finger back at me. Ms. Brenda had taught me from the very beginning that almost every accident was the rider's fault.

In the expanse of a breath, my mind raced through two weeks of memories. On my first day riding with Craig, the groom tacked the horse for me as I hungrily watched and absorbed it all. He put the martingale on and the leather sagged between the reins and the horse's chest, raising a red flag. "Is that how it's supposed to fit? Or is it too long?" I asked. He peered at me for a minute and I wondered if he even spoke English. Was he trying to figure out what I was saying or was he annoyed that the new girl questioned him?

"No, it's fine," he said. I watched Craig and Jessica both get legged up onto their horses with drooping martingales. *It must be fine. It must be different at the track. If it was too long or dangerous, they would have had an accident by now,* I told myself.

So for two weeks I consciously overlooked the excessively long martingales. The day I rode Red, a young horse that liked to gallop slowly with his head low, I asked Craig if I should make him hold his head up or let him gallop low. Craig said, "It doesn't matter, let him go how you want." And since the horse liked to go with his head low, I let him.

And then Red and I tumbled down the track together, and life became before the accident or after the accident. When Ryan/Bryan ran to Red as I scrambled from his tangled legs and tried not to pass out, his hoof was stuck on the martingale. The piece of leather was too long and his head was too low. He literally stepped onto it while galloping, which jerked his head down further and caused him to somersault.

I knew God was and is sovereign and that He would take something bad and turn it into good if I trusted Him, but I also knew I made decisions that caused this accident, and it didn't feel good. It would never feel good.

"Yeah, it was," I said to Mick, looking into his eye. I wasn't sure what else to say. The truth was a chasm between us. *My fault.*

"Well, I'll let you know if I need a rider." He looked me up and down as he spoke, a permafrown set into his face. Other employees of his had paused what they were doing, wheelbarrows full of manure, bridles dangling mid-clean, so they could hear. I wondered if these people gawking had heard of me because of the accident, or because of the article, or if I was just a one-off random interaction that caught their attention.

"Okay thanks," I mumbled and turned away, speed-walking to the security gate and wondering if Mick had any intention of me riding. It seemed like he just wanted to confront me. My neck itched as the blood crept up, creating splotches and turning my face red. Tears threatened to surface, but I looked into the clouds and begged God to help me hold it together. It really didn't matter that Mick knew the truth. In fact, it was liberating. *Maybe Craig will fix his long martingales now and protect his horses*, I whispered under my breath. I hadn't talked to him since the day he pretended to look for my safety vest, so I would probably never find out.

Emails continued to pour in, and Byron forwarded me contact info if I requested it. The dean of the equine department at the University of Louisville sat me down in his office and personally wrote a check to cover the cost of a new riding vest. I never even needed the one Trish loaned me.

A family offered to keep Gideon at their farm for free until I could get back on my feet. People emailed stories of their own dreams and how I inspired them. The list just kept going. Each email, each stranger reaching out became a step that took me from the haze of tragedy and survival. Step by step, I emerged from the fog.

I became human again. I spent time with other students in the equine department computer lab. I made nearly daily barn trips with Sandi. Joey and I visited each other on weekends and talked on the phone all week. We tried out churches and I went to class. My dental visits were further apart, and I looked less like a broken girl and more like a college girl with braces. And through it all, I clung to my God who never left.

Part 2

Chapter 24

The fall semester was well underway, and as my body healed, my mind drifted toward the track. *Maybe I'm ready*, I said to my reflection while brushing my teeth. *God? Is it time? Can we do this?* But how? And where? Even if I wanted to go back to the training track where I started, which I didn't, there wasn't time to get a morning of work in and drive forty-five minutes back to downtown Louisville for a morning class. So the idea continued to dance around in my head and go no further.

The brisk fall air followed me into Equine 101. I dropped my bag, keeping my jacket on for a bit. My ears perked up when I overheard Tara talking about hot-walking. I leaned into her conversation as she mentioned a guy named Ron and his assistant trainer, and how she worked for them at Churchill Downs.

"Wait, you work for a Thoroughbred trainer?" I asked, shocked. How had I known that this girl was obsessed with Gwen Stefani, yet not know she worked at the track?

"Yeah! His name's Ron. He says he's going to take me out and teach me to gallop sometime!" she smiled like she owned the room, and I couldn't decide if she was really that confident or if it was false bravado. Either way, I loved it.

"Really?! I've been wanting to gallop again. I was trying to give my body time to heal after my accident, but I think I'm ready. I just wasn't sure where to start."

"I can talk to him for you!" she offered like it was nothing.

Everything had been an uphill climb for me when it came to the track. This seemed too simple. There was no way he'd hire me based on a referral from a college student, but if she was willing to help, I'd gladly take it. "That would be great!" I told her as the professor cleared his throat at the podium.

We turned to face the front as I tried to control my racing thoughts. *There's no way she could get me a job*, I told myself. But my brain was already cataloging the location of my exercise riding gear and calculating how long it would take to ride in the mornings and still make it to class on time.

God, I can't believe Tara made this happen, I prayed as I stood at the security gate on the backside of Churchill Downs, waiting on Ron Moquett. I wondered if it was real. If he never came to the gate to let me in, it would be fine. I would figure something out.

Simply getting geared up had bolstered my courage enough to take the next step on my own if needed. But within a couple minutes, a guy wearing a hoodie and a goofy grin signed me in at the security booth and stuck out his hand. "Hi, I'm Ron Moquett!" There was laughter in his eyes, as if the world were a big joke and we were both in on it.

"Hey, I'm Sarah. Thanks for this!" I said as I firmly returned the handshake.

"Yeah, Tara told me you wanted to ride! Said something about an accident." He tapered off like he didn't want to talk about the hard stuff. I filled him in as I followed him past rows of bustling barns.

"Yeah. I was riding for Craig at the training track." I glanced up to see Ron nod in recognition and kept going. "They said I was doing really well and it seemed like I was. But a couple weeks in, a horse fell with me. I was trying to give myself time to heal, and I'm not really sure if I'm good enough to be here. I mean, I hope I am."

"We'll get you going!" Ron cut off my rambling with the same confidence in me that Tara had. My heart pounded as I tried to cling to their belief. *This is good. It'll be good!*

"First thing, to ride at Churchill you need an exercise rider's license. Do you have one?" he asked with raised eyebrows.

"Nope." The butterflies kicked up. *What if I need some special certification? What if it's expensive? What if I don't qualify?*

"Okay, well, no big deal. You just head over to the racing office, tell them you'll be riding for me, and they'll get you set up. Go ahead and hang out with us for a bit this morning if you want, but I can't put you on anything until you've got that license. Hey Donald!" he called down the shedrow of the busy barn. Donald, a guy dressed in riding gear, walked up. "This is Sarah," Ron introduced me. "She'll be getting on a few horses for us."

I shook Donald's hand and muttered a shy, "Hi, Donald!"

Tara walked past, giving me a wink. She was holding a leather lead shank attached to a dancing Thoroughbred with bulging neck muscles. "And you know Tara. Hey Tara, after that horse will you take Monster around?"

"Sure!" Tara replied, and I was a little jealous of how at home she seemed here.

"This is my assistant trainer," Ron continued, gesturing to a lady about my size who was a few years older and had a thousand times more presence. I shook her hand and returned to Ron's side. The assistant went back to wiping down bridles. I could feel her sizing me up, and I knew I'd never live up to this woman's expectations.

Within a week, I had a shiny new license that said "exercise rider" across the bottom. Every time I looked at it, I couldn't help but grin, even with the brackets of my braces rubbing sores against the inside of my mouth. I parked in the gravel lot across the street from the backside of the track and followed other people who appeared to work there. As I passed the security booth, I flashed my badge to the officers with a shaky smile and made my way to Ron's barn.

A drum pounded in my chest as I tried to look calm and collected. The training track was a little league field compared to Churchill Downs. This was the major leagues, the home of the Kentucky Derby. *Was it wise to skip straight from little league to the majors?* I wondered. *Probably not but here I am, and I'll give it my best. God, help me with this,* I mumbled.

Barns stretched as far as I could see, all of them with two long rows of stalls down the center and a pathway called the shedrow going around them. Horses munched hay from bulging nets, watching the activity. A few snaked their heads out, mouths gaping open, trying to get a chunk of the other horses and humans walking past. I mulled over the viciousness of it, deciding it must be more of a game than a genuine attack. *But I still need to be careful*, I reminded myself. *Game or not, it would hurt if one of these guys got a chunk of me.*

Other horses stood between barns, one person holding a lead shank while another furiously soaped, rinsed, and sponged off as I walked past. The grooms ran sponges down the horses' legs, squeezed out the water, and then did it again until water no longer dripped from the horses' fetlocks. I thought back to my half-hour bathing sessions with Gideon. Sometimes they went even longer when I meticulously scrubbed every inch of his chestnut coat, spent several minutes hosing off suds and then separated each tail hair by hand instead of running a brush through it and risking pulling a strand out. I couldn't help but laugh, embarrassed at how much time I spent bathing him when apparently it could be done in under a minute with much less water waste.

There must have been a hundred barns all lined up and numbered, with eighty stalls each. Everywhere I looked, the backside buzzed with activity. Riders with short stirrups and knees bent at a harsh angle rode by, their mounts prancing and shooting sideways for no good reason.

I only made one wrong turn before finding Ron's barn.

"Hey, Sarah! Got your license?" he asked. I proudly showed him the piece of plastic. In the photo, my lip looked like I had taken a beating over the weekend and my sun-bleached ponytail hung to the side. The license guy had made me laugh as I tried to keep my mouth sealed together, so I ended up with an in-between smile.

"All right! I've got one horse for you today. He's coming off a layup from being injured and needs to jog two times around. Think you can handle that?" he asked, looking for all the world like he knew I could.

"Sure!" I shrugged. I'd figure it out.

A gigantic dark bay colt emerged from its stall. The groom led him once around the shedrow before pausing in front of me. Ron stood next to the horse, waiting for me to bend my knee so he could lift me into the saddle. "One, two, three!" Ron lifted just as I squatted to jump, creating an awkward and mistimed lurch onto the horse's back. My mount glided sideways, and my heart rate surged, both at the thrill and the fear of it all.

"Oops!" I laughed, mortified at my bad timing. I rushed to tie a knot in my reins like Craig had taught me and prove that I wasn't a complete imbecile. The groom led the horse around the inside of the barn, glancing back periodically to see if I was ready while I adjusted my stirrups. With each glance, I could see impatience building. I fumbled with the leather straps and my face flushed. After two laps, I nodded to the groom and he peeled away, ducking into a stall to prepare his next horse.

Ron strode beside the horse, explaining the three gates to the track. "When you're done you can go out that one by the barn, but when you're going onto the track I want you to go in through the main one in the center."

"Okay," I muttered, trying to soak in everything Ron said while riding this beast of a horse and also marveling at the Twin Spires and bustle of activity.

"We call the entrances to the track 'gaps,'" Ron explained as the nerves I had shoved into the deepest part of my being sprung to the surface. There were a lot of horses on the track.

My originally stalwart mount began to jig. I shortened the reins and listened to Ron. "I just want you to jog him around two times," he reiterated. He stood next to the fence while my horse danced onto the track, swinging his hind end toward the inside of the oval. A surge of panic had me yanking on the reins. *What if he swings his hind end into oncoming traffic and we cause a collision?*

Jogging along the rail felt like driving a taxi through New York City. Riders waved their arms and yelled. Others minded their own business while weaving in and out of traffic, and every horse affected the way the next one behaved. I clung to the rail while horses flew past, galloping loud and fast one after the other in the opposite direction. Each one made my big horse want to do more than the silly little jog Ron told us to do.

I knew I could cause a terrible accident if my mount darted into oncoming traffic. The horse pressed into the bridle, demanding to go faster. I wasn't just risking my own neck by riding on the track—I could hurt someone else. My face grew hotter with each rider who glared, like they could see how new, how clueless, I was.

The racehorse threw his weight into the bit, pulling against my hold on the reins. I felt sure if I released even a hair, he would take off. We were barely a quarter of the way around the one-mile oval and my arms burned. I wondered if I could hold the horse back for the rest of the mile, much less two. Aching, gloveless fingers gripped the reins. Sweat made it even harder to hold on. I knew riding used ab muscles, but never in my life had they screamed so loudly.

It was taking my entire body to keep this horse from running off, and I was quickly learning how weak I truly was. We jogged past the starting gates used in races, but I was so focused on not losing control that I couldn't even cast a lingering glance to see what they looked like up close. Instead, I hung on the reins, praying incessantly that God would help me hold this beast back, that I wouldn't run out of steam, because it seemed I would hit my body's limit and fall at any moment.

We approached the first gap, and I could see Ron watching from the fence. My legs, core, and arms ached. There was no way I could hold this horse to a jog for another lap. I wanted to cry, scream, give up, and just fall off. Instead, I calmly told Ron I was struggling and wasn't sure I could do another lap. He looked earnestly into my eyes. I could see annoyance in his, and he must have seen exhaustion and defeat in mine. His horse needed two laps and was getting only one, but he nodded and said it was fine.

The groom held the horse as I slid off, knees nearly giving out when my feet hit the ground. With a downward lilt to his voice, Ron told me that was all for the day and he'd see me tomorrow before ducking into his office. I lingered for a few minutes, wanting to help, to be part of it all, but I could barely stand, much less contribute. So I quietly slipped out of the barn and shuffled to my truck.

My alarm sounded the next morning well before the sun was up. Disappointment weighed on me, but Ron was expecting my return and I wouldn't waste the opportunity. He greeted me with a mocking smile that made his eyes twinkle as he inquired about how I was recovering from such a hard ride. He reminded me of my brother Nathan, and I laughed at my expense.

"Yeah, I'm pretty tired," I admitted. I had a long way to go to be as fit as the other riders. Ron handed me his car keys and a wad of cash, nodding to the sedan parked by the barn. "Want to make a Hardee's run? I could really go for a bacon, egg, and cheese."

A grin spread across my face. "Oh my gosh, I love Hardees! They have the best biscuits of any fast-food place!"

"Yeah?" he said in surprise. Maybe he expected me to be insulted or disappointed. Maybe I should have been. But I wasn't ready to be dragged around the track again, and I really did *love* Hardees. I was just grateful to be part of things, even if I wasn't on a horse.

I couldn't wipe the grin from my face as I drove Ron's car through the Hardee's pickup window. Then I sat in his office dining on a plain biscuit and hash browns while watching all the comings and goings of a racing barn. Ron asked if I had siblings and told me about his kids. We talked about Tara, who we both agreed was fantastic, and he taught me a little about the operations of his stable.

The next day he put me back up on tall, dark, and handsome, and I sufficiently jogged the two laps around without losing control. My heart pounded through my shirt every time I got close to another horse and rider, which was pretty much the whole time. For the first few days, that dark bay was my only ride. Then they brought out a chestnut for me to gallop.

I wavered between grinning like an idiot and wanting to vomit over the horse's right shoulder as we jogged along the rail to the spot we would stop and wait. When it was time to change direction and gallop, I waited for a gap in traffic, then nudged him forward and aimed for the center of the track. There was no loosening the reins to tell him to gallop. The horse bore down against my hands like the tall bay. I picked up the reins, pulling back as the horse increased to a speed that was surely faster than we were supposed to go. He ignored my hands, so I whispered a prayer and pressed my fists into his neck in front of the saddle. We were cruising. I'd just hold on and hope our gallop didn't turn into an all-out sprint.

By the time I pulled the chestnut to a walk, the blood had drained from my face. *I think it went how it was supposed to go.*

They started giving me two or three horses to ride every day, but when it was time for the dark bay to start galloping, he went to Donald. I wasn't sorry. After all that time off from my accident, there was no way I could have held him back on his first few gallops. The other horses were easier, but not easy. Some days I spent more time driving to Hardee's than riding, but I was part of it all and it filled my cup. *Maybe I can do this*, I thought as I drifted to sleep.

Chapter 25

When I walked onto the backside, the odor of ammonia hit me in the face. I felt a million miles and a world away from the organic chemistry lab at Mississippi College, but that smell brought the lab and the track together.

Walking past barns, I envisioned cleaning test tubes back at MC, squirting acetone into them as the final step in cleaning and drying. I remembered my friends and how we worked together to survive that class. We met in the evenings to study and gave each other hints in lab to figure out how to identify the eleven unknown substances that was our semester-long project.

My stomach twinged, like a chord tying me to Mississippi had been plucked. I wanted to be right here, walking across the backside of Churchill Downs in a safety vest and racing helmet with a pompom on top. I wanted to be chasing this dream, even if I had to wipe crusty tears off my face in the morning before I left the apartment. I just wish I could have my people to chase it with me like we chased those unknowns in lab. Following the ammonia smell of racehorse urine, I passed several barns until I was at Ron's.

The dry erase board had two horses next to my name—the chestnut and tall, dark, and handsome. Electricity swept through my body, making the hairs on the back of my neck stand up and my fingers tingle. *The horse I could barely hold at a jog is on my gallop list. Maybe I'd rather go buy breakfast for everyone.* Before I could get far down a rabbit hole of fear, I reminded myself that I wasn't here to make Hardee's runs. *I've been doing this for a couple weeks now. He'll be fine. I'm ready.*

My mouth stretched into a shaky smile, and I hoped no one noticed the momentary panic. Ron popped out of his office to fill me in. "No big deal. Just take him an easy lap and a half," he said. "Donald's been galloping him since his layoff, and you should be able to handle him by now." I attempted an appreciative smile and nod. *I can do this. It shouldn't be much different from any other horse I've been galloping. Granted, I basically hold on for dear life and pray when it's time to stop, but I'm getting better(ish).*

The groom gave me a leg up. As we walked from the barn, the ground felt impossibly far away on this giant of a three-year-old. The horse behaved well, ears swiveled forward in anticipation of his favorite thing—the track. He was so focused on business that my presence was inconsequential. We went through the gap. There was no silly swing of his bum or excited jig. He set into a working jog, only noticing the horses around us as if they were the frog in that frogger game. With each horse we passed, his body seemed to hum with satisfaction, and I visualized a little green splat on the track.

We stopped at the spot across from the finish pole to wait for an opening in traffic. The smell of stale concession food, yesterday's spilled beer, and fresh manure inundated my senses as my heart pounded in my ears. Other riders sat next to me, some chatting, some yelling insults at each other over my head. Red crept up my face. The horse stood like a prince overlooking his courtyard. When there was a gap in traffic, we pulled out onto the center of the track to start our gallop.

The bay took about two trot steps before he rolled into the faster, four-beat gait. He rounded his neck and pressed into the bit as his speed picked up, hooves pounding quickly underneath me, tossing dirt to the sides. I fought the urge to pick up my hands and pull back as we approached the first turn, reminding myself that it always felt a bit out of control at first. *We'll settle. It'll be fine.* I pressed my hands into his neck, just in front of the saddle, leaning back a tad to use my body weight to communicate. "Whoa buddy," I added my voice into the mix.

He leaned more into my hands, as if angry that I mentioned slowing down. As if he would show me. The exhilarating fast-paced gallop I was accustomed to was turning into something completely different. I squeezed the reins in my fists again, gently telling him to cool his jets and slow a bit, which was met with a defiant lengthening of stride. *How dare you tell me what to do? You're practically a flea.* He didn't need to speak English to make his thoughts clear.

I already had solid, heavy contact with the reins, which strained my forearms, shoulders, and back with each stride, but I moved my hands back a couple inches closer to the saddle, trying to stand up taller and tell the horse that this was too fast. We weren't asked to breeze—just an easy mile-and-a-half gallop.

As we made the first turn of the oval, he continued to gain momentum, striking at the ground in defiance. I picked my hands up and pulled with all my strength, but he countered my request by pressing forward and speeding up. *What if he hurts himself because I can't stop him?* I thought. *What if I ruin this horse?*

The eyes of other riders followed me. They seemed to wonder if I was an idiot sprinting down the center of the track or if I had lost control. I wondered the same. We were quickly approaching other horses, and I had to make a decision. *Should I continue barreling down the center of the track, where the horse knows he's only supposed to be galloping, and put other riders in danger? Or should I steer him to the fast lane on the rail, where he expects to run all out, but we're not risking the other horses?* I didn't want him to think what he was doing was okay, or that I wanted him to run.

A pair of riders in front of us glanced over their shoulders, alerted by the tell-tale pounding hooves of a running horse. We were just a few strides away and I couldn't think of another solution. With a mere glance to the side and a shift of my left hand, the bay moved to the rail where he found yet another gear, stretching his nose out as I leaned back, pulling on the reins with every bit of strength.

God! Help me stop this horse!

A conversation from a couple days before flashed through my mind. Donald had laughed and said, "Oh man, if a horse runs away with me I just chuck the reins at him! Let that bastard run. If he's going to be a jerk and take off, let him run himself out. No way I'm going to stop a horse that really wants to run."

No way I'm going to stop a horse that really wants to run. There is no way I can stop this horse. I have no idea how much he is worth, but if he's training at Churchill Downs it's probably a lot. What if he's re-injuring himself because of me? I can't just chuck the reins. I can't not try. The thoughts kept cycling through my brain along with *dear God, please help me stop this horse.*

In a handful of breaths, we were back to the spot it all started, where we had peeled off the rail hoping for a happy, brisk gallop. We had breezed a mile, and he was still careening around the inside rail with no sign of giving in. Coming around the second lap, I was exhausted. It was a throwback to the first time I jogged this horse, except now we were flying. Surely he was ruining himself and I couldn't stop him.

I looked longingly at the ground and thought maybe I should just bail. Maybe then the horse would stop and I could be done. We had the attention of the whole track now. Heads turned, following us, a mixture of pity, alarm, and anger. As we sped past the three gaps, I looked at them, pleading for help with my eyes. I stood in the stirrups and leaned back, holding the reins like a water skier and using all my weight and waning muscles to pull. The churning of the horse's stride flopped me around like a sock monkey rather than an elegant skier. *How long can he possibly go?* I wondered.

We passed the spot where I normally stood in the stirrups and asked my mounts to stop, finished with our gallop for the day. I wanted to throw the reins at him and give up. I wanted to cry. I wanted to pound his shoulders and yell and tell this horse how ridiculous he was being. I wanted to jump off, leave the backside, and never come back.

The horse didn't care. I continued to pull, the worry over his injury keeping me from completely giving up. But he just ran. We again passed the place where we started, marking a two-mile sprint. My stomach soured.

We came around the bend and the two outriders in their bright red jackets, there to maintain order and help keep everyone safe, galloped up along either side of me. They were like cops forcing a car to pull over. *It's about time*, I thought, hardly able to hold myself in the saddle anymore. The outrider to the left leaned out of his tack and grabbed the bridle of my runaway horse, whose defiance was quickly fading. Once under control, the outrider glared at me as if the whole issue was my fault, and I glared back—angry, humiliated, racked with guilt, and trying not to teeter off the edge of the bay giant.

My muscles screamed. My brain screamed. The trainer and assistant trainer appeared to swallow down screams with every inhale. Their mouths were sealed into tight lines as if the slightest opening would lead to an outpouring of venom, but they kindly held it in. I wanted to melt into nothing. I felt like I was halfway there already as I slid off the horse and tried to stand. The only person who didn't avert his eyes was Donald. Ron and his assistant disappeared into the office, and I stood outside awaiting my fate, like a kid at the principal's door.

"How's he been going for you?" I muttered to Donald.

He tilted his head back and laughed. "Oh, I haven't been galloping him. He wasn't ready! I know the board said to gallop, but I've just been jogging him every day."

I peered into his smiling eyes, trying to grasp what he just said. *He's just been jogging. This was the horse's first gallop in who knows how long. He sits in that stall all day waiting for his one chance to get out. I'm the weakest rider in this barn, probably the weakest rider at this whole dang track right now since I'm so new, and he let me do his first gallop after a layup.* I imagined my fist cocked back, releasing square onto Donald's nose. Him ducking, grabbing his face, and cursing as blood poured out.

"Hey Sarah, come here," Ron called from his office. I cast a scathing look at Donald before shuffling into the room. "What happened?" Ron asked with slanted brows.

My eyes filled and I silently cursed every molecule of saltwater. I threatened to claw my eyeballs out if they dared to spill onto my cheeks. I wanted to tell Ron about Donald not doing what he was told, to cast the fault onto someone else. But I aspired to be good enough to hold my own, no matter other people's actions. I glanced in Donald's direction as if I could see him through the cinder block walls before simply saying, "I couldn't stop the horse."

Ron stared at his desk for a moment, contemplating. I dropped my eyes, wondering what he expected me to say. I'd played enough sports in high school and listened to enough ridiculous excuses about every pitiful thing. Back then, we ran a lot of deep tens. It was a drill where we had to run ten lengths of the gym, and the whole team was supposed to finish in under a minute. Everyone seemed faster and stronger than me, with more lung capacity.

The coach counted down the final seconds as I pumped my legs and chased the finish line, sucking in air that never quite filled my lungs. All the while, the team glared at the weakest link— me—and complained to the coach. I promised myself to never be the girl who whined or complained my way to a starting spot on the team. I'd give it my all and I'd simply be good enough or I wouldn't. Sometimes I was; sometimes I wasn't. Some coaches loved me for it, but most were confused by my silence. Ron seemed a bit perplexed.

My body trembled with the simple effort of standing. *Surely he'll never want to see me in his barn again. I'm not sure I can recover from the shame of it all anyway. Maybe I just won't come back.* "I need to go," I told Ron, *and probably never return*, I told myself, defeat making my already exhausted body weigh double.

A voice broke my string of thoughts. I looked up to find Ron staring into my eyes. This guy who treated life as one big joke was now looking at my very soul like his next words held the weight of my future. "I'll see you tomorrow."

I paused in shock before an excuse tried to push its way out of my mouth. *Surely he doesn't really want me here.* Everything in me said *No. Don't come back*. But he looked me in the eye and told me, "You're coming back tomorrow. It's what we do."

I was taken aback. Shocked. Grateful. For a moment I was twelve years old, lying on my kitchen floor when my brother looked down at me and said, "Don't cry about it, do something. Go talk to Mom and Dad."

Except, instead of Nathan it was Ron. And even though talking to Mom and Dad seemed impossible back then, this was a million times harder. And I didn't miss the way he said "we."

"Fine. I'll see you tomorrow," I mumbled. I dipped my head so hopefully no one would notice the tears stinging my cheeks when I slunk out of the barn, past all the horses coming back from their exercise and getting bathed, past the assistant trainer who watched me go, past the laughing people loving their jobs on the track, past the security gate, across Fourth Street, and to my truck, praying every single step.

I went to class.

I cried myself to sleep.

And I went back to the track the next day.

Because it's what *we* do—as horsemen, as dreamers, as people who lean in instead of giving up.

Chapter 26

I made Hardee's trips, hung around the shedrow, rode some horses, and almost felt like part of the crew. I danced on the fringe, trying to soak in every moment, knowing it wouldn't take much for me to be looking for a new job. Maybe it was my own insecurity keeping me at arm's length, thinking surely Ron gave me mounts as an act of charity. Or maybe the assistant trainer, who never warmed up to me that I could tell, kept me convinced I was one wrong move away from being done.

One early morning, the track was still shades of yellow and gray. Galloping didn't wait for the sun to wake. I finished a ride, thrilled the horse stopped when I stood in the stirrups and squeezed the reins. *What a gem*, I thought. With each successful gallop, this was less scary and more like something I could be good at.

We were nose to butt with the other horses as we made our way along the outside rail toward the gap to leave the track. The horse alternated from a jig to a walk with his head up, and I leaned forward, stretching my arm out to stroke his gleaming chestnut neck. He startled, dipping and spinning to the right, and before I realized what was happening, I landed on my feet next to him, reins held loosely in my right hand.

A laugh sounded beside me and the rider behind us clambered to control his own mount. My sudden appearance next to the horse instead of on his back where I belonged caused his eyes to expand until the white edges nearly glowed in the dull dawn. He flew back and sideways, pulling the reins out of my relaxed hand before I could process the importance of a death grip. The chestnut galloped away with his head up, stirrups flopping against the saddle.

"Well, that was quite the dismount!" I heard a voice say from the darkness on the other side of the rail.

"Yeah! I can't say I've ever done that before," I replied to the stranger, realizing he must have been the source of the horse's sudden fear. My eyes danced with mirth over landing on my feet.

"Well, I can't say I've ever seen anyone else do that either!" the man said. I wondered who he was; maybe an old trainer, a track legend I didn't know about yet. Or maybe just a random person who had connections to get to the backside and loved watching morning workouts.

I watched the commotion my loose horse was causing, wishing I'd tried harder to hold on to the reins. *I should have never let them slip through my fingers*, I chastised myself, clenching my gloved hands into fists. It happened so fast.

Riders pulled up from gallops early as the loose horse siren sounded across the mile oval. Within a few seconds, the outriders in their bright red jackets retrieved the horse, who had quickly abandoned his gallop to stand in the center of the track, bug-eyed with legs braced, like life without a rider might be scarier than the monster by the rail.

The outriders' arrival sucked the joy from my lungs. "This horse belong to you?" one of them asked as he handed over the reins. No answer was needed. I was the only horseless rider standing on the dirt oval. Their faces were set with hard lines and angry frowns.

"Thanks," I said with a weak smile, grabbing my horse. They rode back to their posts and the siren turned off. With a shrug and a smile to the guy by the rail, I made my way to Ron's barn on foot, leading the horse. With each step, I tried to shake off the outriders' disapproval and cling to the feeling of the lovely gallop I'd had, the hilariously unplanned dismount, and the fact the horse was fine. *He didn't even step on his reins!* I told myself. Aside from being made to feel like an unwelcome zit on a first date by certain men in red jackets, it had been a great outing.

"Glad to see you!" the assistant trainer said as I led the horse into the barnyard. She was leaning over a blue bucket, scrubbing it clean while she talked. "I heard the loose horse siren and was worried it might be you." There was a hint of exasperation in her tone, and I pretended it wasn't there. "But here you are!" Relief shone in her features as she held the scrub brush and stood.

I should have just smiled, nodded, and handed the horse to his groom. Of all the times I was unable to talk when I really needed to, today I found myself unable to hold words in. A huge smile stretched across my face as I exclaimed, "It *was* me! He spooked after our gallop when we were leaving the track and I landed on my feet! I almost held onto him, but he got away. The outriders brought him back."

A shadow crossed her face and the muscles of her jaw tensed. She forced an unconvincing laugh. My stomach filled back up with the lead that had momentarily disappeared with my good gallop and successful dismount.

"Hand the horse off, there's no more for you today," she declared, a slight tremor to her voice like waves of anger were rolling through her.

"Okay!" I replied with fake nonchalance, envisioning the whiteboard as it had been this morning, with two other horses next to my name. Apparently someone else would ride them today.

I gave the chestnut a pat as I handed him off, glancing down at my boots and the soft dirt of the shedrow that covered the toes. I glanced down the rows of stalls, over to the whiteboard, and at the closed door of Ron's office before taking a fortifying breath and walking back out into the fresh sunshine of the morning.

"Thanks! Have a great day!" I waved, continuing my charade of simply leaving early and being done for the day as I walked past the assistant.

"Hey Sarah," she started, and I saw tension on her face. I stared at her, taking it all in. This hardworking assistant must be the one who grounded Ron. They rarely talked in front of me, but she seemed like the no to his yes, the stop to his go, the reality check to his wild side. Every crazy dreamer needed one or we'd drift away with no one to reel us back.

Her expression was a combination of emotions. Anger was most obvious, and I wondered if it was all because of me or if there were other things going on in her life and I was simply what tipped the scales. There was exasperation. *She looks like she expects me to have a meltdown and she's going to have to hug me. She doesn't seem like a hugger.* I almost laughed at the thought. With the slant of her eyebrows and softness in her eyes, I saw guilt too. She felt bad for what she was about to say, so I said it for her.

"I'm done here?" I offered with a shaky smile and a lift of my left brow.

"Yeah. Yeah, this was the last straw. We've got to keep the horses safe, you know?" she glanced into my eyes before looking at the ground.

It was odd. It was a dumb thing to be fired for—coming off and landing on my feet. I'd had an actual good ride, possibly my best since I started galloping at Churchill Downs. For a lap and a half around that mile track, I never felt on the verge of losing control or dying.

It sucked to be fired. It sucked to walk away from a job I wanted so badly.

But, ironically, the lead in my stomach lightened. Being let go released a lot of the guilt I carried for every mistake and screwup. Since day one I had wondered why he hired me, and every error made that voice louder and more persistent. Somehow, despite this disappointment, I could breathe easier.

I smiled a bright, authentic smile and the assistant's jaw loosened, her mouth opening a tad in shock.

"Okay, thanks for the opportunity. I really appreciate it, and I get it," I shrugged. And I did. Pressure built behind my eyes, but I refused to release it.

Ron peeked around the wall, his brows furrowed in what appeared to be confusion. Or was it regret? *Does he know what's happening? Did he hear us?* I wondered. For a moment, I contemplated going over the assistant's head and pleading my case before Ron. Surely he'd keep me around. No didn't seem like a word he was too familiar with. But I let the assistant ground me, be the no to both of our yeses. I nodded in thanks and waved as I turned to walk to my truck.

A couple of tears silently escaped while I walked past the barns bustling with activity. Grooms and riders I had come to recognize nodded as they pushed wheelbarrows or got tossed up onto their next mount. Acquaintances called out to me and waved, and I waved back, smiling, pretending my face wasn't wet and that I wasn't taking a walk of shame back to my vehicle. A jockey I'd nearly become friends with approached on his way to breeze a horse. I scraped away the tears with the sleeve of my hoodie, hoping it looked like I was wiping sweat off my brow. Never mind that there was a bite to the air this fall morning.

"Hey, Sarah!" he kept his horse walking as he talked. "You already done for the day?"

"Yep! Finished early!" I smiled and hustled past before he could see the tears spring out of my eyes as I spoke. *Finished.*

Yet, it was freeing to walk without the weight of guilt and a voice taunting me, saying I was only there because Ron was too nice to say no.

I breathed as I passed the intake barn, where they stabled horses who were just in for the day. "Hey sweetie, do you know how to ride a horse from the gate yet?" a gray-haired stranger holding a tacked-up racehorse asked as I strode by. I almost laughed at the irony of it. Would he be asking this if he knew I'd just been fired?

"Not yet," I said, wishing for all I was worth that I knew how. It would have been nice to snag an extra ride.

Who would I ride for next? God, what am I going to do now? I prayed as I walked past the security guys, hoping they wouldn't mention that the sun had only just risen. We tilted our heads to each other and I lifted my hand to bid farewell, rushing past so they wouldn't question me. All while I questioned God. *What's next?*

For the moment, next was crawling back into bed and snuggling Sandi until I had to head to class.

Chapter 27

Later that day, I strode into Equine 101 with my Churchill Downs backpack slung across my shoulder. The bag reminded me of the ladies with pretty hair and form-fitting skirts who seemed convinced I was crazy as they filled my arms with Churchill Downs swag. It made me wonder if I really was crazy to chase this racetrack dream when I'd had a perfectly sensible future laid out in front of me in Mississippi. But it also reminded me that even though nearly every ride felt like teetering on the edge of a cliff in a windstorm, I did it. I galloped racehorses at Churchill Downs. The next step was to do it without feeling like I might die every ride.

Equine 101 was the representation of what I loved about Louisville. Everyone in this class was horse-obsessed. There were three-day eventers, people who had almost no experience with horses but had horse tattoos and folders and were hungry to learn more, and then there were the racetrack junkies. The track kids hung out together—their dads were racehorse trainers, training track owners, and a couple were big-time handicappers. Their names would be on my TV at Derby time for the horses they thought would win, place, and show. It was an eclectic bunch, and I often sat listening to their conversations and learning about other worlds within the realm of horses.

I dropped my backpack onto the '80s carpet next to my seat. Tara was already in her customary spot, up a row right across the aisle. Shame filled my chest. She had gotten me that job, and I had lost it.

"Hey!" I said as blood crept up my neck into my face.

"Hey! How are ya?" she asked, but her pitied expression told me she already knew.

"Ron's assistant let me go today." The heads of the track junkies swiveled. My neck itched and my face heated as I fought the urge to scratch at the nervous splotches.

"What?! What happened?" she exclaimed in faux shock. *She won't be winning an Academy Award for acting,* I joked to myself, but I didn't sense judgment. There was no shadow in her eye or twinge to her voice saying she thought I was an idiot or a crap rider. I scanned the eyes of the racetrack crew and noticed a simple curiosity.

"Actually," I said with a chuckle, "I fell off a horse. But it was crazy!" The shame I'd felt a few seconds before was replaced with a wide grin as I recounted the story. "I had just finished a gallop and we were walking along the fence, and the horse spooked and spun so fast that I landed on my feet next to him!" I laughed as the track junkies' eyes bulged. "It was pretty epic!" I smiled. "But when he ran backward, I didn't hold onto the reins tight enough and he got loose. I'm pretty sure I could have held on too, but I was just so shocked." I shook my head, my eyes still crinkled in the corners.

"Oh, man!" Tara said. "They let you go over that?"

"Kind of. I mean, it wasn't just that. I've screwed up several times. It's okay," I shrugged. "The assistant never seemed to really like me, anyway. Who knows? Either way, I've got to figure out what to do next."

"You could freelance," one of the track kids piped up.

"Really? What's that?"

"You just go from barn to barn on the backside and ask if people need a rider. Some people work for specific trainers, but a lot of riders freelance." He said it as if it was totally normal, although I couldn't recall seeing any exercise riders walking from barn to barn. I was probably so stuck in my own world I just didn't notice.

The lack of judgment from my peers peeled the final vestiges of shame off me. I could see the respect shining in their eyes and figured it had something to do with putting myself out there and riding the big, insanely strong Thoroughbreds. *God, thanks for this tip. I guess I'll be getting up early again.*

"I'm getting up early and going to the track," I told Joey on the phone that night. Sandi and I were sprawled across the fuzzy blue couch, her head resting on my lap and my roommate's black kitten climbing the back of my dad's hand-me-down chair. I had visited Gideon after class. It was a long, full day.

"Okay, well, be careful," he said.

"I will," the words dutifully and automatically rolled off my tongue while my brain shouted: *Nothing about this is careful!* But I didn't need to remind my boyfriend about that. He seemed fairly risk averse.

"I'm going to bed since I'm getting up early."

"Okay, goodnight! I love you." His voice lilted with the words, and it lifted my heart.

Joey Hickner loved me. By the calendar our relationship moved quick, but living it felt like a waltz.

We went on our first date the night before Formal. The next morning, my friends loaded into my truck for a road trip. These had been my people since move-in day freshman year. We had been inseparable for a while, but sophomore year was different. Our schedules no longer lined up, extracurriculars filled our days, and my friendships were reduced to friendly waves and passing hugs. *This day will be like old times though*, I told myself as the truck doors slammed. Austin put a mixed CD he'd made just for the weekend into the stereo.

We ate Funyuns, and drank Coke from glass bottles. The sunshine reflected off the glittery blue hood of my truck and I donned my cheap, oversized sunglasses. *I'm going to Kentucky soon*, I reminded myself, my heart clenching. Gosh, *I love these people. I love our friendship. Well, I loved it last year.* We tried to go back there as we sang along with Broadway and boy bands.

We checked into the hotel. There was a girl's room and a guy's room with a door in between, which we left open. The girls yelled across the doorway with blow dryers, curling irons, and makeup brushes flying in every direction while the guys lounged, draped across beds with tuxes already on and jackets strewn over the backs of chairs.

Mom had bought me a blue beaded dress, and it felt glamorous enough to wear on the Grand Ole Opry stage. Butterflies took flight in my stomach. I undid the zipper and stepped into the dress. My friend Lacy Lee appeared behind me and pulled the zipper up. We both stared at my reflection. Blue waves of beads curved down my body, changing from dark blue to light blue to pearlescent silver. Pink hair, a stunning dress, and a bright, if not fully authentic, smile.

"I'll help you with your makeup!" Lacy declared before pulling out a bag overflowing with tubes and compacts and dabbing stuff on my face.

When I walked into the guy's room, there was a stutter in the energy. I looked into each person's eyes, trying to decipher the reason for the pause, and found ceramic smiles and shadows. Things were changing. Invisible walls were growing, but I couldn't pinpoint where they were coming from. Was it me, them, or an outside force we had no control over? Chewing the inside of my lip, I returned their expressions with a smile that didn't reach my eyes. My date held out his arm and I crossed the room to him, grateful for an escape.

We walked past the double doors into the grand resort ballroom and paused. My stomach dropped. So many cheerful people who belonged, and I wasn't sure if I had a place in this crowd.

I imagined my date's stomach performing its own flips next to me. He was more introverted than I was. I held his arm a little tighter as we approached the check-in table, pulling my shoulders back so no one would notice my loneliness or lack of confidence. We got our table number, and I decided to take a cue from my dress and channel my inner ocean princess, striding into the room like a wave unapologetically surging to shore.

My date chivalrously pulled my chair out for me. I took my seat, smiling graciously at him, and tried to scoot up to the table. The rug clung to the legs of the chair until he helped me lurch forward. I noticed red splotches on his neck that likely matched my own. He took his seat, and I was grateful for his steady presence. We greeted our friends already at the table and checked the name cards to see who else would be with us.

Someone passed the basket of rolls, and my stomach groaned in anticipation. I scanned the multiple pieces of silverware, replaying a scene from a movie I had watched way too many times in junior high: start on the outside and work your way in. I grabbed my blunt knife, pressed it into the stiff butter, and attempted to mush some onto the roll. It refused to spread, stubbornly sitting in a clump.

Hunger pangs gnawed my self-control, and I tore into the heavenly bread, lump of butter and all.

I sat back, savoring my first bite of real food in hours, thanking God for the comfort of my date, and knowing that in a few seconds my belly wouldn't be eating my insides. I casually looked up, and straight in front of me with two round tables between us, was Joey Hickner. Our eyes snagged on each other and I gasped at the shock of it, then giggled. He grinned like he had been staring, waiting for me to realize he was there. Somehow, not a single person blocked our view.

My date looked at me, then at Joey, and I felt a tad guilty. *God, is this a joke?* I whispered. *This is going to be so awkward.*

The rest of our crew arrived, and we snuck bites of dessert until they served the main course. We ate and chatted, the aroma of dinner and bread filling me, and every time I looked straight ahead, there he was. My stomach did flips. Annoyance was clear in the eyes of a few friends. They missed me like I had longed for them. They wanted all of me for the night, like old times, but I had a feeling they would never have all of me again.

The band started playing and before I finished eating, Joey stood and grabbed his beautiful date's hand, leading her to the dance floor. Envy bubbled up as I watched them smile and move with the music. Her hands were in the air. Their bodies touched. It was the same way I had danced with guys for years, with no interest in most of them. It was how kids who grew up in the '90s danced. But I couldn't bear seeing Joey close to another girl.

My drive to be out on the dance floor, showing Joey up, was stronger than my need for dessert. I grabbed my date's hand and dragged him away from our chocolate cheesecake with raspberry drizzle and onto the tile dance floor. We had a shared love of dancing, so I didn't feel too bad.

The beat moved through us with our arms in the air and bodies moving. Sweat trickled from my hairline and my thighs burned from exertion. The music took me away and I glanced up to smile, only to see Joey pressed up against his girl with a huge grin. His eyes cut to me. The music was too loud to talk, so I put my hand on my date's shoulder and poured my competitive siren spirit into outdoing the only other people I could see on the dance floor. Joey's shirt was untucked, and he added a cowboy hat to his non-cowboy head. It was a dance battle, Joey vs. me, and I wasn't sure if the people with us were our partners or our victims.

When the band called it quits, we awoke from the trance of the dance floor to find most everyone had left. The banquet staff was cleaning up. Lacy grabbed my hand and dragged me off the floor, but my eyes lingered on Joey, who stared back with a wicked grin on his face. We grabbed our shoes and my purse, giggling. I glanced at Joey once more and my face flushed. We rushed back to our room, sweaty and blissful.

Two hotel rooms of people crammed into a king bed to watch a movie. The other side cracked jokes and yelled at the characters on screen. Lacy pelted the TV with bits of popcorn. I laid wedged between my friends, enjoying being back with my people, even if my mind was elsewhere. A buzz on the side table had me lunging for my phone. Who on earth would call this late? My screen lit up with "Joey."

"I'll be right back!" I blurted as I crawled over people to get out of bed. I ducked into the hall in my T-shirt and pajama pants and unfolded my phone with a breathless, "Hello?"

"Hey, sorry to call. I know you're with your friends, but I just wanted to hear your voice," Joey said on the other end. The butterflies nearly stole my breath.

"Oh no, I'm glad you called, really!" I tried not to sound too eager, but I was so happy I could have laid down and slept in the hall with the phone pressed against my ear. "It looked like you were having fun tonight," I said, allowing a bit of playful envy to seep into my voice.

"Yeah, well, it looked like you were having a lot of fun, too." A huge smile stretched across my face as he continued, his voice rumbly and low from the night on the dance floor and trying not to wake up his roommates, "Well hey, I'll hang up. I just had to hear your voice."

I didn't want him to hang up. I didn't want to go back in the room with my friends who I knew were unhappy with this development. Taking a deep breath, I imagined sitting in the hall all night just talking to Joey. I released the fantasy and finished the conversation. "Okay, thanks for calling. Have a good night!"

"Goodnight." I could hear his smile through the phone.

Back at Mississippi College, my parents wanted to meet for dinner, and I invited Joey to come along. The drive was approximately six minutes. He slid his hand across the gearshift and intertwined our fingers. My heart leaped. I wondered if he felt the rush that made it hard to talk, or even breathe, when we touched. I glanced up, hoping to see what he was thinking as my body hummed. How can something so small feel so big?

He glanced at our hands and then looked into my eyes and smirked. "I didn't like seeing you with another guy last night."

I paused, trying to decide how much to share, but the truth spilled out. "I really didn't like seeing you with another girl."

"Yeah?" He said it as a question but didn't wait for a response. "Maybe we should just be officially together now and not do things like that with other people." His eyes twinkled when he said it.

The car suddenly seemed depleted of oxygen, so I was a tad lightheaded when I said, "You really mean that?"

"Yeah." Happiness filled his voice, me, the entire car.

"I'm in," I replied with a half-grin and quirk of my brow, like I may as well have been saying I'd take cheese on my burger, or yeah, I'll go on that fair ride. But I knew in the churn of my gut, the staccato pounding of my heart, the lack of breathable air, and this weird peace that settled over me like a blanket, that I might be saying yes to a wedding gown. To forever. Because as crazy as it all seemed, I could see God's hand in every single detail of what was happening.

Minutes later, we walked into Applebee's and he met Mom and Dad.

Sandi's collar jingled as she settled into bed, then lifted her head and thumped her tail as if to say, *Come on, Mom, it's bedtime*! But my left hand was still tingling from the memory of the first time Joey grabbed it, weaving his fingers between mine. God was all over that night, over us, and this thing we were becoming. Maybe God's hand was on this track thing, too. It was a hope. A prayer.

I responded to Joey on the other end of the phone, "I love you too. Goodnight!" I flipped my phone closed and crawled into bed. *Tomorrow I'll put on my helmet, boots, and safety vest and go from barn to barn at the track. Hopefully I'll find some horses to ride. We can do this. Right, God? Are you in all this too?*

Chapter 28

The amount of self-control it took to roll out of my warm bed before the sun rose, to head to a track with no one expecting me, was nearly more than I had. Sandi slept under the covers as my personal heater, creating an even stronger pull to stay put. But the longing that had pulled me across hundreds of miles of interstate, away from my family and friends, pulled my sleepy self out of bed. It was gnawing and incessant. *Chase the dream.*

Never mind that riding racehorses hadn't felt like "the dream" since before the accident. The two weeks I'd had gave me a taste of what it could be like. It was a drip of water on my tongue as I roamed the desert in search of an oasis.

God, please help me with this, I muttered as I tied my boots. The idea of talking to people I'd never met and asking them for a job I wasn't sure I'd survive was too much, so I focused on one thing at a time. *Boots on. Crate Sandi. It'll probably be chilly, so I need to grab a hoodie. I'm not hungry yet, but I need to eat something. I'll just have a little milk. Okay, my stomach should be fine. Vest and helmet are in the truck. Where are my keys?... Okay, got my keys.*

I tiptoed down the creaky stairs that adjoined the other units in the building, slipped out the door, and was greeted by the rising sun. Horses would already be on the track; horses I could have ridden. *This will have to be good enough,* I told myself, knowing I should have pried away from Sandi's warm body when the alarm went off instead of hitting snooze.

The security guards nodded when I flashed my badge and walked onto the bustling backside of Churchill Downs. The first break of the morning, when they closed the track to drive the tractors around it and smooth the dirt, was in twenty minutes. There was almost no way I would get a mount in time. I had to find a trainer who would say yes, have a horse ready to go, and get around the track before it closed. *I should have woken up earlier. But at least I'm here. It's a start.*

Barns stretched out in front of me. Some horses were having leg wraps removed while others stuck their noses into the water hose, soaking their handlers with the frigid back spray. Grooms hustled to finish caring for one horse and get the next ready to go. The air seemed thinner this morning. I closed my eyes for a second. *God, please help me.*

The only way this will work is if I stop pretending I have some place to be and actually approach a trainer. I attempted to pep myself up. A couple barns later, I spotted a target who didn't look too intimidating and made my move. Walking into the doorway of the barn, I stretched my hand out for a shake. He grasped it, and though surely insecurity poured off me in waves, I tried to feign confidence. "Hi, I'm Sarah," I looked straight into his eyes as I spoke, "I was wonderin' if you have any horses that need riding."

The trainer looked me up and down. "I'm sorry, sweetie, but we're all set here. Feel free to come back another time, though." The gainfully employed stuck their heads out of stalls or blatantly glared while cleaning bridles.

"Okay, thanks!" I poured on an extra dose of southern sweetness to cover the sting of rejection and the nervous tremor in my voice. Probing stares followed me, burning holes in my back as I attempted to blend a casual stroll with a desperate run. *I can't believe he called me sweetie. Why does everyone around here treat me like I'm a little kid?* The anger bolstered my resolve, and soon I was at another barn, talking to another trainer.

And so it went for weeks. Most days I'd get at least one ride. Trainers paid me anywhere from $10–$15 per ride, and thankfully my parents sent enough money to cover my cheap downtown rent and board for Gideon. Work at the track paid for groceries and other necessities. It was a good thing I genuinely enjoyed rice for dinner and knew at least three restaurants where I could eat a delicious meal for under five bucks.

When I did get rides, they seemed more on edge than everyone else's mount. They were less inclined to keep their feet on the ground when we were supposed to be walking or jogging, and their brakes weren't as good when it was time to finish our gallop. The trainers acted like they were doing me a favor, which technically they were. I needed rides if I wanted to chase this dream (and eat). But trainers were nothing without their riders.

As yet another horse stood on his hind legs underneath me, pawing the air with his front hooves, I nearly rolled my eyes and sighed. If I wasn't concerned about causing a major accident, I would have. Instead, my hands trembled in anger, frustration, and possibly another emotion I refused to accept as I envisioned falling off and lying in the dirt. My worst fear unfolded in my mind—a horse taking off, crashing into another horse and rider, and killing them.

There was a good chance the trainers were bringing me the rogues of the barn that no one else wanted to ride. But they would always say things like, "This one's a barn favorite. He's an easy ride." As the horse carried me out of the barn, they'd call out, "You be careful out there, okay?"

The barns and horses were all different. The common denominator was me. I mulled over it as my mounts pogoed their way around the track, narrowly missing other horses, drawing glares from riders. *I'm not scared. Would someone who's afraid get up every morning and ask to get on these horses? I love to ride, and I'm brave.* I could taste the lie, but the truth wasn't allowed. Fear and racehorses were a dangerous combination.

A few weeks into my freelance career, I made my way to the farthest side of the track. Normally I gave up and headed to class before getting this far. My bravery had grown and I no longer cherry-picked trainers based on how friendly they looked. Every barn had horses, so I started about halfway in and went to each one. It was my seventh or eighth attempt. The back-to-back rejections were piling up and I was losing my resolve, imagining crawling back into my warm bed. *Just four more and then I'll go,* I told myself as I walked up to another trainer.

The corners of his lips turned down when I asked the question. The trainer was older, near my grandad's age. "Well, I've got a horse I can put you on. Wait right there and we'll get him ready." He stepped into the shedrow and yelled out some words in Spanish, then stood by the door to his office in silence.

I shifted on my feet, glancing at the horses poking their heads out of their stalls. I stepped into the sun to soak up its rays, willing them to chase the morning chill and jitters away. *Where is this guy's regular rider?* I wondered. *Maybe he gave everyone the day off.* My mouth felt stuck in a frown, worn down at the corners by all the rejections. *Wherever this guy's regular rider is, at least I'm getting on one of his horses.*

A beautiful dapple gray walked out. White rubber-coated reins hung down on either side of his neck. His ears perked toward me, and he chewed the bit and danced sideways. "This here is the easiest ride I've got," the trainer said. Like he knew I wasn't good enough for an average racehorse.

"Thanks." I barely hid the offense in my voice while eyeing the jigging horse, skeptical of his sainthood.

Do people talk about how bad I am? Does my reputation precede me? The groom approached with the horse, and I had to remind myself that I couldn't control what people did or didn't say. *It is what it is. I'll keep going either way.*

I silently walked over and stood by the stunning, tall horse. The groom grabbed my shin as I gathered the reins and some mane. "On three?" he asked. I nodded before being boosted into the saddle.

The handsome gray jigged around the barn while I lengthened the stirrups and tied the reins in a knot. The trainer followed, explaining what he wanted and finishing with a very serious, "Be careful."

"Okay," I nodded, ducking as I rode out of the barn and toward the track. *Why is he so nervous if this guy is so "easy"?*

The horse threw his legs out from his shoulder like a wild cat. His walk was urgent, predatorial, and smooth. I squeezed the reins a tad, asking him to relax before he broke into a trot. "There's no rush," I tried to explain, but he was ready to unleash his pent-up energy.

I wondered how long he was confined to his stall before this, picturing a video game energy bar maxing out after two days of eating, standing around, and dreaming of this moment. He tossed his head, attempting to pull the reins from my hands. "Whoa now," I sang, hoping to relax us as a zing of nerves shot through my body. "Just chill."

We stepped onto the track and turned left, and for a moment I was on Pegasus, soaring through the air. His back heels kicked out, lurching me forward before we landed. My safety vest nearly pulsed from the pounding of my heart. Years of being a barn rat had earned me a pretty solid seat. But we were against the rail with horses crowding us. Worst-case scenarios streamed through my mind as the horse took another leap into the sky.

On landing, I jammed my heels down further to improve my balance and shortened the reins to tell the horse to cut it out. He took serious offense to this and went full-on Black Stallion, standing on his hind feet as I pushed my hands toward his mouth and watched the riders below us speed by. They glared and yelled, "Control that horse!" *Thanks for the tip*, I thought, while I tried to remind myself that I wasn't afraid and held on for dear life. I rolled my eyes when I remembered the trainer saying, "This is the easy one."

Every few steps, he launched into the air like he had wings he was trying to figure out how to use. I gripped the leather strap of the martingale. *I'm riding incredibly well*, I thought, a laugh nearly bubbling up through the nerves as we caught air again. *My riding form is textbook perfect—heels down, light seat, reins short enough to communicate but not so short that it drives the horse mad. That part doesn't seem to be working, though. He's still pretty angry.* This circus was almost becoming normal, but we still had a gallop to get through. *Hopefully he won't run off with me.*

At long last, we arrived at the waiting spot where I'd ask him to stand and relax for a moment. That seemed unlikely. I couldn't stop thinking about what the trainer said. *This is the easiest horse in the barn? Did the trainer lie or am I that bad?*

Pins and needles prickled my skin from head to toe at the mere idea of galloping this guy. He stood like a gentleman for a few long seconds and I scratched his neck, determined there was a good horse inside him. He fidgeted, threatening to lunge forward. There was a slim gap in traffic, so I slackened the reins a half-inch and he happily jogged off the rail.

He started off quick, and I pressed my hands into his neck, reminding myself to chill. By the first turn, he settled into a forward gallop, pressing so hard into the bit I wondered if I could hold him. Every muscle in my body strained, but he stayed steady in that quick gallop, and after a mile and a half, I stood up and he slowed down.

My insides were a torrent of over-extended emotions. I wanted to grin. The gallop part of the ride had actually been lovely. But the desire to smile wasn't as strong as the frustration. *Why can't I just relax like the hundred other riders here? Why does every ride have to feel like I'm a breath away from killing myself or getting someone killed? Did the trainer lie to me about this being the easy horse? Or am I really so anxious that it's turning a perfectly good horse into a dragon?*

Saturday afternoon, Sandi and I rolled up to Gideon's new barn–one much closer to Louisville–to find nearly every horse on the property tacked up and meandering around the riding ring. "Hey Sarah!" someone shouted and waved. "We're having a fun show! Compete with us!"

"I don't know," I hedged, remembering the last barn show we attended.

"Aw, come on! The speed classes are starting soon, and we want to see that barrel horse of yours go!"

The mere mention of it shot adrenaline through my veins, elevating my heart rate and making me crave a run on my horse. I contemplated the shallow footing of this arena, remembering Ms. Brenda lecturing us on the importance of good footing when you run barrels. "You want the dirt to be deep enough to cushion the concussion when they run, but not so deep they get stuck or pull a tendon," she had explained.

Peeking over the fence of the arena, I checked it out. The ground looked a little hard, but I wouldn't push Gid. "Okay," I conceded. "We'll do it!" It would just be for fun. A smile stretched across my face as Sandi and I rushed to the barn to tack up so I didn't miss our class.

Fifteen minutes later we cantered circles to warm up. When it was time to change directions, I sat deep in the saddle with a "whoa," and Gid did a perfect, immediate stop. I laid the reins against his neck and pressed my right leg against his side, and he performed a 180-degree spin. Eyes from around the property followed us, and my chest lifted. We did the same thing in the other direction until his body was warm and ready to run. Then we waited our turn.

Another boarder held the microphone, announcing the order for us to go. Most riders were on gaited horses, which had an oddly smooth version of trotting. It looked like legs flying in every direction, but the rider barely moved in the saddle. One after another they went before me, and I realized why they were so excited to see a "real" barrel horse go. No one here knew what they were doing aside from having a good time. A guy made large, sloping circles around the barrels and I cringed. As the announcer mocked him and told the slow time, the rider thrust his koozie-nested beer can into the air, exclaiming, "At least I didn't spill my beer!" Hoots and hollers erupted as other cans and bottles rose into the air.

"Sarah Bullock, yer up!" My pulse thrummed into my fingertips, and Gid's heart pounded under my calf. The other riders turned their hoots and hollers to cheering for the "real" barrel horse. They were ready for a show, and it simultaneously puffed me with pride and put a weight of fear on my chest. *What if I disappoint them?* whispered in the back of my mind, but I chose to look ahead to the first barrel. Gideon's front feet hopped into the air as we neared the gate. When I could tell he saw the spot we were running to, I pushed my hands forward and clucked my tongue.

He exploded forward. His stride devoured the ground and before I could inhale, we were at the first barrel. Even the crowd seemed to hold their breath. I grabbed the saddle horn, expecting him to whip around it. A well-run barrel pattern happens so fast it becomes a series of reactions ingrained from hours of practice at home. But we didn't whip around anything. Gid went from earth-swallowing strides to rocking back on his hind legs and lifting his front feet into the air. Once, twice, then a third time his front feet left the ground as I tried to wrap my brain around what was happening. I pointed him to where we needed to go to complete the pattern and squeezed my legs.

In a contest where hundredths of a second was the difference between winning a big check or winning nothing, the time we spent paused next to the first barrel became near eternity. I tugged on the right rein and clucked, breaking Gid's trance. He moved into a canter around the first barrel, and I tried to put the hiccup behind us as we picked up speed. Behind the second barrel, I turned my head to aim for our next spot, and my leg made a painful thud against the blue plastic. I could hear the hollow sound of the drum hitting the dirt as Gid's hooves pounded the shallow dirt to the third barrel.

Racing past the timers, I could hear polite hollers, but they were as hollow as my insides felt. *Can we ever catch a break?* I wondered. *Can we ever have a great run? And what was that? Gideon has never reared before. Not that they were big or scary. His feet were probably just a few inches off the ground. But they were there and they shouldn't have been.*

I hopped off Gid and smiled to the other riders before slinking off to the barn, confused and frustrated. Gideon pressed his head against my back while we walked. When I pulled his bridle off, I put my hand out and let him rub until all the itchy spots were satisfied. I had wanted to win. I had wanted to show those people how good we were. I wanted to show the world how good we were. And I wanted to enjoy galloping racehorses, to be good at it. Was it too much to ask for?

Unhappiness stretched from my boots to my ponytail, holding me in place. Gideon bumped his head against my shoulder, breaking the trance and reminding me that just a couple weeks before, what I wanted more than anything in the world was to find this red horse with white legs and a blaze down his face. At least I had that, I reminded myself. "Thank you," I whispered to the One who brought him back.

Chapter 29

The cold of autumn turning to winter leaked into my corner room, and I pressed into Sandi's warmth. She'd nosed her way under the covers at bedtime and stayed there. The grating beep of my phone alarm broke the silence, sending me into a frenzy as I turned to grab it, hitting any button to make it stop.

"Not today, God," I muttered and rolled back over, dropping an arm over my dog. Disappointment left a bitter taste in my mouth, and I squeezed my eyes shut, hoping to drift to a place where things felt right and easy. I envisioned that first gallop with Craig on one side and Jen on the other, the freedom and joy.

What if today is different? a voice whispered in my mind. The hope of what could be swung my heavy legs to the side, and I rubbed dried tears off my face. They were becoming a normal part of falling asleep. I opened my phone to turn off the snoozed alarm, and a text from the night before popped up on my screen.

"Good night. Love you." Joey had sent it while I was lost in dreamland. My chest warmed.

Jeans and boots were waiting by the bed. I knocked back a glass of milk and headed to the track.

The race meet had ended and walking on the backside was like watching fall turn to winter before my very eyes. Barns that had been bustling with horses, overstuffed hay nets, and grooms running from stall to stall with dust cloths and hoof picks just the day before, now stood empty. There wasn't even an eye hook in the wall for a water bucket. The structure stood devoid of life and warmth.

Other barns had multiple stacks of buckets out front. Tack trunks, normally hidden away, sat on the bluestone waiting to be loaded into gigantic horse trailers.

"Where's everyone going?" I asked another rider.

"Now that the race meet is over, a lot of people will head south to warmer tracks in Florida or Arkansas. Some will stay until Churchill Downs completely closes for winter and then they'll head to northern Kentucky. There won't be much left to ride, so most of us will head over to Spectrum," he said.

"Wait, what's Spectrum?" He'd said it like I should know what it was. Like everyone knew.

"You don't know what Sports Spectrum is? It's the training track owned by Churchill Downs. They actually just changed the name to Trackside or something. Anyway, it's like ten, fifteen minutes from here."

"Okay. Maybe I'll go check it out," I replied, without plans to do so anytime soon. I had no idea where this track was, but Churchill Downs was right down the street from my apartment and the University of Louisville. I could go from the backside to campus in under five minutes, which was perfect for 9 a.m. classes.

As winter took hold, curtains were pulled over openings in the sides of the barns to trap heat. Most riders left, so it was easier to find a couple horses to ride each day. One morning I peeked in and said, "Hey, do y'all need help today?"

"Looks like we're riding in the barn," the trainer said. "Track's frozen."

"What? It's frozen?" I asked in disbelief. I would have been more likely to believe a Sasquatch was spotted on the backside.

"Yeah," he deadpanned. The guys standing around laughed at my shock. The trainer kept a nearly straight face and kept going, "So we're riding them in the shedrow today. We could use you for a couple."

"Okay, sounds good!" While I waited for a horse, I found a small pile of dirt and kicked it. Instead of scattering, the particles held firm in a little rock-hard mound. I walked to a place full of hoof-shaped divots, stepping on the high ridges. They remained hard lumps that pressed into the soles of my boots, the hoofprints unmarred. It was tempting to call Mom and tell her about this frozen ground phenomenon, but the sun was just rising. It was a bit early for phone calls.

I understood why we rode in the barn now—taking a horse onto a frozen track would mean broken ankle disasters everywhere.

After riding horses around the shedrow, I headed to the truck. A thin coating of ice covered my windshield, so I sprayed it with wiper fluid to melt it before heading north on Fourth Street. A small puddle of water rested on the wiper, and as I drove it moved up the glass, pushed by the wind. It stretched out like a river, branching into tiny tributaries. Seconds later, it turned to ice before my very southern, very shocked eyes.

Forgetting how early it was, I popped my phone open to tell Mom about all this. I called her again from the mall a few hours later, standing in front of a display of winter coats. We never paid full price for clothes, but there seemed to be no other option. I envisioned my bank account $150 emptier. Then I imagined another morning on the frozen track in a hoodie. The cold stayed with me even though the day had warmed up, and I shivered.

"You need a warm coat, Sarah." She sounded like she was explaining something to one of her students, talking slowly to ensure I got the message. But I could detect a hint of humor in her voice. I felt like the Beverly Hillbillies arriving in the big city, except I was a Deep South girl arriving to winter.

The next morning, I walked onto the backside of Churchill Downs in a crisp new winter coat to find the few trainers who had lingered packing up. It was time to find Spectrum or Trackside or whatever it was called.

The people at Trackside were a looser bunch. I had left the pretentious party with more pieces of silverware than I knew what to do with and arrived at a cookout with potluck sides and red-checkered tablecloths. Some of the crew from Churchill had moved over, but most everyone was new to me.

The plethora of noes was back, but at least the grooms chatted with me, making jokes when I walked by. One extra loud guy wore a uniform of baggy jeans and a jersey that hung nearly to his knees. I could hear him laughing from five barns away, and every time I walked past he counted loud enough for half the track to hear, "One Mississippi, two Mississippi!" My insides warmed even if I was on my seventh no and still hadn't been on a horse. Then he'd say, "You remind me of Julie Krone," with a glint in his eye. The first time, I had to ask who she was. A look of reverence filled his face. "She was an incredible female jockey."

My cheeks flushed with embarrassment and pride and my eyes filled. I'd had so much rejection that morning. To be compared with a female jockey at all, much less one who had claimed such respect from someone working on the track, added length to my spine. *Does he have any idea how the outriders watch me?* But I kept the thoughts to myself and tucked his compliment into my pocket.

Eventually I walked into a barn tucked into a far corner of the grounds. The trainer looked like he'd left his office job that morning to run to the track. I stuck out my hand and said my spiel.

"Are you that girl who had the accident and had her horse stolen?"

"That's me!" I said with a wry grin, shaky from all the rejection and grateful someone was at least willing to chat.

"I figured. From the teeth." He said it so low I almost didn't hear the last part. A hint of redness crept into his cheeks, and I realized he must be worried about hurting my feelings. But the last few months had given me a pretty thick skin.

"Yeah, you should have seen them before I got braces. It was rough," I shrugged, offering him an easy smile.

"You know, I train horses for Terri who works over at U of L. She gave me some of those fliers and I put them up at the Thoroughbred training center where they found your horse."

"Really?" I exclaimed as my smile stretched my face so much my cheeks nearly hurt. "Terri kept trying to tell me he was at a track somewhere as a pony horse, but I was convinced he was at a horse sale. I really appreciate you posting those fliers. The guy gave Gid back and even floated his teeth and dewormed him!" I chuckled. Grateful.

"Is that so?" The corners of his lips turned up the tiniest bit. "I'm glad I could help." He paused, peering into my face for a moment before moving on. "By the way, all the horses have been ridden today, but come back tomorrow before 7 a.m. I've got a couple I can put you on."

"Great! I'll see you at 7 a.m. tomorrow, then. Thanks!" I departed with a wave and a twinge of hope.

My stomach growled as I shuffled between barns, attempting to make eye contact and smile at all the trainers who'd said no. It didn't reach my eyes, and I kind of hoped they noticed. It was a walk of shame, another day with no mounts. But at least there was a promise for tomorrow.

The next morning I arrived at that little barn in a back corner of Trackside and got two mounts. One was an easy ride as far as racehorses went. The other was a little dark bay filly, who danced from the barn to the track on her toes like a ballerina. Sometimes she darted sideways or spun before I could stop her. I pressed my weight into my heels for better balance and pushed my knuckles into her neck, which had a calming effect on most Thoroughbreds. Once we were on the track, the girl was all business.

Day after day I rode those two, never falling off or being run away with. Yet the nerves never settled and the exhilaration never came.

When I finished with them, I half-heartedly walked to other barns. Three or four "no thanks" later, I headed to my truck.

Sunday mornings, after galloping at Trackside, I rushed to put on my Sunday clothes and catch the late service. Joey and I attended a small church near my apartment for several weeks. On Wednesdays, they treated college students to dinner before Bible study.

I tried to love it, to involve myself, to connect. They cast glances and smiled with shiny white teeth while clutching their Bibles. The people were so kind, striking up conversations over pizza, and asking about school and horses as we stood on the steps to leave. But I couldn't shake the new girl persona.

I wanted to get carried away in worship without feeling curious eyes on me. I wanted to feel at least a little bit like I was home when I walked into church. After weeks with the small congregation downtown, I told Joey I wanted to try the place Dr. Vittitow kept recommending.

The building was impossible to miss as you drove down Interstate 64 past the Blankenbaker Parkway exit. If there wasn't a gigantic cross in the center of the roof, you might mistake it for a basketball stadium in a city that worshipped the sport. I was leery. How many megachurches made headlines for leading people astray or stealing money? I loved a big church, but this one seemed too big.

My chest was tight from a hard morning at the track. Determined to leave it behind me, I sat hand in hand with Joey in a line of cars that backed all the way down the exit ramp of I-64. “Is this traffic all from the church?” The answer was pretty clear, but I couldn’t help but voice the question. Protestors glared into our window, thrusting signs toward us as we edged from the exit ramp onto the parkway.

“Wow,” Joey said, echoing my thoughts exactly.

“Well, it seems the church is at least taking a stand for something if people are protesting,” I said, and we shared a nervous laugh. A policeman waved us past a sign saying Southeast Christian Church.

Volunteers in orange vests directed cars to different parking lots, and we followed the sign to guest parking. There was a shockingly long row of doors, all leading to the same place. People poured in like the national championship basketball game was happening. Some were dressed in their Sunday best, and others wore jeans with holes in the knee, but nearly everyone nodded and smiled, holding doors for one another.

Fingers intertwined, clinging to one another, Joey and I walked into a huge circular atrium. I felt a million miles from a racetrack, and I couldn’t decide if I was grateful for the space or if I wanted to abandon this building crawling with people for the horses that made me feel like I was dancing with death.

Shelves with pamphlets stood tall in the center of the atrium. Banners advertised kid and youth programs, women’s conferences, and more. We followed the crowd up the escalator and toward the doors. Men in suits stood next to signs stating, “section full; please proceed to next section.” Music escaped through the cracks under the doors, calling me in. My heart rate picked up. I just wanted in.

We turned to head up a level and found that the next set of doors was very much the same. “Try the next level,” a man offered, so we kept going up. The anticipation built with each closed section. *Is there even room for us?* The feeling of missing something incredible overwhelmed me and I couldn’t wait to get inside. By the time we found an open section, we must have been on the sixth floor. Joey lunged toward the door and my steps lightened as the music got louder. A wave of nerves hit as he swung open the door.

Walking into the sanctuary felt like stepping into another realm. Cool air wrapped around us, drawing us in, and music drowned out every other thought or sound. Some people bowed their heads in reverence, others tilted theirs back, arms lifted high in worship. A gigantic screen hung from the ceiling, playing real-time footage of the stage six levels below, where musicians strummed guitars and sang. I was familiar with most of the songs from church events in Mississippi and Christian radio, but the words scrolled across the screen. Chills skittered across my arms, raising tiny hairs. I was simultaneously more alive and more settled than I had been since the accident. One word resonated through me: home.

We sang, listened to the sermon, and took communion from little individually packed cups with wafers. The service ended and the band came back on stage. People filed out of the aisles and through the sanctuary doors, and Joey turned to go. I grabbed his hand. "Wait. I just want to sit for a minute." He nodded in understanding and sat back down beside me. Music streamed through the speakers as singers started low, crescendoing toward the chorus. I had heard this song on the radio, and even sang along. But today the words penetrated my soul.

Blessed be Your name
In the land that is plentiful
Where Your streams of abundance flow
Blessed be Your name

Well, yeah, I thought, *definitely praising God here!*

Blessed be Your name
When I'm found in the desert place
Though I walk through the wilderness
Blessed be Your name

I stared at the stage, unwilling for Joey, or anyone, to see the emotions pushing to escape. Eyes full and chest in a sudden vice grip, I soaked in the words.

Blessed be Your name, when I'm found in the desert place. God, this is me. I'm in the desert, trying so hard, but it's just...

I could see the trainers faces, one after another, as they said no. I felt the nerves ratchet my heart rate when I struggled with yet another horse.

I'm in the wilderness, God.

The song kept going.

Every blessing You pour out
I'll turn back to praise

When the darkness closes in, Lord
Still I will say
Blessed be the name of the Lord
Blessed be Your name

"When the darkness closes in, Lord, still I will say," I sang along, now with bold, unashamed tears streaming down my face. *Blessed be the name of the Lord.*

I thought it was enough to say, "It is well with my soul." But there was more.

Something unlocked in my soul. It was a truth that ran so deep I could feel it in my blood from generations before me. It was a truth my ancestors had known, a truth from the origin of time. Bad things, hard things, didn't change God's goodness. It's who He is.

So why had I stopped praising Him?

Blessed be the name of the Lord.

Instead of the despair of Salvador Dali's clock, draped over a tree like a castoff sweater, I melted into God's waiting hands. I raised my hand to the heavens to praise God, and He poured me into a mold of my old self. A self I hadn't seen in months. But this newer version had a core of joy that could only come from my Creator. I glanced at my skin to see if it was glowing, to see if the world could see the change, and then laughed at myself, my heart light.

I sat in my seat and prayed.

When I go to the track and I don't get any rides, blessed be Your name. And when I have the best ride of my life, blessed be Your name. When Gideon was stolen and all hope seemed lost, blessed be Your name. Even if Gid had died, blessed be Your name. When he was found, blessed be Your name. And if I'm in an ambulance again, being toted to the hospital again, blessed be Your name. Or if things come together and it's everything my little dreamer heart could ever imagine and more, blessed be Your name. If I graduate from college and this entire Kentucky thing ends, and what I hoped for never comes together, blessed be Your name.

Even if it never comes together, I said again for myself as much as for God, *blessed be Your name.*

I realized on the sixth-level balcony of Southeast Christian Church that I had been missing something very important. I had hunkered down in despair, sitting on my pile of rubble like Job, determined for it to be well with my soul.

Now I stood up, stretching my legs and torso, lifting my hands and heart to the heavens. It felt so good to stand after being hunched over for so long. I praised God in the storm and felt freedom for the first time in months.

Chapter 30

"Sarah, I have something I need to tell you," Mom's voice said from the other end of the line.

"Okaaay." No conversation starting that way is good. My mind raced down the rabbit hole of potential tragedies.

"Is Granddad okay?" He was the first, most likely candidate, simply because of age.

"Granddad's fine. Your brothers are fine. But your dad had some chest pains on his hunting trip with your uncle last week, so he went to the doctor this morning and there's some blockage." She barreled forward with the news. "They want to do open-heart surgery as soon as possible. They even offered to schedule it for tomorrow, but with Thanksgiving this week we felt like it would be better to wait."

My face was numb. *No weeks of appointments, imaging, bloodwork, and preparation? That in itself says how bad this is.*

She'd said, "Wait and celebrate Thanksgiving with him," but unspoken words dangled in the air—*one last time, in case it's the last time.*

Wait, in case the nurses and doctors who have to work on Thanksgiving aren't all in on the job because they're wishing they were home eating turkey with their families. Which was fair.

But waiting also meant that at any second, the 99 percent blockage could become 100 percent. He could have a heart attack.

"Okay. So, like," I racked my brain for what open-heart surgery meant. "Is this, like, the surgery where they redirect your blood through a machine while they work on your heart?" I learned about it in history class, of all things. The facts were fuzzy. It had seemed genius that a machine could pump a person's blood while surgeons repaired their heart. I read that page of the textbook with sheer fascination. But to hear that *my dad's* blood would be re-routed, a machine maintaining his life, suddenly didn't seem cool or smart. It was terrifying.

I hadn't planned to go home for Thanksgiving. Christmas was just a few weeks later. Leaving the track for even a couple days meant leaving the two horses I was riding consistently, being replaced by another rider.

"You don't have to come," Mom said. She must have been momentarily crazy. I wasn't *not* visiting my dad, in case, well, I wasn't going to think about the in case. I was going home.

I walked upright through the next few days, going through the motions—shoulders back, chin up, ice eyes. *Blessed be your name, God*, I repeated, *even in the darkness.*

I told Joey, Terri, and my professors. When my mind tried to go down the trail of *what if* or *in case*, I'd stop and redirect only to spiral in another direction.

After the accident, the trailer tire blowout, Gid being stolen, things falling apart, people would say, "Well, at least it can't get any worse." It was their weak version of comfort, I guess.

My attempt at a smile probably looked closer to a grimace. "Well... ha... yeah." But my brain screamed, *Are you an idiot?! Look around! Everything that's good could be smashed to bits in a second—a car accident, a natural disaster, another hidden blood clot in someone I love.* In a single breath, things could be so much worse.

I knew this deep in my bones because so many things *had* changed in a breath. My world was right one moment, and the next it wasn't.

Granny was getting ready to go home from the hospital. Blood clot. Gone.

Galloping down the track on Red, he disappeared. My life would never be the same.

Gideon munching hay in a stall, ears swiveling to listen for my footsteps. Stolen.

God is sovereign, but is He good? The question skidded across my mind, and my expression soured. I wanted to slap myself for having the thought. *Is God good? Of course He is! It says it in His word. I felt it so strongly in church.*

He made sure my brothers and I got to say goodbye to Granny. He protected my body as Red and I somersaulted down the track. He helped me find Gid. And He is in every single tiny thing, even the rays of sun that peaked through the window warming Sandi on the corner of the bed. Of course He's good, I told myself.

But my mind kept spinning. *Maybe he didn't send the blood clot to Granny's lungs, but he allowed it. Maybe he didn't lift Red's hoof over the martingale to start the fall, but He didn't stop it either. He didn't take Gideon, but He watched every moment as someone slipped a halter over my horse's head and led him into a trailer.*

I wanted God to feel good, like a warm hug on a sunny day, but when I leaned in He felt more like the wide-open air as I stood on a ledge at the Grand Canyon. Beautiful, breathtaking, dangerous.

As I packed my bag to visit family, my heart tumbled like an unbalanced washing machine. *What am I supposed to think about this?* I asked God. *I know I need to trust you. I'm trying to trust you. But this is my dad. What if you say no? What if you take him, too?*

My eyes reddened, filling up, and Sandi stood from her warm spot on the bed, wriggling her body from side to side and sticking her nose in my face. I put my hands on her head, relishing the smoothness. I rubbed her ears, studying the little gray heart on her forehead, and let her remind me of God's goodness.

Sandi wasn't the dog I had planned to take to Kentucky. It was supposed to be Flash. My eyes drifted closed at the memory.

In high school, I worked for a small animal vet. I was sweeping the floors of the waiting room when a guy brought in one of the most beautiful dogs I had ever seen. He was lean, with long legs and a chiseled face framed by floppy, silken ears. His coat was a grayish color with red ticking in it. "What kind of dog is this?" I asked once the owner was gone.

"Oh, that's a German shorthaired pointer," the girl behind the computer responded, the screen giving her skin a blue glow.

Golden retrievers, huskies, and whatever else I had fantasized about owning dropped off my list. There was only one dog I could imagine taking to the barn, on trail rides, and snuggling with at night. I wanted a German shorthaired pointer.

I loved our family dogs, but my parents only wanted smaller breeds. To have a GSP, I'd have to be out of the house and out of the college dorm. In Kentucky, I'd have an apartment. No one could tell me no. For the first time in my life, I could have a dog of my own.

For months, I displayed Flash's image proudly on my computer screen in my Mississippi College dorm room. He was stunning. A German shorthair rescue close to Dallas, TX approved my adoption application, and as soon as sophomore year was over I would head there to get him.

Every day, through tough classes, the utter loneliness when Joey was traveling for baseball, and his weeks of mulling over which grad school to attend, a decision that would affect me almost as much as him, the picture of Flash comforted me. I looked at his photo and remembered, *soon I'm going to Kentucky. Soon it'll be me, Gideon, and Flash chasing a dream.* Even as my friends distanced themselves, something I figured was a natural response to my impending departure, Flash reminded me it was worth it.

Sitting with my parents over Sunday lunch, Mom asked when I was going to get Flash and who was going with me. "I haven't really thought about it yet," I admitted. "I just figured one of my friends from school, or maybe Joel would go once we're moved out of the dorms."

"I'll go with you," Dad said from across the table.

I narrowed my eyes a tad, studying him. "Are you sure, Dad?"

Going to get the dog was like a nail in the coffin of his Mississippi College dreams for me. Having a dog meant no dorm living. At MC, no dorm living meant losing part of your scholarship. A dog meant I for sure wasn't returning. *Could the person who wants me at MC the most be the one who helps me take this huge step away?*

The corners of his mouth turned down, but he kept his voice light. "Yeah. Yeah, I'll take you. It'll be good to see my brother! We can spend a couple of days there."

I looked at Dad, then at Mom, who looked at me, then to Dad. Dad was pretending like a quick trip to pick up a dog that sealed a fate he had fought against for so long was normal. My eyes pricked, knowing it was his way of giving his blessing for me to go to Kentucky.

"Okay! I'll reach out to Flash's foster family and tell them we're coming."

The entire way to Dallas, we pretended nothing was changing. We ate Beef Jerky and sang oldies—a father-daughter duo covering hits from the sixties and seventies. When "Unforgettable" came on, he sang Nat King Cole's part and I sang Natalie Cole's, and we swallowed back tears.

An hour from Dallas, I dialed Flash's foster family to inform them we were almost there. My heart fluttered. *This is really happening!* The lady answered, sounding distant and serious. But I refused to let her tone dampen my soaring high.

"My husband wants to speak with you," she said.

"Okay." I glanced sideways at my dad and then stared out the window while I waited for the lady's husband. As we exited right, making a wide loop onto a new interstate, the man picked up the phone.

"Hi. My wife informs me you want to adopt Flash."

"Yes sir," I responded, not sure what else to say, since "I just drove six hours to pick him up, you nitwit," would be entirely inappropriate and not in line with the southern manners my parents instilled in me.

Is something wrong? It can't be. I've been approved. Maybe his resting voice is angry.

"She says you ride horses and want to take him when you ride."

"Yes sir!" I responded enthusiastically.

A girl taking a dog who loves to run out into the open country was perfection. We were made for each other! I reminded myself.

"Well, Flash has a lot of hunt in him. In fact, we've lost him twice when he's run off. This is not a good fit. You can't take him out off-leash. I'm sorry, but you're not a good fit and we are not letting you adopt him."

I filled my lungs with air and held it in. *Do not panic. Do not look at Dad. How am I supposed to tell him the dog we just drove six hours to get is apparently no longer available? At least, not to me.* The window was cold against my forehead and the low Texas bushes and faded green fields zoomed past in a blur.

Even the most chill person would be incensed, and my dad had the hottest temper in the family. *God, what do I do?*

I replied, trying to disguise my mental spiral. "Okay, yes sir." The man mumbled some apology I didn't hear and hung up.

"So they're not letting you get your dog?" Dad said in a cool voice. A vein popped out on the side of his head, but he wasn't losing his temper.

I guess he heard.

"No sir." The blood had drained from my face. *Think, think, think. God, please help me think, what do I do?*

"I'll call the adoption agency. There are more dogs." I tried to sound nonchalant, sure of this idea. *None of them on the website were as pretty as Flash. None of them were young like him. But I need to at least try.*

I found the lady's number on the adoption papers and gave her a ring. "Don't you worry! I've got plenty of dogs at my house. You just come on over in the morning and we'll see if we can find you a match."

"Thank you so much!" I tried to sound cheery, but my heart had deflated.

"I need to leave for work at 7 a.m., so you'll have to come early."

"Okay, thank you so much. We'll be there by 6 a.m.," I assured her before ending the call. A delicate silence settled in the car for the final hour to my uncle's.

We rolled into Dallas and had dinner with family. Dad recounted the harrowing story of how I'd dreamed and planned for this dog only for it to be stolen from me, and how I was now supposed to be at this lady's house an hour away at 6 a.m. to look at what was available. With zero hesitation, my cousin Jon Paul piped up, "I'll take you!"

"Really?" I couldn't believe anyone would volunteer to take me somewhere at 5 a.m., especially not with a laid-back smile as if such an early morning was no big deal.

We watched the sun rise over rural Texas from his truck the next morning. *I can't believe JP is doing this for me* repeated over and over in my head.

The lady lived in a small ranch-style home with a fenced backyard that stretched further than I could see. A pack of mostly cream-colored dogs raced around the yard. She stuck her head out the door to wave us in. Crates lined her living room and dogs were everywhere—lying on couches, begging at the back door, and wriggling at thigh level, hoping for attention. Jon Paul kept himself a couple steps behind me, thumbs in his belt loops, comforting and protective.

The lady's kindness calmed my frayed nerves. She introduced us to the dogs and explained how her rescue took on English pointers and German shorthair pointers. From the looks of things, she mostly rescued English pointers. "Take a look at all the dogs in here, and then you can step into the backyard and meet everyone out there," she said as she rushed past me, still getting ready for work.

Nothing inside met my criteria. *She probably doesn't have what I want. Do I compromise just to have a dog, or do I go home empty-handed? How frustrated will Dad be after he drove me here? And do I go to Kentucky without a dog?*

The lady rushed back into the kitchen and threw open the back door. "There are lots of lovely animals back here. I'll leave you to get to know them," she said before disappearing again. We strode outside and stood on the doorstep. A pack of giddy dogs rushed me, jumping and barking in their excitement over new people. My eyes scanned the pack. In a sea of mostly cream-colored English pointers and mature, gray-faced German shorthairs, there was a little speck of dark brown with salt sprinkled into her coat.

She sat obediently with soul-searching eyes while the others lunged and jumped, clamoring for attention. The ruckus faded out of existence as I stared into the one dog's eyes, a stunning combination of olive and gold.

The lady stuck her head out the door. "Everything okay?" she asked.

"Yeah! Can you tell me about that one?" I pointed to the one that held my gaze.

"She's a nine-month-old female German shorthair. Her name is Sandi. Her family gave her up because she had too much energy and I think they had a new baby. I'll be right back."

"Sandi!" I called, and the wiry pup stood up, coming toward me. She whipped her tail from side to side as she stretched her nose up my leg, hoping for a pet. A couple others jumped at me, but when I ignored them they lost interest, running back into the yard. Sandi's mesmerizing gaze followed them for a moment, but she stayed with me. My head went light when I reached down to stroke her head.

"I want this one. Sandi," I declared when the lady came back outside. JP smiled and nodded.

"Are you sure? Do you want to look at this dog? Or maybe that one?" the lady asked.

"No." I was resolute. "This is the one. I want her."

Sandi sat at my feet, studying me like she was trying to learn everything about this girl who called her name. Like if I chose her she would give her everything to me, forever. I filled out the adoption papers, a nervous buzz filling my ears. I kept glancing at this dog I was committing to.

By 7:05 a.m. the adoption lady rushed off to work, and Jon Paul and I sat in his truck with Sandi in the back seat. She panted, mouth open, the corners pulled up as if she was smiling, but I knew she was anxious. I pretended she was a nervous horse and practically ignored her, determined to be a calm, steady presence.

Every few seconds, I glanced into the back seat. *Not Flash. Sandi. God, did you do this?* I mused. The world glowed and I floated through it. I barely knew this dog, but it all felt right.

Back at my aunt and uncle's house, I went up for a nap, bringing along my new partner. She curled into a ball against my stomach and sleep came easily. *Thank you, God,* I chanted until dreams took over.

How could I have survived these last few months without my dog? I wondered as I stared into her eyes. Simply her presence was a whisper from God, saying, *I am good. I may not give you what you think you want, but I have something better for you. I am good.*

Sandi

Okay, God. My breath shook. *I trust you. You are good. Help us through this mess with my dad.*

I don't remember how I got home. I don't remember Thanksgiving, seeing my brothers, hospital waiting rooms, or if I stared at a phone on the wall while waiting for the doctor to call and say whether everything was good or bad.

I remember visiting my friends at Mississippi College. I walked through the cafeteria that had been my place, memories playing out like ghosts. Friends who had been my people rushed to greet me before heading to class, but the old warmth and joy were missing. And I realized none of it was mine any more than I was theirs.

I remember walking into Dad's hospital room after surgery. I had always been proud of my toughness. I had reveled in being able to look at blood, help with surgeries at the equine hospital, wrap legs, or work on proud flesh. But then I saw my dad.

His skin was discolored in places, either from bruising or the iodine they'd used in surgery prep. *Iodine or bruise?* became a temporary obsession for my spiraling mind. The skin that wasn't bright with color was the complete opposite: pasty, like a corpse. More tubes than I could make sense of connected him to machines filling his side of the room.

"Sweetie, maybe you need to sit down."

I shuffled closer to my dad, Mom next to him. They talked. He cracked jokes. *Was that iodine or bruising?*

"Sweetie? You should probably have a seat."

Who's she talking to? Not me. I'm tough. I swayed.

The hospital room transformed into a battlefield. I stood in the center with no weapon and no will to fight, faint with the realization that we could all be taken down at any second. *God*, I prayed. *Dad was hit. Will he make it?* I wondered. Steady hands led me to a chair and Mom's eyes followed me from her spot beside the bed.

"Sweetie, he's fine. I know it looks like a lot when they come out of surgery," the nurse crooned next to me like I was a child who needed coddling.

I'm tough, I said in my head, as I lost feeling in my face.

"How are you doing, Dad?" I asked, hoping to sound normal but wanting to hold the seat cushion in front of my head in case a flaming arrow was being aimed at me.

"Sarah," Dad said in his little kid voice. It was his go-to when he wanted sympathy. "They sawed open my chest and cracked me wide open!"

"I know, Dad," I said with a single halfhearted chuckle. "Maybe you'll take care of yourself after this."

"Yeah, your momma will keep me in line. She's feisty, you know."

"I know, Dad." I checked the time on my phone. "I've got to go catch my plane." The statement flipped over an hourglass, filling my heart slowly with sand. I didn't want to leave my family. I didn't want to go back to the struggle. But I didn't want to give up on the dream. I was in too deep either way. The only way through was forward.

I stood to walk out, and the nurse rushed to my side to offer a steady presence. "Sarah?" my dad's voice called out.

"Yeah, Dad?"

"I hope you'll go to med school to become a brain surgeon."

I grinned. He was well enough to try to plan my future. He'd be fine.

"No thanks, Dad. I don't want to be a brain surgeon. I'm going to keep working with horses. But I love you," I called over my shoulder as I walked through the door.

"Hasta Luega, Muchacha!" he yelled while the nurse closed the door behind us.

Okay, God, I prayed. *He seems fine! Please help him through the road of recovery, though. Love you.*

Chapter 31

"Where have you been?"

The trainer maintained his usual calm demeanor, but there was an undercurrent of frustration in his question. The dark bay grabbed hay from the net outside her stall, jerking it out with a fury that matched her aggression on the track. Her liquid eyes stared at us, like a girl in the high school cafeteria watching drama go down.

"I went to visit my family for Thanksgiving." My mind filled with a memory of Dad in a hospital gown, tubes everywhere, and "hasta luega, muchacha." At that last part I almost laughed, heavy and desperate, but still a laugh.

"Well, horses don't take holidays. At least not at the track," he said. "I told you I'd need to replace you if you left. I got another rider a couple days ago." There was a hardness to his voice, but the softness of regret in his eyes. A new face with a black and white pompom helmet atop it peeked from behind a wall and then disappeared. Maybe *I should have just told him about Dad,* I chastised myself.

"Yeah. You're right. Sorry about that. I guess I'll see you around." The row of stalls became cold and unwelcoming. I stared at the dirt in the shedrow, inhaling the scent of fresh hay before turning and walking away.

"Sorry, Sarah," the trainer said to my back.

"It's okay," I waved and mumbled, the reality of the next step feeling like a lead weight on my shoulders. I could leave with my tail between my legs, grab a Hardee's biscuit, and crawl back into my warm bed with Sandi, or I could drum up some mounts. I started walking to random barns, asking people if they needed help, my courage momentarily boosted by my favorite groom yelling, “One Mississippi! Two Mississippi!”

A handful of rejections later, I dragged the heels of my boots through the dirt road that led from the barns to the parking lot. As I crawled over the low bar that separated the backside from the parking lot, a car pulled up. The window of the passenger seat lowered. *This feels like the moment I get abducted if my life were a movie*, I thought, but if I stayed a few feet back I figured I had space to get away. I ducked to see into the car and lifted my hand to shield the sun from my eyes. A large man sat in the driver’s seat. *Well, I’m pretty sure I can outrun him*. “Hey there!” He interrupted my thoughts with a robust greeting.

“Hi!” I replied with icy politeness. *God, what is he doing? Should I be running?*

“I’m a jockey agent,” he said with a good-natured grin. “I’ve been seeing you around. You remind me of Julie Krone.” My forehead crinkled together as I tried to take this in. *A jockey agent says I, a girl who can barely find trainers willing to put me on horses, remind him of Julie Krone*? His arm stretched across his passenger seat, a little white rectangle between his puffy fingers. I hesitated a second before reaching through the window and grabbing it. “If you ever want to be a jockey, call me. I’d love to represent you.”

“I doubt I’ll ever be a jockey,” I confessed. It had been on my list of potential career choices when I made a career board for a sixth-grade project. My three options were model, jockey, and veterinarian. If I grew tall and thin, I could model. If I stayed short, I could ride. And if all else failed, I’d help animals. At five-four, jockey was my best choice from the first two, but it wasn’t looking good. “I’m 117 now. It’s the smallest I’ve been since eighth grade,” I told the guy. It didn’t seem like oversharing since this was the basics of his career. “I’m pretty sure I’ll never be able to make weight and also be strong enough to ride races.”

I could make weight, I thought, *but I’d be a husk of a person with no muscle. And if I got stronger, I’d be too heavy. Maybe I could force it,* a wistful part of me imagined for a moment.

“Yeah,” the agent said, “You’d probably need to be around 107 or 108 starting out.”

“I just don’t think I could hit that and still be strong,” I shrugged.

"Well, give me a call if you change your mind." There was a hopefulness in his eyes that left me perplexed. He waved and drove off. I studied the card, flipping it over in my hands as I walked to my truck. *Does he know I didn't even get a mount today?* I wondered as I drove to Hardee's. *At least somebody sees something in me*, I mused, trying to decide whether he was legit. I chose to believe someone saw talent in me.

The truth was I had come to Kentucky thinking I might decide to pursue being a jockey. If I didn't do that, maybe I could be a racehorse trainer. But I saw the early morning grind of the track, the danger of it every day, and the way living creatures counted on you in a way that made something like vacation nearly impossible. And through all that, I was starting to have doubts about becoming a vet too. That was something to worry about later, though. Right now, I would take the classes I needed to keep my options open and try my best to enjoy these two years in Kentucky.

Before my feet even touched the dirt at the farm where Gideon now lived, Sandi catapulted over me and out of the truck. She loomed over a cat who stubbornly stood her ground, hissing and swatting at my dog's nose. Sandi slapped the ground with her front paws, yelping until urgency overtook her and she bayed like a hound who had found a fox. Woowoowoo! was the only thing I could hear. It would have been cute if it weren't so loud and obnoxious and if I didn't pity that hard-as-nails cat just a little.

"Sandi!" I yelled, hiding in my truck for a moment. It was so warm inside, and the winter wind was brutal. Sandi paused, her ears lifted and head tilted at an angle. When she realized I didn't actually need her and I wasn't leaving the truck, she darted around the cat before slapping the ground and baying again.

This new barn had been another gift of Byron Crawford's article. It was a family of horse lovers who had their own place. One of their daughters, Erin, was a couple years older than me and the other, Lindsey, was a year younger. The mom had been in a horrific riding accident a few months before and nearly died. She was back on her feet and in the saddle, pretending things were normal, but the shadow of it still lingered in everyone's eyes.

They read the article and offered for Gideon to live rent-free with them while I got back on my feet. It was incredibly helpful for my college budget and sparse mounts at the track. And it became more than free board. It was a safe place with a family who cared about me and my animals, a haven of support.

Before long, I knew the stories behind all their horses and the old dog. These people loved deeply. Like many of the barns in Kentucky, theirs was originally intended for tobacco and was repurposed for horses. One side was partitioned into stalls and the other was left open for storing hay and a tractor. A large rectangle of land was churned up and fenced off to create an arena for practicing barrels and giving riding lessons.

Gid stood in front of his stall, ready to be groomed. I picked up the bag of store-brand Frosted Flakes and the loud crackling of plastic grabbed his attention. He strained against the rope holding him in place, his red ears perked forward. His head bobbed up and down, hurrying me along.

These moments were better than any spa day, expensive meal, heavy drink, or whatever else normal people did to forget their troubles. As Gideon gobbled up his favorite treat and loudly sucked his tongue, making cringeworthy mouth noises, all my troubles melted away. With Gideon, I lost track of time. An hour that crept by in class would pass before I even had him tacked up.

Sandi gave up on the cat, or maybe the cat realized Sandi had no intention of eating her and made a run for safety. My crazy dog sprinted laps around the old tobacco barn, ears flapping in the wind, releasing the energy she stored as she slept the day away in my apartment. While I curried Gid, removing the crusted dirt and dead hairs, Sandi flashed past the barn doors every few seconds. Lindsey was there grooming her tall, chestnut colored barrel mare.

Sometimes we worked in companionable silence and sometimes we talked barrel racing or swapped stories from the track. Lindsey and her sister spent some years working with and learning from the legendary racetrack trainer Nick Zito. She was more of a Thoroughbred nerd than I was. I just wanted to ride, but she could spout off bloodlines and explain how the offspring of different stallions behaved.

"Wait, his offspring are all known for flipping on the track?" I yelped as we steered our chestnuts to the top of the hill. *Who on earth would want to ride one of those? Geld that stud right now! Cut off his balls! We don't need any horses that produce purposeful flippers. The accidental ones are bad enough.*

"Yeah!" Lindsey said. "I used to ride one. We were mid-gallop one day and she just suddenly flipped backward." She said it like it wasn't that big of a deal.

"She just flipped? While you were galloping?" I marveled. I mean, Red had somersaulted when I was riding him too, and it changed the trajectory of my entire life.

"Yeah! I just kicked my feet out of the stirrups and pushed off when she was going back so she wouldn't land on me." She said it nonchalantly, but her chest puffed out in pride. She deserved it. If it were me, I'd have a T-shirt made and add it to my email signature. It would say, "I'm legit a good rider and can even handle horses that flip mid-gallop." I couldn't believe this girl. I loved her and her scrappy fighting spirit, her tomboyishness that made me look like a diva, and I slightly envied her ability to fearlessly ride on the track.

Turning in the saddle to watch Sandi sprint in a sloping circle around us, I spied the top of Gid's tail lifted an inch or so from its normal resting position. Reaching back, I ran my hand along the dorsal line from the back of the saddle to the top of his tail. Every time my hand got to just above the tail bone, he pressed his tail down like he was trying to squeeze it between his legs. When I picked my hand up, he lifted his tail back in the air. I giggled and did it again. Gid picked up a trot, lurching me in the saddle from the sudden change of speed, forcing me to face forward and leave him alone. "Okay, I'll stop," I said with a laugh, scratching his neck.

The sun attempted to warm us as it angled down from its late afternoon spot in the sky. I stuck my left hand into my jacket pocket and tried to pull my right into my sleeve, using just my fingertips to hold the reins. "It's c-c-c-cold," I chattered to Lindsey.

"This wind!" she said. "Sometimes the cold isn't that bad, but the wind is going straight through my jacket."

As I pulled Gideon's saddle off a few minutes later, my phone buzzed. "It's snowing in Lexington!" Joey's voice came through the speaker.

"What? It's freezing here, but there's definitely no snow."

"They said we might get snow later," Lindsey piped up, "But Louisville doesn't get it as often as Lexington. I think it's because of being close to the river or something."

I repeated this to Joey, who continued to go on about the white flakes falling from the sky. He talked about how big they were, how thick it was on the ground, and all the things that made me want to be in Lexington with him. And snow.

As I flipped my phone closed, I reminded myself that Louisville was much closer to Joey than Mississippi. Gideon bumped me with his forehead as if to say, "I'm here too, and I'd like some Frosted Flakes." In the morning, I'd wake up and go back to the track to chase that dream.

CHAPTER 32

I STROLLED FROM ONE barn to the next looking for rides. A blur of a human rushed by in my peripheral vision. "Come with me." The small man didn't slow as he glanced over his shoulder, "You're looking for rides, aren't you?"

"Uh," I responded, warring between the desperation of needing a yes and running the opposite direction in case he had ill intentions. *God? Should I follow him?* I lifted my eyebrows and stared at the wiry man who couldn't weigh twenty pounds more than me, who was on the verge of disappearing beyond the next barn. I had to jog to catch up. We arrived at a barn to the side of the training oval, an area I'd never ventured to before.

He was small enough I figured he'd been a jockey at some point and made the plunge into training, buying himself prematurely gray scruff and permanently slanted eyebrows. It wasn't lost on me how the stress of keeping a string of racehorses going and paying the bills was aging a lot of these trainers. He rushed around in his helmet and safety vest, commanding a groom and hot-walker. Another rider appeared next to me. *Does he actually need my help?* I wondered. A horse walked by and I pressed against the wall, leery of the playful games of a bored racehorse. It wouldn't be too difficult for him to play *tag the human* and get me with a back leg.

"Hi, I'm Keith," the trainer offered as he stuck out his hand. "And this here's Steve," he nodded toward the other rider.

"I'm Sarah," I replied, shaking both their hands. The other rider had a warmth like he already liked and accepted me. It was easier to breathe around him.

Keith looked me up and down with as much concern as Steve had acceptance. "You're trying to get rides, right?"

"Yep."

"Well, I've got one or two I can put you on." What he didn't say out loud but I imagined was rolling through his mind was, *because you're desperate and I've seen you walking from barn to barn. Because you're struggling but you're horse hungry, and I've been there.* He yelled down the aisle and left me standing next to Steve, waiting on horses to be brought around.

A dark bay filly was led up, bobbing her head and chewing the bit in anticipation. "This is WhySoShy," he said. "She goes around twice."

"Okay, got it." I gathered my reins as the groom boosted me up. A deluge of feelings hit—nerves from being on a new horse and wondering if I could hold her back, excitement at getting a ride, and the joy of her warm energy. The groom led us around inside the barn while I adjusted my stirrups and knotted my reins. He held onto us, leading the prancing filly all the way onto the track, and I smiled as I called her "tiny dancer" in my mind and gave her a calming pat. The groom unhooked the lead rope when we entered the training oval. I turned her left to start our jog.

Riding WhySoShy was like riding a kite. Any bit of wind, whether from the brisk morning breeze or other horses galloping by, had us flittering about. When we turned to gallop, she pressed down into the bit, I pressed my hands into her neck, and we flew. After her gallop, as we jigged toward the exit of the training oval, the groom grabbed us before we could flutter away.

I held my breath when she danced, swallowing down the fear that tried to steal the joy of the moment. But when the guy snapped the lead shank onto her bridle, we smiled to each other and I stroked the filly's neck. For a few minutes each day, this little dark bay and I belonged to each other.

Joey visited me at work on Sunday morning before church, and I asked Keith to take a picture. My blue hoodie puffed out from under the safety vest and Joey wore a ragged baseball cap. We clung to each other and grinned. A few minutes later I leaned over WhySoShy's withers and galloped past while Joey snapped another photo. Then we headed to the apartment so I could change clothes for church.

Joey visited me at the track.

Galloping by on WhySoShy

I stood on the balcony at Southeast Christian in a dress. The smell of ammonia and dirt still lingered in my mind. "Blessed be your name, when the world's all as it should be," I sang, feeling for a moment that things were finally good, grateful I'd learned to praise God even when the world wasn't as it should be. *Thank you, God, for Joey next to me. Thank you for my rides. Thank you for WhySoShy, Keith, and Steve and everyone else in that barn.*

I'm not sure how long it lasted. Two weeks? Or two months?

My tiny dancer was light on her toes after a good gallop on a brisk morning. It was so cold I had pulled some borrowed snow bibs over my jeans. The groom wasn't standing at the rail to grab her, probably held up finishing her stall, but her barn was close. *We can make it on our own*, I told myself. I could see our destination from the track and eyed it, knowing we only had a few more seconds to the safe zone and another successful ride.

The outriders sat on their mounts to my right, chatting with a couple trainers. A blob of horses and riders came toward us. They *must all be trying to get a ride in before the tractor break*, I thought as a mass of unpleasant butterflies took flight in my stomach. *Just act normal,* I told myself, *I'll just push my hands into her neck.*

We were a single horse and rider with a herd of horses coming at us. Traffic on the track was supposed to move similarly to traffic on the road, but they weren't on the track yet and my left turn was just a few paces away. They were spread out, pairs from different barns who just happened to arrive at the entrance together. My filly and I were dead center. It was a happenstance gang surrounding an innocent, unsuspecting victim. *Act normal, it's probably fine*, I told myself.

We were seconds from the turnoff to her barn when WhySoShy's steps faltered. She paused, and I imagined her eyes doubling in size as she took in the gaggle of horses coming at us. I squeezed with my legs, reminding her to go forward, hoping we could keep it together long enough to make it to the turn. The riders coming toward us laughed and chatted, but I watched the smiles melt off a few faces as they registered the problem.

I expected her to dance sideways, throw a buck, or maybe spin and take off in the other direction. I could already see us careening down the track in a panicked run, me pulling with all my strength to get her back to me. Instead, my tiny dancer stood straight up on her back legs. I would have been proud of her for choosing fight over flight, if I didn't slide straight off her back like a kid on a greased water slide.

I landed in a confused heap just behind her back hooves. *What in the world? I've never fallen from a rearing horse.* From my place on the ground, I could see the outriders' contorted faces, eyes bulging like they were witnessing a horrifying accident. *Why are they freaking out? It's just another mishap that I'm in the middle of.* I seethed over the idiocy of falling off a rearing horse. *What in the world?* I wanted to scream.

It was the horse version of being slammed with an unexpected wave in the ocean. For a moment nothing made sense. The sky was blocked by dark brown legs, course tail hairs, and a rump. Scrambling, dirt flying, men yelling, all while I waited for the filly to move forward so I could stand up and grab her before she ran off. As things began to clear, I heard, "Call the ambulance fast!"

In the midst of it all, any fear attempting to rear its head was quickly pushed out by bubbling anger. *It's always me,* I thought as the filly got back on her feet and away from me. Her groom rushed out to grab her. "You okay?" he asked.

"Yeah." I was still in a crumpled heap on the ground. "I'm fine. Go ahead and get her back to the barn." He nodded and took the filly home.

Stunned riders and their mounts parted like the Red Sea to get around me, needing to keep their horses moving before a chain reaction started. Men surrounded me, panicked and concerned. "Is the ambulance coming?" a large man yelled.

"Should she stay down until the ambulance gets here?"

"Maybe we shouldn't move her."

"I'm fine," I spat, trying to figure out why it mattered so much. Riders fell every day. They shared a look. It appeared like some sort of unspoken agreement was made.

"Honey," one of the men spoke slowly, "We saw that horse fall on you. You have to see an EMT." They left no room for argument.

Voices piped up all around me, and I would have been touched by their concern if it wasn't *me*. Again. The center of another incident.

My jaw clenched as I stood, glaring at the men and daring them to challenge me. I would *not* lay in the center of the only entrance and exit to the track and become even more of a problem. Horses needed to get in and out. I was fine. I'd wait for the ambulance, but I wouldn't be going anywhere in it. An ambulance ride was $500. I knew because every month I received a bill, and every month I called to tell them to send it to the insurance company. This ride wasn't necessary and I wouldn't be taking it.

The medic shined a light in my eyes, bent my arms, and tapped my knees. He asked questions. I repeated, "I'm fine, nothing hurts," while the men hovered, taking turns telling the medic they saw the horse fall on me.

Rage boiled in my chest and brain, one clear thought continually breaking the fog, *I'm fine. They saw the horse fall on me? God, is this you again? How did they see a horse fall on me if I felt nothing?*

The medic released me. The innocent victims of my scathing looks and curt words scattered. I checked in with Keith, then stomped to my truck. *Why is it always me, God?* I demanded. *Why can't things just go right?* Then, *they saw the horse fall on me, yet I'm fine. God, is this you again?*

I pressed the accelerator with excessive force and again had the sense that a battle was waging around me. It was as if there was another realm I couldn't see, but if I could step through a doorway into it, I'd be on a battlefield. Instead of soldiers in uniforms, it was otherworldly creatures—Heavenly beings battling demons. Somehow, for some reason, I was in the middle of it. And I was over it.

As I scanned my debit card at the gas pump, an image of an angel diving between me and WhySoShy's body took shape in my mind. The angel used its own body to shield and save me. I unscrewed the gas cap and jammed the pump handle into the fuel pipe.

God, I'm grateful for the rescue, I whispered, *but I'm tired of needing it, of drawing the attention of the outriders and other trainers.* "I can't believe I even slid off her," I mumbled, shaking my head at the idiocy of it. The pump clicked to a stop, and I shuffled back over to grab the handle. The swishing of the snow bibs triggered a realization. *These dang snow bibs are why I fell off*! I rolled my eyes at how ridiculous it was. A sharp twinge of pain shot up my arm when I squeezed the pump handle. Maybe I was a little hurt. "I'm never riding in snow bibs again."

The fear that gnawed at my insides every time I rode seemed to only go away when I was in real danger. How did that even make sense? And how had they seen a horse fall on me when I hadn't felt a thing?

Face hot with anger, I drove to my new apartment. When someone broke into my truck by the downtown place, my parents demanded I move out of the city and into the suburbs. Luckily Haley, the girl I met at polo, had become a friend. When I told her my predicament, she invited me to move into her dining room since she only had a one bedroom.

Two wriggling dogs greeted me when I walked through the door. It was hard not to smile at the sight of Siler and Sandi together. They made as good of roommates as Haley and I did. "Such goobs!" I laughed as I bent over to give both dogs head scratches, then twisted to avoid Sandi's tail whip.

"Oh, hey!" Haley said from the kitchen. "When I came home from work, there was another empty bread bag on the ground." Warring emotions rolled through me. I focused on the bread bag.

"Again?"

"Yeah! And it was brand new! I'd only eaten one slice and had pushed it all the way to the back of the counter." She held the empty bread bag up as evidence.

"Sandi and Siler!" I scolded. Both dogs tucked their tails. Sandi hopped onto the couch, ears laid back and head dipped in submission. Siler ran around the corner. It was impossible not to laugh.

"Did you have a fall today?" Haley asked as she caught a glance at my dirt-covered clothes.

"Yeah. We were leaving the track and all these horses were coming toward us. The filly panicked and reared, and thanks to these snow bibs I slid straight off." I tried to chuckle, but pain shot up my arm and my cheeks heated in embarrassment.

"That's why my boss doesn't let me ride in snow bibs or anything bulky," she said. "Even when it's freezing, I can only wear riding pants or jeans." Glancing down at her work clothes, she said, "Obviously I choose jeans."

My jaw clenched and my chest turned into hot knots at the mere mention of her job. "Apparently he's right. I'm never putting these snow bibs on again. I'm going to change." I rushed down the hall to the bedroom.

"Okay, I'm heading out to the polo barn to get some practice in. You should join us!"

"I've got class. Thanks though. Have fun." I swallowed back tears and closed the door after Sandi slipped through. Gulping for air, I dove onto the bed, clinging to Sandi.

Oh, God. Ever since Haley had gotten the racehorse gig, a festering lump had taken root in my chest. *I couldn't have even taken the job,* I reminded myself. *She works until two and I have class. Plus, I wouldn't last three days with her boss' junior-high-style relentless teasing. The guy has no filter.* But it felt like another layer of failure.

God, why is it so easy for her? I cried, seeing my own ridiculousness, which only made me feel worse. *God, this is my dream. This isn't her dream. Why does it all come together for her and it's all so hard for me?*

I cried over the unfairness of it. I cried because Haley was my best friend here and I hated having these hideous feelings every time I was around her. I cried because I wanted things to work, to be easy for once.

God help me through this, I prayed. Immediately, a thought popped into my mind. *This is envy.*

I bit the inside of my lip as it began to sink in. *This is envy.* It was one of those basics I learned in Sunday School before I could read—one of the Ten Commandments—"Thou shalt not covet." Even through the tears, I inwardly eye-rolled at the old-timey language used when reciting the Ten Commandments.

I'd always heard that one and thought, *what's the big deal? Envy, or coveting, or jealousy doesn't hurt anyone. I mean, "Thou shalt not murder" makes sense, but what's the big deal with envy?*

The problem with it was becoming real. I couldn't genuinely smile at my favorite person in Louisville because every time I saw her, I saw what she had and what I didn't.

Glancing at the clock, I knew I needed to wash the dirt out of my hair, pull myself together, and get to class. First, though, I pulled out my Bible, read a little bit, and spent some time with my Creator. It was a prayer of gratitude for protection, a prayer of repentance for the problem eating away my insides, and a plea for help.

I want to be happy with what you've given me, and grateful for my journey. I want to be happy for Haley and for all the good things that happen for her. A hiccup made me pause and I grabbed a tissue. *God, just please help me,* I begged as I got out of bed to take Sandi out for a quick potty break.

Chapter 33

I SURVIVED A FEW more weeks at Trackside and made my way back to Churchill Downs as spring approached and trainers returned. For a couple weeks I rode for Ron again. His assistant trainer and I struck out from the barn together on fillies—a dark bay and a chestnut. Our conversation was stilted, neither of us sure what to say. A piece of straw blew across our path and in a single swift movement, my filly dropped her shoulder and spun. I rode it out, then steered her back to the path.

The assistant gaped at me and I looked back, quirking an eyebrow. Her expression morphed into something I never expected to see from her—respect. I took it in stride, another tiny step toward making a place for myself here.

"One of these fillies flipped with me last week," she said as if we talked all the time.

"Are you serious?" My eyes about popped from their sockets. I tried to grapple with this information and couldn't. "What did you do? How are you not hurt?"

"These fillies from Canada are flippers. I don't know what their deal is." She rolled her eyes in a funny combination of deadpan and dramatic. "She went backward and I just stepped off."

"You *stepped* off?" I repeated, shocked at how simple it was for her. I could sit a spin, but these things happened so fast. How did people have the mental capacity to step off? As we made our way onto the track, the insecurity I always felt around this woman began to dissipate. A new feeling was taking over. I didn't want to hide from this lady anymore. I wanted to learn.

I showed up to Ron's a couple mornings later, but he didn't have any horses for me. With a shrug and a "see ya later," I turned on my heel. *I'm here, I may as well see if I can find some rides. God, please help me find some rides,* I prayed.

A handful of noes later, I eyed a big, green "ML" sign hanging on the side of barn thirty-four. "Mike Lauer," I whispered into the crisp air, recalling someone in class talking about how mean he was. I walked the length of the barn deciding whether I should listen to the warnings or ask this Mike Lauer guy if he needed a rider.

A car pulled slowly toward me, stopping when the front bumper was level with my knees. The man inside leaned into the passenger seat and gathered up his newspaper. The door opened and the man unfolded himself, tall and foreboding. A deep-set permafrown marked his face, reminiscent of an intimidating coach who only communicated in barks.

I replayed my friends' complaints about what a tyrant this Lauer guy was, but when I glanced into the barn the horses looked as happy, if not happier, than at any other barn on the backside. I put my shoulders back, grinned, and stuck out my hand. "Hi, I'm Sarah. Do you need a rider?"

"Hi there, Sarah," he said as he looked from my lace-up boots to the pompom on my green and yellow helmet. For once it wasn't a look that made me want to hide. He shook my hand, firm but not crushing, and I figured if he could size me up I could do the same. This intimidatingly tall man wore khakis, a barn jacket, and tennis shoes. I imagined his wife picking them out from Belk. "Hang around," he said. "Let me see what I've got up for today, and I'll let you know if I need you."

"Okay!" I replied. I watched him disappear into his office, heard him bark at his employees, and observed his horses hanging their heads out of stalls, eager for a peppermint and their turn on the track. His employees eyed me warily as they went about their work.

"You said your name is Sarah?" he called from inside the office. I peeked around the corner to see him sitting behind a desk.

"Yes, sir." Silence followed as he shuffled papers around and paused to scan some of them.

"I've got one you can ride today," he said, before yelling down the shedrow, "Get that horse in nineteen ready to go before break!"

I rode to the track with the barn's main rider on one side and Mike on the other, giving instructions. At the entrance, he turned to the trainers' observation deck and I steered the horse onto the rail. The familiar nerves kicked in as horses swerved around us and the pounding of galloping hooves echoed. But it was a good ride. We galloped one and a half around and jigged off the track. Mike appeared next to us for the walk back to the barn, asking me how the horse felt and how his breathing sounded.

"See ya tomorrow?" he asked as I turned to leave.

"Yep! See you then!" I smiled.

Mike never said, "Be careful out there." He never questioned my abilities or whether I'd get his horse back home in one piece.

A couple weeks into riding for him, I stood in the shedrow waiting for my second ride of the day. "You're going to breeze this one."

Energy jolted to my fingertips and down my legs. My heart picked up at the mere idea of dropping a horse onto the rail and letting him fly. "Okay!" My smile was shaky, and when the groom threw me onto the horse, I pulled my stirrups up shorter than usual so I could get a good crouch over his withers. We made our way to the track, did our warm-up jog, and then turned to gallop. At the pole where Mike told us to start the breeze, I steered the horse to the rail, bent my knees into a low crouch, and blew him a kiss.

The horse's center of gravity dropped low, and he exploded forward. His legs folded underneath him, grabbing the ground just enough to launch into another huge, leaping stride. Other horses on the track were blurs as I focused on this little horse's bobbing ears and the dirt in front of us. My hands moved back and forth, following the movement of his head, and we flew. In just a few seconds we passed the square pole that marked the finish line, and I stood tall in my stirrups to tell the horse we were done. He continued a brisk gallop around the turn, still rolling along, and I imagined him folding in his wings.

"How'd he feel?" Mike asked as he walked along next to us. I attempted to act normal, swallowing down the exhilarated grin that threatened to consume my face.

"He felt great! His breathing sounded normal, and he didn't need any encouragement."

"This horse holds a speed record in Indiana," Mike said with a sparkle in his eye. I couldn't tell if his expression was pride in his horse or joy at giving a girl who obviously loved fast horses the chance to fly. It made me think of Gideon. This horse was fast, but I was pretty sure Gideon was faster. As I waved to everyone at the barn and traipsed toward the truck a bit later, I wondered, *was that horse faster than Gid?*

"I think I'm going to breeze Gideon today," I told Joey, who was in town for the weekend and had accompanied Sandi and me on our barn trip. "I just really want to know who's faster."

"Okay, sounds good! Just tell me what you want me to do," my ever-supportive boyfriend responded. But Joey's body became slightly stiffer, his movements mechanical. I could tell this idea was pushing his comfort zone, but I could also see the gleam of excitement. He wanted to see Gideon run as much as he didn't want to see me get hurt.

I greeted my handsome boy in his stall, blowing gently into his muzzle. His nostrils widened as he sucked in my scent and puffed a sweet-smelling breeze of his own. I slipped him a peppermint I had grabbed from the stash in Mike's office. Gid crunched the candy and blew in my face again, a combination of grass, horse, and mint overwhelming my senses. "Someone should make a candle like this." I closed my eyes and inhaled.

While I groomed and tacked up, I explained to Joey what would happen. This was no wild run through the woods. Gideon was too fast, too nervous, to take a breeze lightly. This would be regimented and purposeful. Otherwise, every time I rode Gideon for the next six months, he'd be crow-hopping, expecting to breeze again. I strapped his barrel-racing saddle onto his back and buckled all the pieces with such familiarity I could have done it blindfolded. Gid stood patiently, occasionally bopping me with his nose or blowing peppermint breath into my face. Then I swung onto his back.

We trotted and cantered a few circles to warm up. When he felt ready, I took him to the end of the longest, straightest spot I could find that hopefully had no hoof-eating holes in the ground. I'd been on a somersaulting horse one too many times to ignore proper footing. Gideon knew my intentions as we neared our take-off spot. His neck arched and his front feet lunged into the air, running nearly in place. He wanted it. He was ready.

I stuck my hands forward, leaning over the saddle horn, and Gid launched. His back legs were his engine, propelling his front end into the air and onward. I pressed my weight into my heels for better balance, stood in my stirrups, and clucked my tongue against my teeth to say, "Faster! Faster!" The wind whipped across my face and stole my breath. The only encouragement he had needed was a single thought, "run."

Mere seconds passed and we were almost to the fence. "Whoa," I leaned back and gently pulled on the reins. Gid slowed and I turned him in a sloping circle to the right as we both attempted to come down from our runner's high. Tears streamed from my eyes to my hairline, a gift from the wind. Joey stood by the fence, Sandi next to him, her whole body wriggling from side to side. Joey's expression nearly made me laugh. "That was fast!" he said with rounded eyes.

"Yeah!" I tried to contain my smile, reaching down and scratching Gid just in front of the saddle. "He was faster than that racehorse!"

Gid was faster than the fastest racehorse I've ever ridden, I repeated to myself. I couldn't stop the mental image of us at the National Finals Rodeo, competing with the best barrel racers in the world.

"I've got two going to the gates today," Mike said. "Y'all are going out together so you can work the horses next to each other."

"Okay," I grinned, my eyebrows raised in nervous excitement. I'd never ridden a racehorse out of the gates before. Craig had said he would teach me, but we never made it that far. In the past, other trainers I rode for would have my name on the board. Then they'd ask if I knew how to break a horse from the gates, and when I shook my head regretfully, they'd wipe away my name and write another one. Mike didn't ask, though. *He must know*, I told myself, deciding to keep my mouth shut. Maybe he figured I was a good enough rider, and how do you learn if not by doing?

Mike peeled off to tell the timer guy to clock our rides, and as soon as he was out of hearing range, I admitted to the other rider I'd never broken from the gates before. "It's easy," he said.

"Okay, so what do I do?" I needed to know this. I needed to not screw this up.

"Just do what I do. Follow my lead. Tell them we're going together. They'll shut the gates. When they open we'll drop onto the rail and breeze them out."

"Okay." It sounded simple enough. I'd just do what he did. We jogged our horses to warm up. The trembling in my knees was unavoidable but I begged for the horse to not notice, or at least not hold it against me.

God, please protect us, I prayed. *Please keep us safe and help me to not screw this up*. My heart pounded so hard I thought surely it could be seen pulsing through the safety vest. A flash of heat reddened my face as something like deja vu hit. A year before, I had prayed for safety only to somersault down the track with Red. I had grappled with that so much and pelted God with questions. *He did protect me*, I reminded myself, *but he still let the horse fall.* My stomach soured at the thought.

The pair of riders in front of us exploded out of the gate. We were the next to go, and my stomach did flips as I grappled over this prayer. *He won't always keep me safe how I want,* I decided, *but I'm going to trust Him anyway. Besides, I certainly can't keep myself safe.* The instances where it was quite clear God, an angel, or something protected me flashed through my mind. *I couldn't have protected myself when the horse fell on me. I'm trusting you, God* was my final thought as the gate crew grabbed my horse's bridle.

Two men ushered us into the gate so quickly that neither the horse nor I had a moment to process or hesitate. As the metal door clanged shut behind us, I remembered seeing these guys work the gates for the Derby on TV. *These guys are good*!

The other rider sat, so I followed his lead, sitting calmly, or at least it looked that way on the outside. I held onto my reins and wrapped my ring finger and pinkie around the martingale strap for extra support. Suddenly, a loud bell was ringing in my ear. I had heard this bell every morning from far away. Walking around the track, waiting at barns, on the backs of horses I was galloping. But it had been background noise I never considered. Now it was in my ear as the angled, padded metal doors in front of my horse flung open.

The horse dropped inches underneath me. My mind took off on its own trail. *We saw a video about this in class. The horse drops up to four inches before launching out of the gate. They weren't wrong.* I marveled at all the thoughts that could pass through my mind in a fraction of a second.

I grasped for a chunk of mane, but only got hold of some sparse strands. The other horse shot in front of us as mine stuttered, confused that his rider was sitting on his back instead of hovering over it. Once he saw the other horse go, mine launched out of the gate to catch up. I was a flailing mess, more of a potato sack than a rider, with my weight on his back and my hands in the air. Within four strides I collected myself, crouched over his withers, and kneaded my hands along his neck. We were one horse-width off the rail, and even with the slow start, we edged up next to his stablemate's hind end.

The other rider turned his head to get a glimpse of me. We ran down the stretch, my horse's nose even with his mount's flank. I urged my horse to catch up, clucking him along, pouring belief into him to make up for the lost moment coming out of the gate. Just as my guy's nose reached the other's shoulder and I thought, *we're going to do it!* we passed the finish pole. Both of us stood in our stirrups and let the horses gallop out for a quarter mile before gently tugging the reins and pulling them down to a slow jog, all of us gasping for breath. "You got left behind!" the other rider immediately started in. "Did you not see the light?"

"Light? You never told me about a light!" I barked back. *No freaking wonder I wasn't ready.* I wanted to be mad, but after that experience it was impossible.

"Yeah. The light turns green and then they open the gates. That's how you know to get in position."

"You never told me," I defended myself.

"Well, I thought you knew."

"How was I supposed to know? It was my first time!"

A gruff voice piped in as the horse's hooves clip-clopped on the road back to the barn. "Sarah, you got left behind! What happened there? Was that your first time breaking from the gates?" Mike must have power-walked from the trainer's stand to catch us.

"Well, yeah." My cheeks flushed and I didn't feel so clever. I must have misread him before.

"Why didn't you tell me you had never worked the gates before?" He huffed, but it felt like he could never be truly angry with me, just extremely irritated.

"I thought you knew," I claimed in an innocent voice, "And whether you knew or not, I had to learn somehow. No one ever lets me work from the gates because I've never done it before."

"Well, you got left behind. It messed up his time." He cocked his eyebrow.

"Sorry," I said, resigning myself to giving no more excuses.

I was regretful about being left behind and messing up the horse's time. I had no idea what trickle-down effect that would have. Would it keep him from qualifying for a race? Or would it just show up in the race program and confuse bettors?

But I didn't regret doing it. *That was freaking epic! God, thanks for keeping me safe*, I prayed as we got to the barn. I hopped off and gave the horse a grateful pat, handing him off to the groom, who snuck him a peppermint. I couldn't wipe the smile from my face for the rest of the day.

Chapter 34

"Hey, I was thinking," Joey said as we rode in the car together, fingers intertwined.

"Yeah?" I laughed. "That's good!"

Joey plowed forward, ignoring my gibe. "What if we go look at rings?" My face flushed. "I mean, it's a big deal, and I don't want to surprise you with something you don't like. Let's just go look around so you can show me things you like. Give me an idea."

I wanted to crawl across the center console right into that boy's lap. I wanted to grab his face, run my fingers through the wild curls he'd grown since we left Mississippi, and mold my lips to his. I wanted to feel his arms wrap around me and hold me close. But we were driving, so instead I reached over with the hand that wasn't already holding his and grazed my fingers along his knuckles. "I'd like that." My face stretched into a crooked smile.

In all my life, I never imagined getting married right out of college. I thought I'd be the girl who lived on her own for a while, built a career, and did her own thing before deciding to get married. But then I sat across from Joey Hickner in the library at Mississippi College and had a niggling feeling that God's plan was different.

"Where should we go?" I asked, realizing neither of us was the sort who frequented jewelry stores.

"I guess Shane & Co," Joey said with a shrug. We both laughed over the number of times we had complained about the plethora of Shane & Co ads on the radio.

"It seems like their advertising works," I said with an eye roll before pulling out my phone and shooting Haley a text. "We're looking at rings!"

The display case was endless, and right away I could see most of the rings were too delicate for my horse-girl lifestyle. "I need something durable," I told the sales guy, so he pulled out a handful of rings and set them in front of us. I tried to imagine sliding my riding glove over them, the fabric catching on the diamond. I envisioned pressing my fists into a horse's neck with a ring underneath my glove. The prominent setting would feel like a lump. "Really, most of these are too high. Can we get something that doesn't stick out so much?" I didn't know the lingo, but I knew my life.

"She rides racehorses," Joey's chest seemed to grow as he said it, and my own warmed even as my thoughts went in another direction.

Well, I try, I wanted to say, but instead I explained the mechanics of tight riding gloves and about the time I helped a friend sift through shavings for hours in search of a diamond that fell out during barn work.

I showed Joey my favorites, and then we dined at McAlister's like everything was normal, dipping chips into chicken tortilla soup and drinking a sweet tea bigger than my head. In a way, things were normal. Picking out rings was new, but looking forward to a future with Joey, *'til death do us part*, was the only future I had wanted or expected for a while now.

Later that week, we chatted on the phone like we did nearly every night before bed.

"How was your day?" Joey asked.

"Fine. I got on two horses and didn't die. Then I had class, went to see Gid, and rushed home in time for Haley and me to race to polo. Now I'm trying to get to bed because I need to be at the track early."

Joey nervously started in. "Are you? Do you? I mean, how are your classes? Do you, maybe, need to study?"

"Classes are fine! Doing good. Everyone's struggling with this Econ class, but the teacher literally uses the exact practice test in the back of the book. Like, do the other students not open their textbooks?"

"I don't know," Joey said, but I could tell he didn't believe me. I had spent hours a day studying when I was a biology major. Now I barely had time to crack a book, but thankfully the business classes weren't so demanding.

"Hey, in a couple of weeks it's our twenty-one-month anniversary, and I want to take you out. Don't schedule anything for that Friday night, okay?"

"Okay," I responded slowly, thinking how silly it was. We hadn't celebrated a month anniversary since probably number three or four. I wasn't even sure I remembered the date anymore. *But we did go ring shopping*, I reminded myself, *so I won't question him*. "It'll be fun to go on a fancy date! Maybe I'll get my hair done!"

"Yeah!" I could hear the shaky smile in his voice. "Get your hair done, maybe get a new dress. It's going to be really special! Just don't schedule anything that night, okay?"

I booked a hair appointment with Haley's guy and was left with $70 in my account, but man did my hair look good! I found a teal halter dress with a gauzy fabric on the clearance rack, and was down to $35. *Good thing I've got parental support money coming in a couple days*, I told myself. But instead of the draining zap of stress, birds took flight in my stomach. I called Joey as I left the department store.

"So, what are we doing on our special date?" I teased, knowing he was determined to keep it a surprise.

"You'll find out soon!" He sounded excited and a bit nervous, and I wondered if he knew how clear it was over the phone. "Did you get your hair done?"

"Yep! And I got a new dress too! Down to about $35 in my account, but Mom will send money in a couple of days and Mike should pay me soon. I'll just eat rice 'til then," I joked, calculating how many $4.75 sushi rolls and $5.25 McAlister's kid's meals I could eat without hitting zero.

"It's worth it," my normally reserved boyfriend said, and I knew beyond a shadow of a doubt that this date was more than a celebration of however many months we'd been together.

Haley hung around the apartment until Joey picked me up, and when he arrived, her presence was like a mom on prom night. "Y'all be safe now! And don't go doing anything I wouldn't do!" We all laughed because I was by far the biggest prude of all our friends, her included.

We backed out of the parking lot, and I waved to Haley, birds going crazy in my chest now. I held Joey's hand, and it was warm and comforting. Home. "Did you see that Pat Day's retirement ceremony is tonight?" I asked. It was all over the local news while I got ready.

"Yeah! Do you know where it's at?"

"No, but I figured it's downtown somewhere. Maybe at Churchill Downs? It's amazing how much this city loves a jockey. He's like a celebrity here!"

"Isn't he a Christian too?" Joey asked.

"Yeah, he's always doing things to support wounded jockeys and working on education programs for the backside workers and stuff. He seems like a really good guy. I kind of wish we were going to the ceremony," I mused.

"That would be great, wouldn't it?" Joey grinned in a way that made me think, *wait... are we going? I mean, I'm pretty sure he's popping the question tonight, but maybe we're going to the retirement ceremony first?*

"Are we going?" I blurted with excitement.

"You'll just have to see!" he teased.

I stared out the window at Louisville, mesmerized by this life and this town I was getting to be part of. *Thank you, God.*

The car was taking a very familiar route, and with each turn, my mind raced through possibilities of where we could be going. As we turned onto the road Churchill Downs was on, my heart rate doubled. "We're going to the track! Are we really going to his retirement ceremony?" I nearly squealed, and Joey's entire face stretched into a gigantic, somewhat shaky smile. *I cannot believe we're going to Pat Day's retirement ceremony!*

The frontside of the track was huge, and on my tour after the news article, they had shown me extravagant banquet rooms. It would be the perfect location for a jockey's retirement ceremony.

Joey flipped on the blinker while we were still driving alongside the barns on the backside, then pulled up to the same security gate I walked through every morning. Things stopped making sense, like I was using pieces to the wrong puzzle. We wouldn't get to a banquet room through this gate.

Joey kept talking about the retirement ceremony like it would be on the backside with the horses. He was running with it and I was letting him. I smiled a weak, confused smile, not buying the lie but curious and nervous to see what was actually happening. Joey got out of the car and spoke to the security guards. I stared, feeling awkward at such a familiar place with none of the familiar early morning people. Joey pulled his car through the gate and hooked a right, parking against the fence.

God, what is going on? I mumbled, hating this unknown but also thrilled by it. It was like I could see the end of the book, where I was pretty darn sure I'd have a ring on my left hand, but couldn't figure out the plot that would get us there. We had taken a literal, unexpected left turn.

Our fingers stayed interlocked as one of the security guards pulled up behind the car in a red van and told us to hop in. He didn't smile, and I would have thought we were being abducted if Joey wasn't so at ease. He turned and looked at me, his brown curls looping around his head and blue eyes sparkling in the setting sun. The smell of horse pee and dirt was an odd juxtaposition to our fancy clothes.

The fragrance of the track made me long for it, my emotions confusing me. It didn't make sense to long for something I had. Maybe it was because reality hadn't yet matched the dream. Or maybe my heart already knew that soon enough I'd finish college and walk away from this place to start the next phase of life. Summer had officially given way to fall, and fall marked the beginning of my last year in Kentucky. Maybe I already missed it.

"Come on," Joey said, tugging me into the van. Those dang birds started flapping in my chest again, and I would have jumped into the vehicle if I didn't walk like a newborn foal in my high-heeled shoes.

The guard slid the door closed and climbed into the driver's side, awkward and quiet. We drove through the tunnel that burrowed underneath the track, a place I'd never felt allowed to or even considered exploring. At that moment, I regretted not getting to know every nook and cranny of this place. I gaped at the concrete walls of the tunnel, realizing I rode horses over it every day. The van climbed the ramp and I held my breath as we emerged onto the track.

In all the ways I'd visited Churchill Downs—on a private tour after Byron Crawford's article, as a racing fan, now as a horseman—none of them had been like this. The van bumped along and Joey made another retirement ceremony comment. I just nodded, gaping at the grandstand to my right and the infield with the Kentucky Derby winners' circle, odds board, and video screen on the left.

When we were almost to the spot where I stopped the horses every morning to wait before we galloped, the vehicle was put in park and the security guard opened the door. The guy nodded toward something, his stern face bulging over his too-tight collar. I climbed out, stepping down onto the surface I had only ever ridden a horse over and my heels sank into the rich dirt. Joey wiped his hands on his pants, and when he grabbed mine again, they were clammy. His carefree smile shook, and I distantly wondered if the retirement ceremony was happening somewhere in that massive building as I tried to figure out what was going on.

The wind blew my hair across my face, chilling my bare shoulders. Revelers at some corporate party bled out onto a balcony, and I could tell we'd grabbed their attention. I followed Joey, who pulled me to the infield side of the track, past a flowery horseshoe shape in the manicured grass, and up to a small podium overlooking the horseshoe. "Do you know where we are?" His voice was reverent as he asked.

Looking around, it clicked. "The winner's circle?"

"Yeah." The corner of his lips tilted into a lopsided smile that set the birds in a flurry again. "The winner's circle for the Kentucky Derby. It just felt really appropriate because this is why you came, and it's been such a big part of our story."

Joey went down on one knee. He held my hand, looking up into my eyes as I tried my hardest to focus on him, to hang on every word. But it felt like that moment in the movies when the camera pans skyward. My awareness lifted, and I could see the entire scene from above.

The rowdy partygoers on the other side of the track leaned over the balcony rail and whooped and hollered. There were the Twin Spires of Churchill Downs and empty grandstands. The dirt on the one-mile oval felt almost sacred. It reminded me of how big and good God is.

I saw the Kentucky Derby winner's circle, a place people worked their whole lives to get to for just a moment. The cheers from the spirits of those who went before us, the ones who ran the race and held the trophy, were at once silent and deafening. I saw Joey down on a knee and me, standing there with dress and hair billowing in the wind, a strand of hair stuck to my lip gloss, staring into his eyes.

I recalled that day that felt like a lifetime ago, sitting across from him in the library, when I had to step outside and yell at God because he was letting me fall for someone when I was leaving. For a second I was sitting at a table in a sparkling blue dress, surrounded by friends but only seeing Joey. I saw the mundane things I knew would forever be us—him complaining about my messiness, us loving Sandi, him being overly worried, me not worrying enough, our hands hooked together, the way it felt to rest my head on his shoulder or wrap my hands around his waist and feel his arms envelop me. And I saw that all along, without any doubt, God had his hand on us.

One day in Mississippi, I had taken him riding with me. Our relationship was fresh, not even really official yet, and we started talking about what we wanted in the person we would marry.

With an ease that came from being on Gideon, my happiest place, I said, "Yeah. I have a list of guys who meet the requirements."

We turned a corner, leaving the woods and walking out onto the carriage road, and I twisted in the saddle to see his face. The corner of his mouth had pulled up into a smirk. "So who's made the list?"

I turned back around to watch where we were going. The carriage road stretched out in front of us, covered in thick grass up to Gid's knees. I paused and then laughed awkwardly, "Well, currently it's just you." My heart rate kicked up a notch at the uncharacteristically bold proclamation that was as much a shock to me as it probably was to him.

He was it for me, and I was it for him.

And in the way it would probably be for the rest of our lives, I missed most of what he said. It was probably something about undying love. There was a tiny twinge of guilt knowing he had worked hard on the speech and meant every word for me. But I meant it too when I said, "Yes! Of course!"

He lingered on his knee for a second, like he didn't expect that answer and wasn't sure what to do next. Maybe he hadn't planned the next part, or maybe I did something out of order since my mind was in the clouds, but I grabbed his hands and pulled him up, demanding his arms around me, the arms I would rest in until death do us part. And then he lowered his mouth to mine.

"Thank you, God," I whispered as the drunk guys cheered and Joey yelled back. We floated back to the red security van, awkwardly smiling and clinging to each other as the security guard said, "Well, did you do it?"

"Yep! And she said yes!" Joey replied, shoulders sagged with relief, face lit with a smile bright enough to light up my insides.

Then we headed to dinner at a restaurant with black and white horse-racing pictures all over the walls. We watched the recap of Pat Day's retirement ceremony on the news that evening.

Chapter 35

Burrowing cold hands into the front pocket of my hoodie, I traversed from the parking lot to Mike's barn. Across the backside were stacks of buckets, tack trunks, and bags full of horse blankets and leg wraps. "Make sure you get all the eye hooks!" someone yelled from inside the barn.

The magic of fall was ending, winter was blowing in, and the trainers were packing up to leave. My insides twisted over this. Every day, a bit of the tension and fear had chipped away. If things could stay like they were, maybe soon I would feel good, even great, on a racehorse. If we could keep going all the anxiety would fall away, and I could truly enjoy galloping.

"Sarah, come in here," Mike called from his office as I walked into the shedrow.

"Hi!" I sighed, enjoying the warmth from the heater.

"We're packing up this afternoon." There was a hint of regret in his eyes. "We're heading to Turfway."

"Okay!" I'd never been to Turfway Park, but I knew it was far enough away that I couldn't make it work. The twist in my gut tightened but I tried to cover it up, acting like this is just what happens. Because it was. Everyone went somewhere in the winter. A lot of riders followed their trainers to Arkansas or even Florida, but I wasn't a career rider.

"You're welcome to come with us." He looked up, clearly expecting my rejection.

"Nah. I've got school." I glanced down at the diamond sparkling on my finger. "And I don't want to be even farther from Joey. Thanks though!" I wanted to tell him thank you for treating me like a real exercise rider. For saying, "I think we can put you on something," and then continuing to do so every day since. But my tongue felt thick and couldn't form the words, so I smiled and swallowed back regret.

We galloped like usual that morning, but between sets, grooms hustled to pack.

"Come back tomorrow in case we have something for you," Mike told me. "But after that, we'll be at Turfway."

I shuffled to my truck, imagining another winter at Trackside. I remembered the days when the track froze and we had to ride the cooped-up, high-energy Thoroughbreds around and around inside the barn. Most rides were more like stunt shows than pleasant walks. I ducked from the ceiling beams and tucked my knees in when a rambunctious filly launched us too close to the wall.

On the first track outing after the ground thawed, I prayed every stride that I could hold the dragon back. Days trapped in a barn made them lighter on their feet and heavier in the bridle. *But before I can even have the pleasure of such an exhilarating experience*, I reminded myself, *I'd have to walk from barn to barn asking trainers if they need help, getting ten noes for one yes.*

Two red lights before the turn to my and Haley's apartment, I hooked a right into the Ruby Tuesday parking lot. I walked in and submitted an application to be a server.

Back in my truck, I closed my eyes, tears clinging to my eyelashes.

Hey God, I started my prayer, then laughed at myself over the casualness of it, like I was talking to a friend. A hiccup escaped as I cried harder, the realization hitting me. The Creator of the universe was my friend. I was suddenly aware of the air filling my lungs and how every single simple breath was a gift from God. *My friend*. I kept going with my prayer.

This dream was yours to begin with, God. You planted it in my heart, and you helped me get here. I've tried and failed and tried again, and I'm tired. I'd really like to gallop racehorses like that vision I have in my head. Like it was for those few days before the accident. But it's in your hands. I'm stepping back. In my mind, I held my dream on a tray that I lifted up to God. *It's yours.*

I went to the backside one last time and jogged a horse around twice before the groom took her to prepare for the move. It was done. The other horses had already left or waited for their journey with shipping wraps padding their legs. I waved to Mike, filling my "thank you," with as much sincerity as possible, and nodded to the grooms. Walking past the security gate with a last farewell, my chest, legs, arms, everything was heavy.

The next morning I snuggled Sandi, her body and steady breaths warming me until the sun streamed in my windows. I thought about the few horses at Churchill out for their morning gallops. It was late enough that there wouldn't be many horses left to go. Sandi and I went for a quick walk before I grabbed a glass of milk and drove to U of L. Between classes I escaped to the equine department's student computer lab and sat quietly, trying to focus on schoolwork while my friends talked. Twisting the diamond ring around my finger, I struggled to focus on one thing for more than a few seconds.

A buzz had me grabbing for my phone. I couldn't decide if I was glad for the distraction or annoyed that yet another thing had stolen my brain power. Stepping out into the hall, I flipped it open. "Hello?"

"Hey Sarah, this is Chad from Ruby Tuesday! We got your application, and I wanted to give you a call."

"Okay, great!"

"I'd love to have you come in for an interview," he said, and we scheduled a time two days out. The relief shocked me as I flipped the phone closed. *Why do I even care about this job?* I asked myself, and I couldn't help but laugh. *Maybe because I want to eat more than bowls of rice occasionally*. My rent had definitely increased since moving into the burbs with Haley, and the check to the rental office every month took nearly all my parental support funds. More income was necessary.

Ruby Tuesday offered me the position of server. I bought some non-faded jeans and black restaurant shoes and found a white button-up shirt in my closet. I expected a heaviness to accompany me to this new job; a dread over walking away from my dream and walking into something so many people complained about. Horror stories about rotten customers and disgusting kitchen conditions filled my head. But as I walked in on the first day, my body hummed with nervous excitement.

The managers introduced me to the other servers and the kitchen staff. Everyone was friendly and seemed genuinely happy to be there. I sat in the corner by the bar and watched videos on food safety before shadowing an experienced waiter for the evening. At the end of my shift, Chad reappeared. "Are you hungry?" he asked. "Your first meal is on us!"

A free meal felt like a golden ticket. "Sure! But I never eat here. I'm not sure what's good."

The menu was basically burgers and a salad bar, neither of which excited me.

"Have you ever had a bison burger?" He rapped his knuckles against the bar.

"No. Is it? I mean, it doesn't sound very…"

"You've got to try it then. It's delicious! And I'll add some onion straws." Chad tapped on the monitor to input my order, and I wavered between being excited about free food and dreading getting two things I didn't really love. Minutes later, a plate appeared in front of me, the smell so rich with spices and meat that my salivary glands went into overdrive. I picked up the burger, adorned with bacon and cheese, and took a bite. My eyes closed while I savored the flavors. *This is what a burger is supposed to taste like? Yum!*

Chad sat across from me for a minute. "It's good, isn't it?" His smirk said he knew exactly what was going through my mind, and his eyes shone with pride.

"This is delicious!" I put the burger down to try an onion straw. My dad loved onion rings, so I'd had my fair share growing up. They were always too much crisp, and not enough onion. Something I ate but didn't love. When I popped the onion straw into my mouth, the flavors exploded—salt and spice. Then I bit into it and the sweetness of the onion took over. "Oh, my gosh! There's more onion than breading!"

"Is that a good thing?" Chad looked nervous.

"Yes! I normally don't like onion rings because it's all breading and barely any onion. This is perfect! Plus, I love the spices!"

Chad beamed. "I knew you'd like it! Hey, I gotta get back to work. See you tomorrow for your next shift?"

"I'll see you then!" I smiled as he ducked back through the kitchen door, and I focused on finishing this incredible meal.

The money wasn't great, but the food and people were. Regular customers requested to sit in my section, and I became friends with other servers. In accounting class, I'd catch myself dreaming of a bison burger and onion straws. There were no horror stories—no roaches, mice, or food transferred from a finished plate to a new one. Just good, clean, well-prepared food. And the customers who made me want to accidentally bump drinks into their laps were well outnumbered by the ones I truly enjoyed serving.

My phone buzzed as I walked across the business building to class one day. Robert's name popped up on my screen and I flipped it open. "Hey Robert!"

"Sarah!" He nearly shouted into his phone, and I could hear buckets banging in the background. "I've got a proposal for you."

"Okay?" I wasn't sure how to respond, but he plowed forward anyway.

"I've got this filly. She didn't do well on the track. She's just sittin' around here on the farm, and I need to move her. What if I brought her up to you next time I'm in town and you could train 'er and sell 'er?"

My heart fluttered. "I would love that, Robert! There's just one thing. I really can't afford board for another horse." My face flushed at the admission, but he couldn't be surprised.

"You figure out if you have a place to put her where your other horse lives and see how much it'd cost. I'll pay her board, plus give you a little extra for training her. And when she sells, you'll get a percent."

I could hardly speak. This was a dream. "Okay, Robert! I'll get back to you on that." He started to hang up, but I jumped in before he could. "Wait, Robert! What's her name?"

"Her name? We call her Tippo. It's Tippo Bayou. I name all my horses after places in Mississippi."

"Okay, thanks! I'll get back to you." I sighed dreamily as I hung up.

It took all my willpower not to doodle *Tippo* on the edges of my notebook in class. *Tippo Bayou. A horse is coming to Kentucky for me to train*!

Two weeks later, a long trailer drove up to the barn where Gideon lived. The family stood with me, hands in back pockets or thumbs poked in belt loops, eager to see the new arrival. A small, dark bay filly stepped off the trailer. Her fluffy winter coat made it hard to see how she was really put together, but I could already tell why she hadn't done well on the track. She was still growing and learning how to use all her parts. Robert released her into the stall and she cowered in the back.

I introduced Robert to the family, figured out the paperwork, and as soon as the trailer was driving away, I ran to see Tippo. She stood against the back wall, looking warily at me. Every time I moved, she flinched. Her halter looked nearly grown into her face, and I made it my mission to build enough trust to remove the halter before heading home. The process started by pulling a chair up in front of her stall and taking a seat.

She got used to my presence in the chair, and eventually I stood and inched my way closer. Once in her stall, I used a lead rope as an extension of my hand, flicking it at her until she no longer flinched but stood there with curiosity, an ear turned toward me. Soon I was close enough to use my hand instead of the lead rope, and I stroked her shoulder, then her neck, and then her rump. Little Tippo never took her eye off me, but the wariness she arrived with dissipated.

Slowly, I worked my way back toward her head, rubbing and talking until she let me touch the top of her neck and her face. I grabbed the buckle to the halter and tried to undo it slow and gentle without her noticing, but the dang thing was stuck! She jerked back, eyes wide, and I gave the piece of nylon a hard yank before letting go. It dropped to the ground and Tippo cowered in the corner again.

It took a couple days for Tippo to grow from afraid of being touched to part of my little herd. She picked up brushes between her teeth and gave them to me for grooming. Her favorite game was grabbing the zipper of my jacket between her teeth and running it up and down, miraculously never biting me or hitting me with her face. Sandi slapped the ground with her front feet and darted from side to side, wanting to be part of the fun. Gideon gave us the side eye, obviously thinking we were crazy. I laughed, heart full, not even thinking of the track for a moment.

At times the unresolved racetrack dream I'd come to Kentucky to chase felt like the missing piece to a puzzle. This puzzle was turning out more beautiful than I'd expected, but I wondered. *Maybe I'll just have to have an unfinished puzzle. I don't know. It's in God's hands now.*

When Haley came home in her exercise riding gear, my chest burned with envy so much that sometimes the heat moved up into my face, and I was sure I resembled a red cartoon devil with steam coming out of my ears.

I'd close my eyes, pretending it was just a tired long blink, inhale, and beg God for forgiveness for this envy that could so quickly sucker punch me. *God, forgive me. I don't want to feel this way. Please help me not to be jealous of Haley. And by the way, I'd like to gallop again. Like how it was in the beginning, if that's cool with you. But if not, okay. I still love you.*

Occasionally, when the weather was nice and I wasn't exhausted, I put on my riding gear and went to Trackside to see if I could get some rides. It was good to see familiar faces. We laughed, and I told them to come see me at the restaurant and grab a burger. But for most of the winter, I let them deal with their cooped-up horses without me.

Without the track, I became engrossed in polo, training Tippo, and chasing the vision of Gideon and me taking over the barrel-racing world. Joey and Sandi sat next to me in the cab of my blue pickup and Gid rode behind us in the horse trailer. People gawked as I backed Gid down the ramp. I felt their stares when we loped circles for warm-up, and when the announcer called our turn, I knew we were good enough to win the whole thing.

But we never did.

At first, it was random incidents—a bad turn, a bumped barrel. We practiced at home and came back ready for more. In the middle of our most perfect run, someone's loose dog ran across the arena, forcing me to pull up. A couple shows later, my horse, my partner, stopped going into the arena when I asked. He ran backward and someone on the ground helped drag him to the alleyway, where he exploded forward like the barrel-racing superstar I knew he was. *Nerves,* I thought.

One show, after a perfect and fast first and second barrel, we turned the third to head home. As his back legs tried to propel us through the last part of the turn, they slipped and our fall was cushioned by the deep arena footing. It was simultaneously the cause of our fall and the reason I felt like I landed on a cloud. Gid clambered back to his feet and we kept going. Before the next show, he was mysteriously lame and on stall rest. The family he lived with let me take one of their horses. But it wasn't Gideon.

When Gid was sound again, we got back to showing. When it was our turn to run, I clucked him toward the alleyway. The whites around his eyes grew as he raced backward before a helping hand gripped his bridle, pulling him forward. It took three people on the ground to get him into the arena, but once we were in he was off like a rocket. We got to the first barrel, ready to whip around it. Instead he paused, front feet in the air. I clucked him forward, pointing to our spot next to the first barrel, but I felt his panic. He went into fear mode, where he no longer registered anything I asked, and ran sideways out the gate.

My heart felt like lead. I had this vision of the two of us winning barrel races and going to the National Finals Rodeo. Gideon was the fastest, best barrel horse I'd ever sat on, and I knew he was good enough, but run after run was a failure. I couldn't get Ms. Brenda's voice out of my head, telling me to take him off the barrel pattern. "But he's so good!" I wanted to scream at the voice. Sure, there might be other horses out there I could pursue a barrel-racing career with, but I wanted it with Gideon or not at all.

Funds were low, classes were hard, and polo was taking a lot of time, but I forced another barrel race into our schedule, dragging Joey and Sandi along. When I signed the papers and handed over the check, the registration lady said, "Looks like you'll be going around ten p.m."

"Uh, okay." I was hoping to be home at a reasonable hour, but they couldn't help how busy they were. "Thanks!"

At nine-thirty, I threw Gid's saddle on and strapped his protective boots around his legs, then we went to warm up. "Excuse me, folks," the announcer came over the loudspeaker. "We're going to take a bit of a break. Drag the arena, eat some dinner because we haven't had a break all night. We'll be back."

We ambled back to the trailer. Around eleven, I thought surely it was almost our turn. I put Gid's bridle back on and went to warm him up. Then again at midnight and two a.m. Joey and I sat in the back of the truck contemplating sleep, but not wanting to miss my turn.

It was after four in the morning when I finally rode through the gate for our run. Frustration ate my insides as people grabbed the bridle to help get my horse in. *Why won't he just go?* I wanted to cry. In the arena, Gideon launched forward, running down the first barrel. I grabbed the saddle horn, ready to turn, when instead he paused, his front feet lifting into the air. Steering him back to his path, I went through the motions and tried to finish a solid, beautiful pattern, but my heart was somewhere else. Because in a show with that many riders, you didn't win by pausing at the first barrel.

Chapter 36

A NOTICE WENT OUT to the equine business students that a local Thoroughbred breeding farm was hiring a vet assistant. It wasn't a track job, but I was hungry to learn anything I could about the industry. I submitted the application and got called in for an interview. It wasn't long before I turned in my nonslip restaurant shoes for boots again.

It was foaling season. The mares' bellies bulged with babies that would arrive any day. We drove from barn to barn, checking grumpy or apathetic mares to see how the foals were growing and to try to predict when they would arrive. I held tails to the side with one hand and lead ropes in the other while the vet shoved his gloved hand inside the mare all the way to his shoulder. It only took a couple days to realize I wasn't sure if this was the kind of vet work I wanted to do.

I prepared vaccines for the hundreds of horses on the property, popping plastic caps off new needles and twisting them into syringes. When it was time for the stallion at the farm to breed, I stood in the doorway, not experienced enough to be helpful. I watched as two men held the mare and two more held the stallion to make sure neither horse was hurt in the process. Frankly, I was glad they didn't want my help.

The vet taught me how to pack his x-ray plates into heavy canvas bags, and then how to hold them so he could get pictures of all the yearlings' legs before they went to the auction.

Some mornings I arrived to harrowing tales of the births from the day before. One mare was being led back to her stall after a few hours in the paddock and the foal fell out of her onto the barn floor. I gawked and stuttered, "Was...is the baby okay?"

"He's fine!" the vet laughed. Another broodmare, carrying a highly anticipated foal, had been waxed over for weeks, keeping everyone on high alert. She was limited to one hour of turnout, and when the guys went to collect her from the field, there was a tiny foal at her side.

The men talked and I listened, absorbing everything I could and parsing out things on my own, like what "waxed over" meant. Apparently when it was almost time for labor, wax formed over the teats of the broodmare.

I secretly hoped I could witness this thing everyone referred to as a miracle, but they always happened in the afternoon when I had already left for class, or in the darkest hours of night. *It has to happen while I'm here at least once,* I told myself. *It's a mathematical impossibility for it not to.*

Weeks into my job, we pulled up to a barn to check the mare. The farm manager, Bryce, jogged out to greet us. "We've got one in labor!" he exclaimed. My heart rate kicked up a notch, expecting the panic everyone showed on TV.

Dr. K's mouth battled between a grin and a frown. I imagined he was annoyed that our schedule for the day got interrupted, but maybe he still loved this part of the job. "All right. Sarah, grab that bag in the corner. Leave the ultrasound machine. We won't need it here." Then he strolled into the barn, gripping his cup of coffee in one hand.

If they weren't panicking, neither would I. I lifted the back hatch of the SUV, grabbed what Dr. K requested, and strolled in behind everyone else, just slightly faster with flushed cheeks.

"Here's the bag." I lifted it toward him. He was already in the stall with the mare, checking her over.

"Thanks. Just set it down there," the vet nodded toward the door.

I tiptoed forward to set it down. "Need anything else?" I asked, not sure what help I could offer. Everyone around me was so much more experienced.

"Nah, just stay nearby in case I need you to grab something from the truck."

Stable workers crouched on the floor outside the stall, each holding a different piece of equipment and waiting to be needed. I retreated to a spot directly across from the action but outside the hum of activity.

For as snarky as these guys could be bantering back and forth all day, I found myself entranced by them. "Hand me the gauze and scissors," Bryce said, stretching his arm toward the door. One of the guys tossed a white roll of gauze into the stall. Bryce kneeled behind the mare. I held my breath as he stroked her tail so all the hairs laid down smoothly. He wrapped the gauze around the top—over, under, over, under—taking care to be diligent, like this wasn't just another of the fifty births this year. This horse wasn't a box to be checked. She was a mare, struggling with the pains and process of labor. Dr. K stroked her sleek coat, and I bit the inside of my lip, wondering if I should be doing something helpful or productive while on the clock, but my feet wouldn't budge.

The mare groaned as two little points emerged from just below her tail. "I see some feet!" Bryce exclaimed in a low voice. He grabbed the tiny legs, the mare pushed, and the baby surged further, almost indiscernible within its sac. Another push from the mare and the foal spilled out onto the straw, legs all over the place. The placenta, veiny and reminiscent of an alien, ripped and fell to the ground. The mare's head rested on the straw, recovering from her effort, and Bryce held the foal's nostrils to his face. "He's not breathing! We need oxygen!"

My heart rate kicked back up. I wanted to help. Did I need to run to the truck? Get something from the office? Should I hit my knees right here and pray for this foal? In two long strides, one of the stable workers delivered an oxygen tank with a cone on the end. They nestled the cone over the tiny muzzle, and Bryce massaged the underside of the baby's neck. The corners of my mouth turned down. *This isn't much of a miracle. This is terrible. God, please*...

"Okay, he's breathing! We're good!" Bryce exclaimed before I could even finish the prayer.

I watched the foal gulp a lungful of air and open his liquid eyes, which seemed too big for his tiny head. He blinked, looking at the people around him as if grasping to understand what just happened and how he got here. We lingered to make sure the mare and foal connected, and then most everyone dispersed, getting back to whatever work they were doing before. Dr. K picked up the placenta, stretching it so he could look for missing pieces. Then he tossed it in a bucket and asked me to take it to the truck.

For the rest of the day, I worked in silence, doing whatever Dr. K asked, but pondering that moment when the foal was born, those seconds that he didn't breathe. A few days later it happened again, almost a carbon copy of the first. Bryce yelled, "Oxygen!" and a few seconds later everything was fine.

What is it that helps foals, or any living thing, transition from swimming in their mother's womb and depending on another body for everything, to taking that first gulp of cool air? I pondered while I snapped caps off syringes. I'd heard so many times that every breath is a gift from God, and now I understood. I could practically see God blowing in that foal's face, giving him his first gulp of air. That was the miracle I buried in my heart.

From work, I went to class, and from class I went to polo or to see Gideon and Tippo. Eventually the polo team opened its own barn, and I moved my horses there so I wasn't driving so much. Guilt weighed heavy on my chest for leaving the family who had opened their home to my horses, but I was stretched in too many directions. Days grew longer and warmer, and Haley and I picked up a side job grooming for two members of the Louisville Polo Club.

In the middle of all this, I heard about the Kentucky Derby Princesses program. Every year, five young women were chosen to represent the Kentucky Derby at social events and even on media like the *Today Show*. They were invited to all the Derby festivities and were given prime seats on Derby Day. I figured if I couldn't gallop racehorses, maybe I could be a Kentucky Derby Princess and have a front-row seat to it all. *Surely they'll choose me after everything I've been through.*

I sent in the application, fully expecting a callback. I wasn't disappointed. A few weeks later, donning a skirt suit Mom bought me for a pageant in high school, I strutted into one of Louisville's finest hotels. Chin up, shoulders back, and determined not to let this suit's previous failure discourage me, I sat in a room full of other girls my age. Most had their moms with them. They were beautiful and chatty, with perfect hair and makeup, and we had all made it to the final round of interviews.

I pulled out my phone and texted Mom, "Waiting for my turn at the interview!"

"Good luck!" she sent back.

"Sarah Bullock," a lady with a clipboard called out. My head snapped up and my neck started itching. *If I can ride a racehorse, I can talk to a panel of judges,* I told myself. Striding into the room, I smiled warmly, nodded to everyone, shook hands, and then sat, knees pressed together so hard my muscles threatened to cramp. *Why are ladies expected to press their knees together? This is a freaking workout! I'd rather just cross my legs.*

But to the judges, I smiled, laughed, and swooped my hair out of my eyes. They asked about me and my experiences, and I saw their eyes sparkle as I wowed them with my tales. *I'm actually doing a really good job! I've so got this*! Then a guy looked at his notes and back to me. "If you were a condiment, which one would you be?" His eyes glimmered when he asked.

My chin began to quiver and I chuckled at the ridiculous question. I remembered my pageant training that had never worked before—repeat the question to buy time to think. It was a good tactic since I wasn't one to come up with witty responses on the fly. "If I were a condiment, which one would I be?" I laughed when I almost said condom instead of condiment. "I think I'd be, hmmm..." *What would I be? What would I be? Oh crap, come on Sarah, come up with something.*

"I'd be mustard." I blurted. *Face palm.*

"Really?" the guy responded. "Why would you be mustard?"

"I don't know!" I said with a confident, casual shrug, knowing I was failing. "It's good. Not many people like it that much, but I'd rather dip a fry in mustard than ketchup. Everyone's into ketchup but mustard's better."

"Okay! True! Most people do prefer ketchup!" I noticed the spark had left some of their eyes as they moved on to the next question. "What's the difference between a woman and a lady?"

I stumbled through, describing the traits of a lady in detail since the actual words for those traits had left my brain. It reminded me of cell biology, when I could have walked my professor through the entire cycle of a cell, but the specific terms for the parts vanished from my head.

I smiled and thanked the judges, wishing I could dive out the door directly into my truck. Instead, I casually wobbled away, crossing the ocean of beautiful, polished young ladies who separated me from the elevator. They watched me and I smiled back, lifting my chin. As the elevator doors were closing and I was celebrating the moment I could drop this façade, I heard a ding. *Crap on a stick*! A radiant mother/daughter pair stepped into my safe haven.

As I pretended to be happy to share my ride to the lobby, every word I'd said to the judges became a study of how good or bad I was at interviews. *Mustard? Really? To these judges, I probably was a lot like mustard—not as well-loved as ketchup.*

But even if a couple of the questions didn't go great, none of those girls had my story. None of them had my grit. I didn't read the paper, but probably none of them had been featured in the Courier Journal. I went back to my apartment, exchanged the suit for jeans, and held onto hope. *God, if I can't gallop, it sure would be cool to be a Kentucky Derby Princess.*

I was watching my time in Kentucky tick away. After the semester ended, I would take one final summer course—an intensive that would be so time-consuming I wouldn't do much else. Then it would be time for my next adventure—marriage and moving to DC with Joey. I had always known the track would be a two-year thing. These two years were quickly coming to a close.

Chapter 37

Finished with my morning work, I sat in my equine class wondering if the Kentucky Derby Princess people would call. If I was chosen I would hear back in two weeks. The image of me parading around in a poofy ball gown played through my mind and it seemed ridiculous. But it could be a fun experience to end this whole Kentucky adventure. *God*, I prayed again, *I'd really like to do this Derby Princess thing if I can't gallop*. It became a chant.

I eavesdropped on the conversations around me. One of the track guys mentioned that a trainer at his dad's barn was looking for a rider. Then, as if realizing I was a rider and I was right there, he turned to me. "Hey Sarah, are you looking for a job?"

"Well," I paused to think as the racetrack crew stared. I had a job at Hermitage and had technically committed through the end of breeding season, which was three more weeks. Normally I finished every commitment I made, but right now a huge clock hovered above me, counting down my days in the Bluegrass State. "Yeah, I'd be interested." My heart did a little leap as I said it. *God? Is this you?*

Four days later, I stood outside a barn in my half-chaps and pompom galloping helmet. The trainer, Ian Wilkes, was quiet, observing. The farm manager, Bob, did most of the communicating. "You rode for Mike Lauer, huh?"

I racked my brain to remember if I'd told him this during our brief phone call. "Yep! How did you–?"

"We asked around," he said, and I could have sworn his face reddened.

"I rode for Ron and a few other guys, too. I spent a lot of time freelancing." My own face heated at the memories of walking from barn to barn, feeling like a liability. A charity case. I had always wondered what stories were whispered behind my back. *Whatever they were, these guys either don't care or they weren't bad enough to stop them from giving me a chance.*

Bob kept chatting, drawing me from the spiral of insecurity. *I've got nothing to lose,* I told myself. *If I muck this up, no big deal. I've probably got too much going on to take on a gallop job anyway. God, help me with this. I don't know how I can finish my classes with all these papers and exams and do this job. I don't even know if I'm good enough to ride here. This is all you. I'll just do my best and trust you.*

"So when the horse comes out, just take him around two times. We usually start at the half-mile pole," he instructed.

"Okay!" I pushed my shoulders back. *Liability is a big thing, so they're totally going to give me the easiest horse in the barn. I wouldn't be surprised if they threw an exercise saddle on the pony horse. I've got this.* This was the most relaxed I had ever been before getting on a racehorse.

I had all but given up on this dream of galloping before I left Kentucky. I pictured the time I held my hands out, palms up, and literally gave the dream to God outside of Ruby Tuesday. If I got the job, it was an unexpected gift from above. If I didn't, I'd finish out at Hermitage, complete my degree, and maybe get this Derby Princess thing.

They led a black colt out of the stall. *He doesn't look like a track pony.* The center of my chest hummed in eagerness and a giddy smile expanded across my face. I swallowed it down, trying to look serious. I grabbed the reins and sparse mane on the horse's neck and Bob gave me a leg up. The groom led me around a circular path in front of the barn while I knotted my reins and adjusted the stirrups.

Bob and Ian walked to the stand overlooking the track so they could watch. Curious faces silently peeked out the end of the barn. I wasn't concerned. This was the easy horse. He felt good underneath me.

"Listo?" the groom asked. I adjusted my final stirrup.

"Listo," I nodded. He unhooked the lead shank and released us. The training track smelled like spring grass with the slightest hint of manure. There was no heavy ammonia smell like at Churchill where so many horses are packed into a tiny space. The wind tickled my arms, and I gathered the reins short enough to control my mount, but not so short as to annoy him. The path went toward the training platform before turning left and running parallel to the fence. We had a bit of a walk from the barn to the opening of the training oval. Eyes followed me and the horse as we approached the platform. I looked up to Bob and Ian, giving awkward yet polite acknowledgment.

"Just take him around two times," Ian reiterated in his Australian accent. I nodded, hoping I didn't get the poles confused. With no warning body language, ear twitch, pause, or any other indication, the horse dipped and spun left in less time than I could take a breath. One second we were on the path; the next we were fifteen feet away and facing the other direction.

I pressed against his side with my left leg, and steered with the reins to get him back on track, noticing the raised eyebrows around me but not giving it much thought. *No big deal*, I reminded myself. *This is the good horse! That was a fluke.* We got back to the spook spot and again, he spun so fast my stomach nearly stayed where we had been a half-second before. The observation deck got quiet, and I knew if I turned I would see other faces gawking out the end of the barn.

Chuckling inwardly, I thanked my first horse, Misty. She had been a professional at introducing me to the hard ground, scooching and spinning whenever my guard was down. Thanks to her determination to get out of work, I eventually learned to stick to a naughty horse, most of the time at least. Tightening the reins a tad and giving the horse a swift kick, I got him moving forward and gave a nod to the trainer's stand as we passed. They nodded back, and I wondered if they were holding their breath. *Maybe they're worried about liability or something*, I laughed.

It was liberating to ride a horse without others crowded around me. We could hop sideways all he wanted and wouldn't cause a collision or put someone in the hospital. *I can breathe out here. I can ride.* I held the reins just short enough to feel his mouth and communicate that it was time to behave. I hugged him with my calves, the gentle pressure reminding him he was safe, and we were moving forward. He walked down the path and onto the track without another incident.

As he stepped onto the soft dirt surface, we struck out into a floating jog. I looked at the poles —short green and white ones and larger red and white ones—trying to remember which were which. Some were quarter poles, marking a quarter of a mile. *Those are probably the red and white ones since there aren't as many*, I figured, counting back from the gigantic pole that must be the finish line. Bob had told me to start at one of them, but I wasn't exactly sure which one he meant. *Will I not get the job if I stop at the wrong pole?* I wondered and decided all I could do was my best.

The trusty black colt toted me around the track until we got to the spot where I was pretty sure they wanted me to stop. I squeezed my hands and sat deeper into the saddle, and he obediently relaxed to a walk and then a stop. He was calm with a steady heartbeat under my leg. *Truly they've given me the easiest horse in the barn. The spook must have been a fluke. This is every bit as easy as I expected*, and I gave him an appreciative scratch just in front of the saddle. He swiveled his left ear to listen and turned his head enough to see me with his left eye. We shared a knowing smile. "Thanks for the lovely ride so far, buddy."

We waited for a handful of heartbeats. I gathered the reins and squeezed my legs, encouraging him to go. His neck gleamed in the sunlight as he dropped his head, relaxing onto the bit and galloping forward. We came around the turn and my body, breath, heartbeat, everything moved in unison with this horse. *What a gem*! We galloped past the trainer's stand, and I pretended not to look at Bob and Ian. I told myself I didn't care what they thought. This was a picture-perfect ride and if they weren't happy then I wasn't the right fit.

We came around the next bend with another lap to go when a loud "whoooo whoooo" sounded. It took four strides before I understood what it was—the alarm for a loose horse. I looked around confused, forgetting we shared this space. For a moment it was *our* piece of Heaven. I wasn't exactly sure what to do, but I knew I needed to try to stop.

Pulling up a racehorse at the end of a gallop could be nearly impossible. I was convinced that sometimes God's hands alone slowed them to a walk because my little 117-pound body surely couldn't do much for a horse that wanted to go. Trying to stop a horse when we weren't even halfway through the gallop was absolute insanity. But I leaned my weight back, tugging gently on the reins, and the horse slowed to a canter for a few strides, then a jog, and a few steps later, he stopped.

We stood, facing the loose horse. He was a tiny speck running around the other end of the track, his head straight up in the air as toy-sized people hollered and approached him with their arms stretched wide. Soon the horse was caught and the alarm went silent. I wasn't quite sure what to do. *Should we be done? Or do we keep going? Do we go extra because we took a break?* I put my leg on and we jogged back to the center of the track. After another strong squeeze, the black colt picked up his gallop and we finished our work.

My new friend was sweaty as we came off the track. He alternated between a walk and a happy jig underneath me, and I beamed as I rubbed under his mane. It was a spot where Gideon always got itchy, and I figured this horse would like it too. *Maybe I won't get the job*, I considered. *After all, this is the easy horse. But we had a good ride. This would be a nice farewell to my crazy Kentucky experience.*

Ian and Bob followed me into the barn, and I hopped down as the groom grabbed the reins. They whisked him away for a bath and I regretted for a moment how the track worked. I wanted to bathe him myself, a thank you for an exceptional ride.

"You've got the job," Bob said, and I studied his white hair and friendly face for a moment, processing as my stomach did flips.

"Wow. Thanks!" A hesitant smile stretched across my face. *Is this really happening, God?*

"Just one thing," Bob inserted. "When there's a loose horse, always make sure you face away from it. That way if it comes toward you, the horse you're on can get away. There have been accidents where a loose horse runs head-on into another horse."

"Okay! That totally makes sense," I replied with an enthusiastic nod, hungry to learn more.

"When can you start?" He cleaned his glasses while he talked.

"I need to finish out this week with Hermitage; I can start next week though." My lungs squeezed knowing I'd be cutting out on Hermitage, and that I'd only be in Kentucky for a couple more months. If these people knew I was leaving town, surely they wouldn't hire me. My face flushed at the omission as we set up my start day.

Less than a week later, my alarm blasted before the sun was up. My sluggish mind sparked with a reminder: *you're going to gallop racehorses.* I threw on my jeans and boots and raced out the door.

There were two other riders, and we quickly became friends. The little black colt was part of my regular string of horses. When I rode, Bob and everyone else expected me to be good enough, capable.

I never heard, "Now, Sarah, I want you to be careful out there." No one said, "Are you sure you can do this?" They believed in me, and I flourished under their belief.

One day, the three of us stood waiting for the grooms to bring out the next set. My black horse was led out and I smiled expectantly. He stopped in front of another girl. "Aw man, I'm stuck with him?" she complained.

"What?" I exclaimed, my own disappointment coming through. "He's the easy horse! He's my favorite one to ride!"

She laughed. "No way. We all hate riding him. That's why you normally get him."

I can't believe this! my mind screamed as we went back and forth.

"No," I told her. "He's the easy one. That's why they put me on him for a trial ride. Because they're not going to put me on a hard one and risk the liability of me getting hurt."

"Sarah," she looked me in the eye and almost stopped laughing, "I swear to you, we all hate riding him. Several people came out to try for the job and he dropped them all. We couldn't believe you stayed on."

I laughed, imagining them watching me when he did that oh-so-hard and completely unexpected spin. It didn't surprise me a lick that people fell off as he spun right out from under them. And along with that laugh, my insides swelled. I could have floated away like a balloon in the wind. I really did earn this job! And they weren't just giving me the easy horses.

I didn't hear back about becoming a Derby Princess, and every time I thought about it I smiled, replaying that prayer in my mind. *I'd really like to do this Derby Princess thing if I can't gallop.*

"Thank you," I whispered. "I prefer galloping."

Days were filled as full as a fat tick with senior-level classes, final papers, polo, riding Tippo and Gideon, wedding plans, and preparations to move. I stood on the deck after my rides for the day, enjoying the warm sun and time at the track. A Bible verse popped into my head. "But those who trust in the LORD will find new strength. They will soar high on wings like eagles. They will run and not grow weary. They will walk and not faint."

And I knew God was keeping His promise. I was trusting Him, and He was giving me the energy to enjoy and thrive in my final weeks in Kentucky. Even so, my insides clenched every time I drove the tree-lined sideroad to the training track. Each day was a countdown to my last.

What was likely monotonous for my new friends was a daily adventure for me. Each horse led out of the stall, each leg up into the saddle (sometimes still mistimed on my part) was a fulfillment of things that had played in my imagination for years. I relished it. When my rides were done and the others kept going, getting more mounts than me because they were more fit, I stood on the deck and watched, chatting with my new friend Bob.

God's goodness and provision surrounded me as if I were swimming in it. Final papers for my hardest classes would normally have me hunkered over a keyboard for hours, but I worked on them in small pieces between classes. I rode my horses, helped take care of the polo herd until the sun went down, then stayed up late finishing schoolwork.

The sun rose new every morning and so did my energy, no matter how little sleep I'd had. When I was with Haley and Joey, I was *with* them, laughing and living, Sandi at my heels or sprawled across my lap on the couch. I felt life flow through my veins more in those final weeks in Kentucky than ever before. The stories piled up.

There was the day Awshuganow, previously one of the easiest fillies to ride, returned from her first race with a nasty habit of balking. I swore I could get her moving and they let me get on her. Sure enough, she stopped at the walk, then at the trot, but soon I had her rolling into a forward gallop. *I'm good*! I thought, just before I found myself eating dirt. She had pulled a quick reverse, slipping out from under me and sending me flying through the air like a dart. I landed in a heap before I even knew I had been unseated.

Bob laughed until tears dripped from his eyes and he had to take his glasses off, leaning over to wipe his face. For the first few seconds, I stared at him, stunned that anyone could laugh at such misfortune. But then I realized nothing hurt, and when I envisioned what it must have looked like when the mare did a quick direction change and I didn't, I found myself laughing with him as I swiped dirt off my jeans. When the other riders finished and joined us on the deck, Bob recreated the tale using his hands to show us how I projected through the air, and we all laughed.

One day I was riding a handsome bay colt around the circle in front of the barn, waiting on the other horses and riders so we could gallop together. Ian and Bob stood to the side. A horse and rider emerged from the barn, and just as I grinned to welcome them, my colt stood on his hind legs, front hooves pawing the air in what must have been a testosterone-fueled challenge.

I leaned forward, my chest touching his neck. I pressed my hands toward his mouth to be sure I didn't pull the reins and cause him to go over backward. He seemed to linger in the air and I wondered if we would fall. I'd heard tales of horses rearing so high they flipped, and they never turned out good. Ian stepped up next to the horse and I looked down, my bulging eyes meeting his calm ones just as the horse's front feet landed safely on the ground.

"It's fine," Ian said. "Don't you worry about that. Just keep him moving."

"Okay," I squeaked out, anxious to get going toward the track.

The third horse and rider came out of the barn and we headed to the track. As soon as everyone's hooves made it onto the soft dirt of the training oval, we picked up a jog. The three of us rode single file along the rail, my horse sandwiched in the center, and my heart sang. We made it to the spot in front of the trainer's deck where we allowed the horses to relax before our gallop. The other riders chatted with the men on the training platform, and I sat silent, enjoying the vibrant colors and warm sunshine of spring.

Another trainer, Carl Nafzger, stood on the deck. When the racetrack kids talked about him in class, their voices dropped to a near whisper. It was the same reverence my dad had when he talked about Bear Bryant. Carl and Ian worked together some, and when he was within earshot, I clung to every word, hoping to glean some of his wisdom.

I was snapped back to the present when my horse stood straight up, pawing the air again, challenging the world. His front end lifted so high, I marveled at how I didn't slide off. I thought surely if he went up any further, we'd fall back and I'd find myself sandwiched between him and the ground. After an eternity of seconds, he put his front feet back on the ground and acted normal.

"Sarah, you've got to remind him you're there," Carl said behind me. He must have seen the tension in my shoulders. "You're so light he forgets you're there. You can't just sit there and do nothing. Pat him, talk to him, move around a bit. Don't let him forget he has a rider."

"Really?"

"Yes. He forgets about you."

I wasn't so much questioning him as the idea of a horse forgetting he had a rider. I felt quite substantial to myself.

My mind conjured videos of this trainer doing all the things the kids at school talked about. They said he'd been a champion bull rider, and I could see a dust-colored beast emerging from the shoot, kicking his heels in the air before throwing a wicked spin, all while a younger Carl Nafzger hung on, one arm in the air. The image morphed into a young man willing to do whatever was needed around the racing barn so he could learn and have his own successful operation one day. If he'd ridden bulls, racehorses probably weren't too intimidating.

I had never been one to memorize all the prominent racehorses and their records, but even I had heard of Unbridled, whom Nafzger had saddled to win the Kentucky Derby and the Breeders Cup in 1990. Whatever Carl Nafzger told me, I'd take to heart. I reached forward, scratching the horse's neck. Then I moved in the saddle, turning a tad before standing and pressing my heels down to stretch my calves. All through it the horse stood there, calm.

We had a lovely gallop, all while Carl's words played in my mind. *He forgets you're there. You can't just sit there and do nothing. Pat him, talk to him, move around a bit, and don't let him forget he has a rider.*

Classes finished just in time for Derby. In two years, I never got over how the entire city, even the university calendar, revolved around Derby week. It reminded me of the reverence for Mardi Gras in Louisiana and south Mississippi. My parents came up for one final visit to the Bluegrass State. We secured grandstand tickets for the big day, but first they wanted to watch me ride.

Friday morning we stood the horses in front of the trainer's deck, waiting as always, before we galloped. I scratched the horse's neck and played with her mane while Carl talked to my parents. My dad tried to regale him with the harrowing tale of how I stubbornly made my way to Kentucky and all the awful things that happened when I arrived, but Mr. Nafzger had a way of controlling the conversation. Before the story could get out of hand, I heard him tell my parents, "She's got a lot of horse in her."

Galloping past the trainers' deck when my parents visited.

My mom shifted the conversation to how much I had always loved horses, but again Mr. Nafzger said, "She's got a lot of horse in her." Like he wanted them to know, like he wanted *me* to know, standing there in front of them pretending I wasn't hanging on every word of their conversation. The countdown of weeks left in this job had moved into days, and my insides were a mess of gratitude, joy, and sorrow.

It was like finishing a book I loved and never wanted to end. But if the book went on forever, would I have loved it as much? In the final chapter, a legend, one of the great horsemen of our time, saw the horsehair in my DNA. It became a chant whenever I questioned myself. *She's got a lot of horse in her.*

I was so afraid they would tell me not to come back that I only gave them a four-day notice. There was one intensive summer class, some final dental and orthodontist appointments, and it was over.

CHAPTER 38

I ARRIVED IN LOUISVILLE like a wave crashing onto the shore, forceful, demanding, and loud. Breaking apart. Wondering if I could be put back together.

When I left, I slipped away with the tide.

I could have stayed in Louisville—postponed getting married for a little longer, or even for a lifetime. But I chose to chase the next leg of the journey where I could see God's handprints. To go to another shore where I would walk hand in hand with Joey Hickner.

I packed my things and hugged Haley. She kept saying, "I can't believe you're leaving," and like a broken record I replied, "I know!" My face glowed with joy and expectation while my eyes were wet with tears. When I got to Louisville I had imagined all the horses I would ride, and even the classes I would take. I had imagined walking across campus and grabbing lunch in the cafeteria. I had never imagined new friends like Haley, or how hard it would be to leave them.

With Sandi sitting in the passenger seat, my co-captain, I drove to the barn where Gideon and Tippo lived, hooked up the trailer, and led them up the ramp. People had offered to buy Tippo, but I couldn't do it. She had wormed her way into my heart, and I didn't want her to be part of a polo string. She needed a girl who would dote on and love her. So, I'd hold onto her until I found that girl or give her back to Robert if that's what he wanted.

Leaving was an out-of-body experience. This dream I had chased for years, had given up so much for, was done. And it looked nothing like I expected. "Thank you, God," I whispered for the thousandth time. Heart heavy, heart full.

Dr. Vittitow and Dr. Tran had taken my broken pieces and helped put them back together. I sat in their chairs days after Red and I somersaulted down the track. Then again when Gideon was missing and I clung to a tiny thread of hope and the prayers of those around me. I knew that when despair pulled on my heart so hard I couldn't pray, they stood in the gap and prayed for me. Between dental molds, shots, and pliers, I regaled them with the story of finding Gideon, and when the article in the *Courier Journal* came out, they celebrated with me.

There were days I sat in the chair and didn't talk much. I didn't know how to articulate the struggle of wanting something so badly I had been willing to sacrifice everything, yet it was always just out of reach. So many times, my fingers brushed the edge of the dream but I came away empty. I didn't know how to talk about the way God set the dream in my lap and I grabbed it with both hands. It would take me years to process.

Days before leaving Kentucky, Dr. Tran removed the braces, giving me a retainer with a tooth in it, and Dr. Vittitow put the finishing touches on my smile. All I knew how to say were surface things like, "Thank you," and "Wow, y'all have been amazing. I'm so excited!" and "I can't believe I have to find a new dentist and orthodontist in Virginia."

How could I thank them for being the hands of God, loving me when I needed it most? It seemed odd that the love I needed came from people like a dentist, an orthodontist, and a school adviser.

I dropped by the equine business building on my last day of class. How could I ever repay Terri for not only being a guidance counselor for college, helping me cram three years of classes into two so I could graduate on time, but also for bringing me breakfast the morning after my accident? I knew almost no one and I sat in an apartment with my dog, an aching body, and jagged shards of teeth hanging from my gums. I didn't know how to move forward, but a Styrofoam box with pancakes was a good first step. And then she helped me find Gideon with her fliers and determination that he was at a racetrack somewhere. She could have sat in her office and just done her job. That's all anyone expected. But her door was always open.

How could I thank the trainers, other exercise riders, and grooms who laughed with me, encouraged me, or at minimum never told me what I'm sure was on their minds—"This isn't for you, girl, just give up. Stick to show horses." I imagined myself standing on the backside, opening my arms wide as if to embrace the world, and yelling, "Thank you!" at the top of my lungs. But it wouldn't have been enough. They wouldn't have heard over the sounds of horses nickering and buckets banging around in the stalls, and if they did they wouldn't have understood. It wasn't perfect and most of the time it wasn't pretty, but they gave me a chance.

How could I thank Ian, Bob, and Carl? I left them abruptly, rudely, yet they embraced me still. I went back for one more visit, a taste. I stood on the deck next to Bob, watching my friends ride, and he regaled me with the tale of how I shot off Awshuganow like a dart. This time I bent over, covered my mouth with my hands, and my entire body shook with the laugh of a girl who no longer felt the drag of a longing so deep sometimes I couldn't breathe.

There were the Reynolds, who had been a family for my horses and for me, taking us in without even knowing us. And all the Louisville polo people who had coached me in a new-to-me sport and treated me like one of them even though I missed the ball almost as often as I made contact.

I slipped back into the ocean, and things went on without me.

As I drove down the interstate, constantly checking my mirrors to make sure the horse trailer was safely behind me, the story began to unfold. The determination I arrived with, the brokenness after the accident, the desperation and fear every time I sat on a horse (no matter how much I tried to deny it). The nights I cried myself to sleep wondering if I could do this, and would I survive if I did? Then I gave the dream to God, assuming that was the end of it. To my total surprise, as if it were an encore performance, he gave me that last job—the one that exactly matched the dream I had carried in my heart for so long. It was a gift from my Creator.

Gratitude filled my soul and ran in my blood until it fed every cell in my body. I left Louisville in peace, knowing that God had shown me His goodness.

One month after leaving Kentucky, I married Joey in the Baptist church where I grew up. Friends played the music, my brothers read Scripture, and my bridesmaids lined the stairs wearing Derby hats. Some were friends from Kentucky who'd made the trek down to celebrate with us, and others were from my life before.

Afterward, we celebrated at a reception venue on a lake, smiling until our faces hurt and spending so much time with people we loved that we forgot to eat our cake or drink the root beer floats. When it was time to leave, Joey and I clasped hands and ran through a tunnel of friends, bubbles, and cheers. At the end stood two horses, ready to carry us away to a new life.

My maid of honor, Lauren, held onto Gideon's reins. His eyes were rimmed with white, and his nostrils heaved at the commotion and the mysterious orbs floating in the air. When he saw me coming, he took a big breath and his entire body relaxed. I stood next to him trying to figure out how to get into the saddle gracefully in my gigantic dress. He turned his head and blew in my face. I leaned forward and blew back. "Hello Gideon," I smiled and my heart said *thank you*.

I yelled, "Don't look!" before I hiked up my layers of skirts, stuck my foot in the stirrup, and swung onto his back. The crowd roared with laughter as Lauren adjusted the layers of fabric. Joey rode back and forth waving his cowboy hat, eliciting whoops and hollers from the back of a little spotted lesson pony from Winterview Farm. Our friends and family cheered, the photographer snapped photos, and we rode off into the sunset, toward our honeymoon and life together.

Getting in the car to ride to the reception.

Joey and Cosmo working the crowd.

Gideon keeping it together while I arrange all my skirts.

Riding away together!

Chapter 39

Robert offered Tippo as a wedding gift. My heart raced when I sat next to Joey in the airplane to Turks and Caicos and asked if we could take her with us to our new life. Three days after we arrived back home in Jackson, Mississippi, the back of my blue truck sagged with the weight of our things and our two horses, and we made our way to our new home in Virginia.

We lived in a 900-square-foot apartment and every day I drove a nearly one-hundred-mile loop to different hunter/jumper barns for work with Sandi by my side. I had decided to give myself five years to try my hand at making a living with horses. If I didn't have what it took, I'd go to vet school or maybe get a master's in business administration.

Through it all, Gideon was my happy place. Much like a professional pianist might play grand pianos at concert halls but come home to an aged piano that loses tune more quickly than it should, Gideon was my home piano. My imperfect source of joy that reminded me why I pursued a career with horses in the first place.

Sometimes we competed in the flat classes at English shows, always taking home ribbons. We attempted to barrel race two more times. He pleaded not to go into the arena, attempting to refuse, but ultimately never able to say no to me. We flew in so fast it felt like being in a vacuum, but when it was time to turn at the first barrel, he stopped and reared.

It took years longer than I'd like to admit, but one day I realized a horse that lived to please me and loved to run didn't balk at the gate from excitement. He didn't rear at the first barrel from a stubborn streak. It was pain.

During a particularly bad hoof abscess, I had his hooves x-rayed. The vet's eyebrows lifted. "Wow, Sarah," she said. "This horse is tough. He's a good one. That navicular bone looks like Swiss cheese. It's got to be painful. I'm not even sure how he's walking."

When he recovered from the abscess and the barn where he lived was closing, I moved Gid to a retirement home, promising to visit regularly. He deserved to live his best life in a big field with regular visits from Mom.

Every couple weeks I'd drive out to see him with a crinkling bag of Frosted Flakes. I'd try to jump on him, clinging and pulling myself up while he patiently waited. We didn't practice things, exercise to get fit, train, or any of the things I did with the other horses I rode. We just soaked up each other's presence as Sandi ran around in the tall grass. I closed my eyes and felt him move underneath me, his muscles rippling. He smelled like earth and love.

Visiting Gideon in the retirement field.

When a friend wanted to ride the horse I had for sale, Mr. T, I gladly handed the leggy bay off to her and brought my handsome chestnut up from the retirement field. Sandi was busy pointing at guinea hens while we played with horses.

Gideon blew in my face and I closed my eyes, gently blowing into his nose. Then my old barrel saddle was back out. It felt so good to be on Gideon, his tail higher than ever, his neck rounded in joy. I put my right leg against his side and he spun to the left, beautiful, fast. Then I did it with my left leg and he immediately responded. *What a well-trained horse,* I thought, knowing I had done a lot of that.

People say animals don't have souls, but what connects me with this horse so deeply if it isn't a soul connection? I pondered.

"I think I want him!" my friend said, interrupted my reverie. "Will you sell him to me?"

I cocked my left eyebrow because for some reason I've never been able to cock the right. "You want Mr. T?" I asked, amused.

"Yeah, Sarah! I really do! I think he's wonderful!"

"Okay, well if you buy him I'm going to start riding Gideon more. I've missed being with him."

A few days later I skipped out to the retirement field to catch Gid, looking forward to another blissful ride. Holding my hand out to display the treat I brought, he stretched his slightly sun-pinked nose to me. His left eye looked like a gray storm had descended on it, obscuring the liquid brown with a cloud. I slipped his halter on and let him nibble the treat from my outstretched hand, relishing the feel of his lips grazing my palm while considering his eye.

At least once every year he got an ocular ulcer, though admittedly it had never been this large. This looked like something that had festered for a couple weeks, but there had been no trace just four days before. Comforted by a history of eye injuries that had been treated and healed with ointment, I wasn't worried.

After clipping the crossties to the sides of his halter, I called the vet, trying not to grumble over the bill that would be coming. The tip of Gid's pink tongue was sticking out between his lips and he sucked on it, savoring the treats. His ears tracked me as I brought over the grooming box and pulled out the rubber curry comb.

The shine of his glistening coat had been stolen by the sun, leaving the hair yellowed and coarse. I picked the dirt from his feet, marveling how something that looked so perfect could hide a bone the vet described as Swiss cheese and had caused so many issues for us. I pulled out Frosted Flakes and giggled as he grabbed for them, dropping some to the ground before licking the sugar from my palm and loudly sucking his tongue. He stared into the field, watching other horses. I stared at his cloudy eye and waited for the vet.

This probably won't be a big deal, I comforted myself, although it was the biggest eye ulcer I'd ever seen. *Ten days of medicine and he'll be good as new. Hopefully it's not fungus again. I have no idea how I'd get that fungus medicine into his eye seven times a day with my work schedule and him living thirty-five minutes from me.*

Sandi had run off to point at birds. Gid slurped his tongue while I massaged his big red ears, which had tufts of hair coming out the bottom. I always called them old man hairs. He wasn't really old, though. Fourteen. He was five when I got him, and horses live to around thirty unless something bad happens.

My heart still ached over Tippo. She was only six when a bout of colic hit so hard and fast the vet said the only humane thing to do was end her life. Otherwise one of her organs might rupture. It had been so sudden. Gid dropped his head, moving closer so I could reach his ears. I let the heat of his body distract me from cold thoughts. He was a balm that soothed my rough edges.

Eventually I put him in the stall and pulled the blue mounting block in front to use as a seat so we could wait together. He stretched his head down and blew frosted flake and grass breath into my face. I gently blew back, thinking horse breath might be my favorite smell. I wondered if I was his. Did I smell different every day because of what I ate and drank? Did he judge if I smelled like coffee or fast food? Or was there something consistent about my scent that set me apart? He nibbled my hair, and I thought, *no other horse is allowed to do this.* Gideon could do almost anything, and I wouldn't say no.

Dr. B's white truck bumped up the barn driveway. I'd met her first as a rider when we attended an adult riding camp. After a week together, I decided I'd trust her more than anyone with my horses.

"Hey there, Sarah!" she said with an impish smile as she grabbed things from her truck. "What have we got here?"

"Well, he's got a big ulcer on his eye. Like, really big." She started preparing her little test strips for eye ulcers while I talked. "I rode him a few days ago and he was fine. I haven't seen him since, so I'm not sure when it started, but even so it looks pretty big to have just grown for three or four days."

"Let me take a look here." Gid's head was up and alert over the stall door, unsure of this lady coming toward him.

He let her hold his head. “Has he had ulcers before?” she asked as she touched the area around his eye, moving his eyelids a bit to get a better look.

“He gets an ulcer in his eye at least once a year, but it’s never been this big. Normally we just treat it with antibiotic ointment and it goes away pretty quick. One time he got a fungus and boy, that was an ordeal!”

“I bet,” she replied. Her smile was gone. *Probably because she’s focusing.*

She popped her glove off and stepped away. “Well, Sarah,” her normally perky voice dropped in pitch. “It looks like he’s got what’s called Recurring Uveitis. Most people call it Moonblindness.”

My friend’s pony had Moonblindness, I thought. *This is okay. Not a big deal. Her pony was old and may even still be alive.*

But she kept going, “On top of that, there’s a considerable amount of scar tissue and glaucoma. Sarah, you’ve got a decision to make.”

I would have been less surprised if Gideon had stood on his hind legs and started juggling. The word *decision* in vet talk only ever alludes to one decision—to kill your pet or not.

What is she talking about? I yelled in my head to God. *She obviously doesn’t know us. She doesn’t know me. Gideon and I fight. We fight for each other, and we fight to be together. There is no decision to make*!

Her body language had changed. She was making herself smaller, slumping her strong shoulders. The change in energy drew Sandi over and she put her nose on Dr. B’s shorts. I bowed up like a fighter, raising an inch, chest out, jaw tight, ice in my eyes, searching my brain for some kind of response other than “a decision.”

“Let’s talk options,” I said. “What does treatment for this look like?”

Her eyebrows lifted. “Well, for the Moonblindness there’s an ointment you can give him that helps keep it in remission. He’d need it twice a day every day for the rest of his life.”

“Okaaay.” I drew out the word as my mind fired with options, opportunities, angles, anything. If I had my own place, that wouldn’t be a big deal. But I didn’t have my own place, and ointment twice a day would be difficult to impossible in the retirement field thirty-five minutes from my house. “What about a specialist? The time he had the fungus in his eye we talked about sending him to a specialist.”

"Yeah, there's someone who comes up to the area about once a month. We could look at getting him in to see her and see what she says." But I could see it in her eyes. What would a specialist be able to do for such a common disease?

"You know, he's probably had a mild version for a while. That's probably why he's been getting ulcers in his eyes." She said it like it was a white flag, a peace offering in this unspoken fight.

"Yeah," I said. "Let's get him in with the specialist."

"Okay." She began packing her things and writing my invoice. "I'll call the office and they'll be in touch to set it up once we know exactly when she'll be in the area."

I sat in my car waiting for the light to turn green, railing to God. *Who does she think she is? Doesn't she know we don't give up that easily? Doesn't she know we've basically defied death at least ten times by now? This stupid little eye thing is nothing compared to what we've been through!* I took a second to inhale and looked at my phone, wondering who I could call that would get angry along with me.

The light finally turned green, and I shoved the accelerator down as pressure built behind my eyes. *God!* I borderline yelled. *God, what am I supposed to do*?

"Give him to me." I heard it as clearly as I heard the car engine next to mine, but it wasn't my ears that picked up the words. It was my heart.

What? Was that some figment of my imagination or were you just talking to me? I know you wouldn't have said that. You gave me that vision, the one of me as a mom, kids playing on a tire swing, and Gideon old and swaybacked in my backyard. That can't happen if I give him to you.

"Give him to me," I heard again, like a whisper into my chest that traveled to my head. "I have a place for him in my army."

A place for Gideon? In your army? A fresh wave of tears sprung to my eyes, a mixed bag of fear, hope, anger, and a thousand other emotions I couldn't express or understand. I imagined Gid standing out in the big retirement field, wasting away. Then I imagined him, as best I could, in God's army.

The only pictures I could come up with were from a scene in the Bible when Elisha stood on a precipice, surrounded by enemy soldiers with his slave boy panicking by his side. "O LORD, open his eyes so he may see," Elisha had prayed. The Bible says, "Then Elisha prayed, "O LORD, open his eyes and let him see!"

The LORD opened the young man's eyes, and when he looked up, he saw that the hillside around Elisha was filled with horses and chariots of fire." *God's army horses.* I always felt like Gideon and I had warriors' hearts. There were so many times in Kentucky when I was sure I walked through a battlefield. Like there was a spirit realm that coexisted with ours and only a thin veil separated me from a world of blood and carnage.

My heart stuttered. *You want Gideon?*

"You don't need him anymore. I do."

It could have all been a figment of my imagination, a creative conversation with myself. But it wasn't. I never would have volunteered to give my Gid away. We fought for each other.

I called Dr. B back. Called my trainer. Called my mom. I told Joey over dinner, between hiccup sobs that made it difficult to talk. He sat quietly, absorbing my heartbreak.

My heart was a sack of bricks, dragging down my shoulders, the corners of my mouth, the water from my eyes. I vacillated wildly between peaceful and inconsolable, my head leaned against the steering wheel, the horse I was grooming, or the wall of the shower. Grief would sneak up, snatching the air from my lungs. It felt like my insides were being torn out. *How could I? My Gideon?* I couldn't even think the words.

We set an appointment two weeks out. It was excruciating. It was a gift. Every day for two weeks, I visited him before or after work—whenever I could. My friend came out with her camera and took beautiful photos of us. I taught him to wrap his neck around me to get a treat and give me a hug. I groomed him, medicated his little wounds from living outside, and knew in my heart that it was right.

He was retired. His body was broken in so many small ways that added up to this. He didn't live in my backyard where I could walk out every morning and give him medicine. He was dangerous when he got scared. Some horses, like my friend's pony, can live for years in a field, blind some days, seeing fine on others, calmly grazing and following a pasture-mate around to stay safe.

Gideon wasn't that horse. He would impale himself on a tree branch or run through the fence and get hit by a car, and those scenarios would be monumentally worse.

Plus, God had spoken. He'd said, "Shut the window," and I listened. He'd said, "Quit your job," and I didn't. Now he said, "Give Gideon to me." I would obey. This was right.

I relished, marveled even, that I could be with Gideon and smile, knowing what was coming. That was the thing with him: he always made me smile. When it was time to leave, I'd medicate his eye and put him in his field, rubbing the swirl on his forehead and giving him Frosted Flakes. He'd lean into me, and I relished it.

But as I stepped into my car, all the happiness from his presence was stripped away, and I was reminded of the clear reality that I would soon go forward in life without my war horse. Mine and Joey's dinners started fine, but at some point I'd lose myself to the grief. He sat across from me, sometimes quiet, sometimes trying to battle through and continue the conversation.

I sucked in a deep breath, in awe of another truth. Who am I to train a horse for the Creator of the universe? In the logic I tested over and over in my head, that's what I had done. I trained Gideon, cared for him, fought for him, loved him, and now he was going to be in God's army. Is that not the ultimate gift to God and from God for a horse-crazy girl?

I was grateful, but I also hurt. Gideon was my best friend. I had hopes and dreams and still unanswered prayers wrapped up in that horse. When I retired him, it was like they were put in a coma. Somehow death and a coma were so different. When he was gone, the dreams and prayers would be dead too.

It was a beautiful day. The kind where I normally would have rushed to put on my boots and hit the road to my favorite place and favorite horse. We had Gid's final appointment. I didn't want to go. I considered canceling, pretending everything was fine and normal, like Gideon wouldn't go blind off and on and eventually impale himself in a panic. I tried convincing myself I was crazy and that I hadn't actually had a conversation with God about Gideon joining God's army. But what did I learn in Kentucky if not how to discern God's voice? And how important it is to obey.

As much as I wanted to put this off, I also wanted to go early—to soak up every single second with the horse whose heart had connected with mine like no other.

To imprint his rich, earthy smell on my brain, feel his breath on my face, and feed him an entire bag of Frosted Flakes without worrying about colic because it wouldn't matter. I just wanted to be with him.

And so I did.

I groomed him and fed him Frosted Flakes and he savored the flavor, sucking on his tongue and making those repulsive slurping noises, and I relished them. He dipped his head, pressing it into my chest and closing his eyes, and I rubbed my hands on his large cheeks. Somehow this horse always chased away my sorrow, even now. I thought that maybe, just maybe, I was experiencing the peace that surpasses all understanding that the Bible talks about. Because in this moment I had dreaded since the day I met Gid, we enjoyed each other, and I was fine. I even smiled.

A few minutes before the vet was set to arrive, I thought about how strange it was that Gid wasn't suffering before the end. He wasn't in immense pain, struggling to stand, or lying on the ground like every other time I'd said goodbye to a horse. *Maybe this is a gift too.*

I couldn't think of a single reason not to swing onto his back one last time, so I led him to the fence, climbed to the top board, grasped his sparse mane, and swung my leg over. Part of my brain tried to argue that if I could ride him maybe I shouldn't be doing this. Yet it simultaneously felt so right, a parting gift for both of us. He rounded his neck, perking his ears, and lifted his tail as we explored the property one last time, his warm back and high withers implanting itself for a lifetime.

God, when I die and whatever happens happens, I prayed, *maybe Jesus will greet me or maybe my spirit will ascend to Heaven. I don't know. But whatever happens, can Gideon be there to greet me?*

A peace settled over me. The vet arrived.

The grass itched my ankles as I leaned my face into the lifeless chestnut body spread beneath me. Sobs racked me at the realization that my first true love—the animal that had leaped into my heart nine years before—had left the earthly realm to join God's battle forces. I choked on my tears and snot poured from my nose. I laid it all out there, just me, Gid's lifeless body, and the presence of my Creator, settling on me like a rich, deep fog.

I prayed. Words failed me at first. What could I say when he was gone? So I started simple, basic. *Thank you*. Soon words poured from my soul.

Thank you, God, for this horse.

Thank you for us.

Thank you for the day he jumped across the creek and claimed me. Thank you for saving him when he broke his leg. Thank you for the vision you gave me that kept me going even if it's not really happening that way.

Thank you for Kentucky, for teaching me everything you taught me. Thank you for using this horse again and again to teach me to put you first. Thank you for not giving up on me even though I put dumb stuff before you, my God. Thank you for loving me so much that you made this horse for me. I can tell you made him for me. He was everything I ever wanted. Thank you for not always giving me my way or making things perfect. Even though I wish we could have done all those cool things, I see now that your hand was on it. Thank you for having your hand on us.

Thank you. Thank you for your love. Thank you for Gideon. Thank you.

A guy stood by the gate, waiting for me to leave so he could push this lifeless corpse into a hole and cover it up. I knew the body before me was no more my beloved horse than the tree that shaded us, but it was hard to pull away. It was Gideon's body. I dug my fingers into his hair one last time and took in the beauty of his gleaming white stockings, the scar on his back leg, and the white blaze that went from between his perfect ears to his bottom lip, and I whispered my thanks to our Creator one more time.

Peeling myself from the ground and not looking back, I nodded to the guy and made my way slowly to the gate. A thousand strings that tied us together tried to pull me back. I reminded those strings that Gid wasn't there anymore. My hands shook as I undid the chain to the red gate that led out of the pasture, concentrating on each step. Every angle of my foot, lifting my knee, each breath, all required effort, thought. I made my way through the patch of trees, past the riding arena, down the short hill, and past the barn. I had left Sandi at home, and I wanted more than anything to have her by my side.

There was one more field to walk through and I could hide in my car, safe, alone. Two horses stood in my path. I didn't want to look at them. I didn't want to make eye contact, afraid they knew I killed one of their kind. *What if they know and they hate me for it?*

Instead, the darkest bay, a horse that was normally indifferent to my presence at best, walked to me. I paused to see what he was doing, looking at the ground to avoid his eyes. He walked slowly, like I was a small kid he was being careful with, and pressed his head into my chest like Gideon had done so many times. I squeezed my eyes together and leaned into him while silent tears streamed down my face.

Epilogue

"Bye guys! Have fun! See you after service!" Small arms wrapped around my waist before my kids bounded toward their Sunday School rooms. Fingers laced through mine and I turned to smile at Joey. An overwhelming sense of victory filled my chest. "We're going to be on time!" I exclaimed.

We stepped into the sanctuary as the musicians keyed up their instruments. Joey led me to our normal spot in one of the front sections. Taking our seats, we made eye contact and a jolt of happiness spread from my chest all the way to my fingertips. It was good to be back in this place after so much time watching online and while the world was shut down.

Memories from our date the night before filled my mind, and I leaned into Joey. I couldn't believe it had been fifteen years since we walked down the aisle in front of our friends and family. And through it all, it was still easy to choose him every day. "Thank you, God," I whispered, squeezing Joey's hand.

"Welcome to God's house, everyone! Let's stand and worship our Creator." The singer stepped back from the microphone and strummed the intro to the song on his guitar, and a room full of people lumbered to their feet. Joey and I disconnected our hands and stepped apart to focus on worship, and too quickly, we were back in our seats for the last prayer before the sermon.

"Dear God..." the prayer started. My mind drifted away.

The day that bright chestnut horse with four white stockings and a blaze leaped over the wide ditch and into my life, he was called Easy. His name had been changed as often as he had changed hands, which in recent months had been pretty frequent. For the first time, I had a horse that didn't know his name, one I could gift with a name of my choosing.

This was a lot of pressure. It had been years since I doodled names I wanted to give my future horses in notebooks designated:

Horse Lovers Club (if you aren't in the club, you are not allowed to open).

Members: Sarah Ruth

I kept my club small.

By the time this new horse arrived in my life, the notebooks full of names were lost to childhood and I was starting from scratch.

I loved the idea of giving my horse a biblical name and David had always enamored me. He had slain Goliath, screaming, "You come against me with sword and spear and javelin, but I come against you in the name of the LORD Almighty!" Then he buried a rock in Goliath's brain and chopped his head off. Gruesome but epic. David's faith made my head spin and my heart squeeze, and some days my eyes filled up just hoping I could have that kind of faith. Plus, he'd written so many Psalms and was described as ruggedly handsome, kind of like this horse. But "David" just didn't sound right for an animal. That would be like naming him Jeff or Mark.

I called my youth pastor and explained the situation. "I have this new horse, and I want to name him something from the Bible. David is my favorite, but that's a weird name for a horse."

"Let me think on it and get back to you," he said in a bit of a rush.

Standing in my driveway, I closed my phone and whispered a prayer. *God, what should I name this horse? I just, I really feel like he's a gift from you, and I want you to get the glory here.*

A couple hours later, I was on my way home when my pastor called back. "Sarah, I was thinking about it. How about Gideon?"

Gideon, I thought. I liked how it wasn't a commonly used name. It was cute. I thought about what I knew of Gideon's story in the Bible. All I could remember was something about a guy called to lead God's people into battle, a lamb's wool soaked in dew, and him demanding God to prove himself. I had never been impressed with his lack of faith, but I loved the idea that he was a warrior. Maybe it was from keeping up with two older brothers, or the fierce hearts of the women in movies that inspired me, but the idea of fighting battles for my Heavenly Father always pulled my shoulders back and pushed my chin up.

I pulled out my Bible and looked Gideon up. The text said he was the weakest warrior from the weakest clan and that when God chose him to lead, Gideon simply didn't believe it. He accused God of being wrong, and then tested Him over and over, demanding multiple miracles before eventually conceding to God's call. I was losing patience just reading it.

Once Gideon decided to listen, he took an entire pack of warriors out to do what God had promised—defeat the Midianites who were oppressing God's people. But God told Gideon he had too many men, so anyone who was afraid could go home. Twenty-two thousand men left, and ten thousand stayed on the battlefield.

Then God said there were still too many: take them to the water and we'll thin the herd there. Gideon did as he was asked, and the Lord told him to separate those who lapped the water with their tongues from those who kneeled to drink. Personally, I thought that was strange, but I guess I'd never consumed water directly from a stream. The men who lapped water like dogs stayed to fight and everyone else went home. Only three hundred men remained!

That night, Gideon split his three hundred men into three groups, giving them jars and trumpets. They surrounded the enemy camp on three sides, and as the guard was changing, they smashed the jars and blew the trumpets, shouting, "A sword for the LORD and for Gideon!" The Midianite army, filled with fear, turned on each other with their swords and ran. Gideon's army of three hundred men won.

God used this guy, the smallest man from the weakest clan, who doubted and challenged at every turn. Then he used a laughably small group of three hundred men with a bunch of jars and instruments to defeat an army of around 135,000 warriors.

I sat in my bedroom with my Bible in my lap, surrounded by horse pictures, and prayed. *God, please use me and Gideon for your kingdom. God, help us to lead your people and show people how good you are. Help us help others come to know you.*

To be honest, I wasn't sure how a horse and a girl could help God's people. The only idea I could come up with was Gid and I becoming world-renowned barrel racers or maybe jumpers. Whatever it was we were best at, a reporter would put a microphone to my mouth as people cheered in the background. "Tell us about today's competition!" she'd say. When I finished gushing over how amazing Gideon was, the reporter would ask, "To what do you attribute this success?"

I'd smile, glancing up to the heavens, maybe even fist bump my heart, point up, and say, "God is good! I really owe it all to Him," with tears brimming in my eyes. Christians across the world would be encouraged and even people who had never been interested in Jesus might trust Him because when you trust God, you can be amazing like Gideon and me.

Is that daydream embarrassing to admit? Maybe a little. Actually, a lot.

Instead, our story was full of more tragedies than victories. We went to competitions and won a few ribbons, but we also skipped from one injury to the next. Gideon was retired and gone before he hit middle age. When I thought of our story, it was usually with a heavy heart from lost time and unreached dreams. Some days, the grief over saying goodbye to those hopes and prayers was just as heavy as the grief from losing Gideon. I imagined those dreams and prayers woven into his rich red coat, buried the day the tractor dumped dirt over his cooling body.

On rare occasions, God answers prayers in a big way that leaves us stunned and speechless. More often, His answers are simple and we don't even notice. Some prayers go seemingly unanswered, as if the lack of response is a response in itself. I was mostly okay with that.

If I had learned anything, it was to trust my Creator. I had begged God to help me get to Kentucky right out of high school, convinced another two years of delaying my racetrack dream would ruin everything. Against all my efforts and prayers, I ended up at Mississippi College—just long enough to meet Joey. Then in Kentucky, everything fell apart so quickly in ways I had never fathomed. I fought for my dream like a bull ramming his head into a cement wall, determined to get to the other side no matter how it was shattering me, until the day I looked up and handed the dream to God.

God showed me time after time how He can and will work all things for my good when I love and follow Him—even things like horrible crashes or horses being stolen. The good He works out is rarely what I expect or hope for. There's always a lot of growth involved. But when I look back on the hard journey, there's not a thing I would change. I can see God's fingerprints on the circumstances and on the person I've become.

The preacher ended his prayer and rolled into the sermon, but my wandering mind would not be reined in. With mixed emotions, I thought about the decade since I said goodbye to my best friend and the dreams and prayers that went with him—a decade of occasionally hearing an extra set of hoofbeats over my left shoulder and checking to see if I could catch a glimpse of Gid running with us.

From Gideon, my mind drifted to the book I had spent so much of the last year working on. When I started writing the story, I wasn't sure where it would lead. I just knew I was called to write it. It took months of telling God all the reasons I wasn't qualified before I caved and said yes. Then there was a decade of picking it up and putting it down. On January 1 of 2020, I declared it my year to finish the memoir.

I silently laughed. 2020 was over and the memoir was still not done. But I had finally finished the first draft a few weeks before, and I couldn't believe how beautiful the story was. Sure, I had lived it. But writing it down and seeing how God brought it full circle was astounding. I tried to explain it to people, but there were no words. My friends would say, "Well, of course it's good! You worked hard on it." And I wanted to scream, *No! This is so far beyond me. That would be like taking credit for a beautiful sunset because you took the picture.*

My mind drifted to the teenage prayer that I had nearly forgotten—*God, please use Gideon and me for your kingdom. God, help us to lead your people and show people how good you are. Help us help others come to know you.*

The realization hit like an unsuspecting wave on a beautiful, calm beach day. I would have fallen to the ground if I wasn't already sitting. Focused on calming breaths, I bowed my head and tried to look normal. In a single thought, my world changed.

What if the Creator of the universe, the Beginning and End, the great I Am, is still answering my prayer? What if God is so big, so good, so sovereign, that when it felt like my world was ending, He was creating the most beautiful story? What if, years after Gideon's death, God is using our story to answer my prayer?

I wanted to weep at my Savior's feet. I didn't deserve this gift, yet He gave freely. Every inhale filled me with His love, and every exhale carried away my doubts. And there had been a lot of doubts. It was hard to trust a God who gives and takes away. Even the thought brought back the feeling of Gideon being lost, my teeth broken and held in by a metal bar and brown glue. It was a desperation I had wanted to cave into, but I forced myself to keep going, one hour at a time. There are still smells, like the face wipes I used back then, that make me want to run to the nearest trashcan and vomit.

But God could see the whole movie when I could only see the little snippet I was living. He took my worst moment and was using it to answer my prayer.

Whenever I think about being at the Kentucky fairgrounds, walking the length of the barns to look into every stall, asking every person, and coming up empty, I think of how I longed to walk away.

A drive to Mississippi would have been so much easier than staying. I imagined my parents' warm arms and the long embrace they would give me. I imagined the sobs racking my body as they held me up. Sitting in my truck, I had pressed my head into the steering wheel and weighed my options. Surely Mississippi College would reinstate my scholarship. Sandi could live with my parents and Joey could visit me on breaks. I could go back to my old job where I was loved and treated like part of the family, where the horses were safe and fun. Surely someone would have a cheap or free horse and I could just start fresh.

But it wouldn't be Gideon.

Maybe *Finding Gideon* isn't just about a horse, but about the Gideon within ourselves.

If God chose to use the lowest member from the weakest clan, maybe we don't have to be the smartest or fastest or even the most holy. Maybe we just have to be willing to not walk away, to stick around and finish the story, even if we're easily distracted and it takes a decade longer than expected. Even if we're not sure where the story is going half the time.

For my entire life, I thought questioning God was bad. *How dare I question the Creator of the universe?* I even got angry on God's behalf when Gideon repeatedly questioned Him, asking for miracles day after day to prove his calling was legit.

But God never seemed bothered by it. What if He's okay with our doubts and questions, as long as we are willing to persist for a response?

And what if the parts of life that feel inescapable, miserable, and make us wonder how a good God could let this happen are ultimately being used for good?

The more I think about the twenty-year wait for my prayer to be answered, the more I can't help but wonder how many prayers He's still working on. Prayers whispered by people so long ago they pretend they forgot about it. Maybe it hurts to think of it going unanswered, or it just seems impossible.

Church ended, and I realized I spent most of it lost in my own musings. I smiled to myself, knees still weak from my revelation. We picked up the kids from Sunday School and stepped into the warm spring day. "Dad, where are going to eat?"

"I don't know; ask your mom."

Rays of sun cut across the sidewalk and I floated through them, reminding myself to stay present. My kids turned to me, hope and joy spread across their freckled cheeks. "Where are we going to eat?" they yelled, drawing the attention of others.

"I was thinking Santinis?" I looked to Joey. He nodded and the kids ran on ahead. I grabbed Joey's hand, thinking about Gideon and the book, answered prayers, and the way God chooses unlikely heroes.

Thank you, God, I whispered. *For all of it.*

A NOTE FROM THE AUTHOR

GIDEON WAS MY HERO and my first love. I lived for him and the way he gently lipped carrots from my hand, shared his scent as we blew in each other's faces, and touched my arm with his pink, sticky tongue after a yummy treat. He was my joy.

Then the dream of galloping racehorses became my greatest pursuit. I wanted to feel a horse's muscles bunch and release as the wind whipped my face more than I wanted air itself.

It all sounds beautiful. Maybe you smiled when reading about Gideon and imagined what riding a racehorse would feel like when I described the dream. God gifted me the horse He knew would bring joy to my soul, and He planted that dream in my heart. James 1:17 says, "Whatever is good and perfect is a gift coming down to us from God our Father, who created all the lights in the heavens."

The horse and the dream were gifts from God.

The Bible also says in the Ten Commandments, "You shall have no other Gods before me." Before I met Gideon, I thought that meant we shouldn't put Baal, Zeus, Budda, or any other thing humanity considers a god before our God. But when Gideon broke his leg and I thought I would lose the horse that held my heart God spoke to me, revealing a hard truth. Gideon held the highest place of honor in my heart, a place only God should be.

So, as you read in the scene where I sat in my pickup (a truck that saw more emotional breakdowns than any other place in my life), I rearranged things and gave God His place back. Unfortunately, similar to the Israelites who spent a thousand years drifting and returning to God, my heart struggled to keep God in His place. It became comical in the most unfunny way. I'd put God first, but then slowly I'd switch them around and put Gideon right back on the throne.

To someone who's never loved a horse, this may sound silly. How could someone put a horse in front of God—the Giver and Creator of the horse? And I might ask in return, how could someone put money, their career, a goal, the need for security, or even their kids, in front of God? I don't think it's just me. I believe most of us have a tendency to put something before God.

The pattern of putting things before my Creator became even worse when I arrived in Kentucky. For a blissful week, I held everything I ever wanted in my hands. According to the trainer I worked for, people were talking about how good I was, and I believed it. I built my life on the foundation of hard work, determination, and horses, and it was paying off. But when the winds and rain came, they swept me away.

Thankfully, the story didn't end there. I didn't go home, defeated and horseless. God captured me and held me. With grace, He guided me through learning to worship Him even when times were tough. He provided people and a church who spoke into my life, and He taught me how to put Him first. I didn't rebuild perfectly, and the struggles didn't end, but I learned what it meant to have the Creator of the universe as my true foundation and hope.

I've told you my story, but what about yours? Have you seen yourself in the pages of this book?

Have you wondered how a good God could let certain things happen to you? Have you dreamed big dreams or prayed big prayers that seem lost to the wind? Have you struggled with envy or putting other things before God? Hopefully this story has encouraged you to lean into your faith.

If you're wondering how that works, want more details on how to lean in, or even who this God is, go to www.LiveRideLearn.com. I have resources there, and you can also contact me. I would love to chat or point you in the right direction.

If you've read this book, you are now part of my story, and I am part of yours. I thank God for that gift.

Sandi

Sandi moved to Virginia with us and had a good long life accompanying me to different barns. When she was eight, she got an autoimmune disease that attacked her joints. She survived but struggled with arthritis for the rest of her life and had to stay home from trail rides. Even so, she loved to run at the barn until the very end. Her younger human siblings were blessed to get to know her before she left us to be with Gideon.

But who stole Gideon?

I KNOW PEOPLE ARE wondering this. Anytime I tell the story, it's the number one question. The truth is, I don't know for sure who stole Gideon, and it doesn't matter. I can hear you now, saying, "Yes it does!"

But really, it doesn't. Gideon and I found each other, and I didn't hear of any other horses being stolen after that. It seems we were one-time victims of someone who probably just wanted to get rid of us and wasn't brave enough to simply ask me to take my horse and go. Whoever it was, I've forgiven them.

Acknowledgments

Sometimes I'm full of words—enough to write a book. And sometimes there's this feeling that swirls between my stomach and my heart that says so much, yet there are no words to express it; no matter how hard I try to formulate a sentence, it won't come. But I'll try.

First, thank you, Louisville. You're a city of dreams.

Thank you to every single person who played a part in this story. Whether you made it to the page or not, whether we were best friends or barely friends or not even friends, thank you!

Thank you to Byron Crawford who indeed helped turn my story around with an article in the paper. And thank you to everyone who reached out after they read my story. How could I show appreciation to strangers through an email? How could I tell the guy offering to pay my dental bills that I was sticking with my dentist because in my heart of hearts I could tell it's the chair God wanted me in? But I was so humbled and grateful for the offer. How could I tell the people who reached out because I inspired them that I was really just putting one foot in front of the other and nothing felt special or amazing at the moment? If you were one of those people and you're reading this, I appreciate you. Fifteen plus years later, I haven't forgotten the love and hope you gave me during an incredibly difficult part of life.

I feel like I should apologize to the outriders. They'll probably never read this, but those guys are excellent horsemen, doing an incredible job of policing the backside of Churchill Downs, and keeping everyone as safe as possible. I maybe wasn't their favorite person, and they may not have been mine either, but I have a lot of respect for them.

Thank you to my early readers. Writing a book is difficult in a lot of ways. You pour hours upon hours into something with no clue if it's going to be worth reading, so those early readers got the joy of dealing with all my insecurities.

To my brothers, we may not have gotten along when we lived at home, but now you're two of my favorite people in the entire world. Thank you for making me tough when we were young, and dropping serious words of wisdom at perfect moments.

Mom and Dad, I honestly feel bad y'all will read this. Now that I'm a mom, I can't imagine reading about the struggle my kids go through. But I want you to know I'm grateful for all of it. Thank you for making me wait forever to get that first horse. For loving me, guiding me, and sending me to Mississippi College. I'll even swallow my pride and say thank you for the times you said "no." Thank you for letting me spread my wings and chase my dreams. And thank you for not making me come home. That had to have been the hardest thing in the world as a parent. You could probably write your own book about those months when I was nine hours away in a world of strangers with everything crumbling around me.

Joey, when we were newlyweds, I remember feeling like I got to have a sleepover with my best friend (with benefits) every night! It hasn't changed. Thanks for your patience as I spent years on this book. Also, thanks for letting me put our love story in here (and I apologize for not paying attention when you were proposing. I guess the secret is out).

To my horses, who would I be without you? Thank you for letting me press my face into your neck and breathe in your smell. Thank you for carrying me through some of the best and hardest times (even if you do cause at least half of them). Sometimes Joey probably fantasizes about what our bank account would look like if we didn't have horses, but what he doesn't realize is he'd be married to a miserable shell of a woman. And no, the house wouldn't be cleaner.

JJ and Essie, someday you might actually read this, and I can only imagine what you'll think. Thank you for being my best cheerleaders. I am so proud to be your mom, and so grateful for your hugs and kind words. I love the people you are. I hope you trust in the Lord and go for your own God-given dreams, and I pray I'm brave enough and strong enough to support you.

Caitlin, Hope, Amanda, Jennifer, Tricia, Katrina, and Mom (I think that's everyone. I'm really sweating about missing someone here), thank you for letting me talk your ears off about this book. Your courtesy nods, encouragement, and feedback have been so helpful. Sometimes I just needed you to listen and sometimes I needed actual words, and all of you seemed to deliver what I needed. Thank you.

To Danae, my editor, I can feel your urge to delete this. You are so talented with the delete key, removing the excess and honing this story. Thank you for the hours and hours you poured into this story.

David Fassett, I freaking love my book cover. I know I was the worst kind of client, coming to you with almost no vision. But when I saw your web site I knew God would give a vision to you. It's beautiful.

Sara B – thank you for helping spread the word about this story and for taking a load off my plate. Jennifer – you are the queen of the launch team. My left and right hands in the book launch.

Ashley, thank you for writing such an incredible bio! It's so much better than what I started with.

To the people who believed enough in this project to back the Kickstarter – thank you! Writing this book has been a long process of sitting on the couch with God and a laptop. When you believed in this story enough to back it, I felt like all of you had been sitting on the couch with us, cheering.

Nathan, Eric, Kim, Becky, Mary, Hope, Aunt Melissa, Susan, Krista, Lauren, Rob, Quintus, Uncle Carroll, Joel, Josh, Cayce, Alex, Dr. Tran, Cheryl, Cindy, Kay, Mom and Dad, Mrs. Carol and Mr. Joe.

Thank you.

And finally, thank you to my Creator, the first and greatest Storyteller. Thank you for the gift of this story. Thank you for pursuing me and this call for me.

Photo Album

A few gems before everyone had cameras in their pockets.

The first documentation of Sarah's horse obsession.

The first horse I ever rode, Ms. Ann. She was thirty-something and grouchy. I was eleven and on cloud nine.

Henry, my second horse. I was around thirteen.

Summer after tenth grade. Gideon was my new horse and I was helping with Winterview Farm's summer camp.

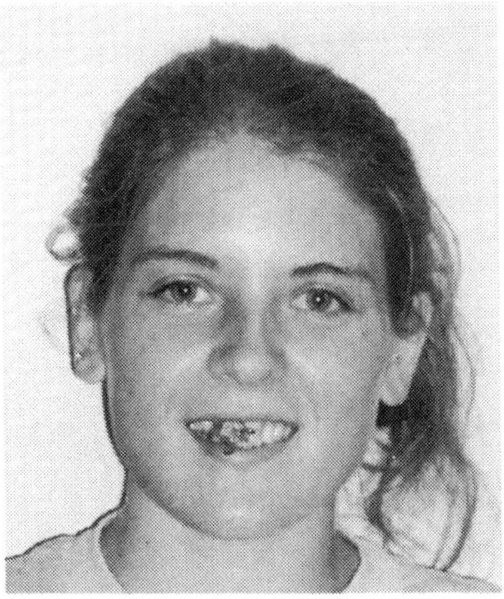

The day Dr. Tran removed the bar and gave me braces.

Our first Kentucky Derby! We bought tickets to the infield and found a spot by the fence where we could see a bit of the final stretch.

The only documentation I have of nearly two years playing polo.

Haley loaned me some show clothes and we competed on the University of Louisville western show team.

Sandi came with us to the show and got to stay in a hotel!

Visiting home after Hurricane Katrina hit and demolished the woods behind Joey's parents house.

Joey visiting me at Ian's barn.

Mom and I at my final Derby as a Louisville resident. (Dad and Joey were there too, they just didn't make the photo.)

Riding Gideon under the lights at Winterview Farm the month we were in Mississippi to get married.

Bridal photos on my noble steed.

One more!

Adult riding camp with Tippo in Virginia.

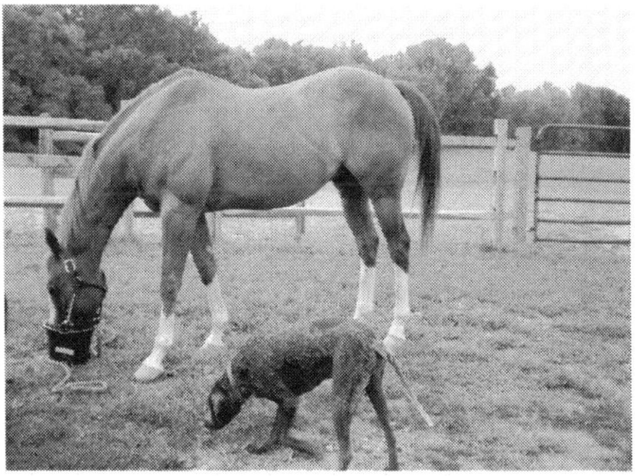

Gid and Sandi in Virginia.

An attempted family photo in 2020.

The photo used on the cover. I wanted "pretty pictures" with Gideon, so I drug my mom to the barn and she took three. We got a winner! This was sometime pre-Kentucky.
My friend, Amanda, said this perfectly captured the feeling of the book, and I think she's right.

MORE FROM SARAH HICKNER

A journal for horse lovers

Short stories from before Kentucky

A journal for storytellers

www.LiveRideLearn.com/books

About the Author

Hickner was born and raised in Mississippi and began riding when she was 11. At 19, she followed her dreams to gallop racehorses in Kentucky. The next two years became a wild ride of epic highs and (quite literal) hard falls as her world came crashing down around her. The pieces came back together to create a story worth sharing.

Sarah has been fueled to share this part of her life because she believes that strength can often be found in the broken parts of our stories. Her journey is a living testament to one of her favorite Bible verses, Romans 8:28 "We know that in all things God works for the good of those who love Him, who have been called according to His purpose." Sarah wants to share this message of hope with her readers. When it feels like the sky is falling and nothing good could come of the situation, GOD CAN work it for good, and He always does.

When Sarah isn't writing or at the barn, you'll find her cheering on her kids at one of their many activities or trying to maneuver around her tiny kitchen with her husband, Joey.

Now all glory to God, who is able, through his mighty power at work within us, to accomplish infinitely more than we might ask or think. Glory to him in the church and in Christ Jesus through all generations forever and ever! Amen.

Ephesians 3:20–21

Made in the USA
Middletown, DE
14 January 2024

47556475R00196